MW00513588

Options Trading (3 Books in 1) : *Options Trading Crash Course* + How To Build A Six-Figure Income + Stock Market Investing for Beginners

Nathan Bell

Options Trading Crash Course: A Complete Beginner's Guide To Learn The Basics About Trading Options And Start Making Money In Just 30 Days.

Nathan Bell

The information herein is provided for educational purposes exclusively and is universal. The presentation of the data is without contractual agreement or any kind of warranty assurance.

All trademarks inside this book are for clarifying purposes only and are possessed by the owners themselves, not allied with this document.

Disclaimer

All erudition supplied in this book are specified for educational and academic purpose only. The author is not in any way in charge of any outcomes that emerge from utilizing this book. Constructive efforts have been made to render information that is both precise and effective; however, the author is not to be held answerable for the accuracy or use/misuse of this information.

Foreword

I will like to thank you for taking the very first step of trusting me and deciding to purchase/read this life-transforming book. Thanks for investing your time and resources on this product.

I can assure you of precise outcomes if you will diligently follow the specific blueprint I lay bare in the information handbook you are currently checking out. It has transformed lives, and I firmly believe it will equally change your own life too.

All the information I provided in this Do It Yourself piece is easy to absorb and practice.

Table of Contents

INTRODUCTION

Searching for a tremendous beginner-level book on options trading can be extremely frustrating because we have many people with different perspectives.

On the other side, consider that options trading as a fertile specific niche for originalities. This book, nevertheless, was written to take full advantage of clearness and readability, all while providing a comprehensive look at the principles of options trading. You should be ready to make your first few trades after reading this book.

In addition to helping develop a financier's portfolio, options trading involves a series of strategies that will permit financiers to incur considerable revenues at their designated convenience level.

How does one become an active options trader? Well, this is an excellent book to begin. Beginning with the basics, this guide to options trading will take budding investors through the definition of options, Infos on the various types of options, go through different strategies that can be implemented while trading, and set out an essential step-by-step guide to success, pointing out mistakes to prevent, and figuring out the investment terminology that frightens numerous prospective investors. Traders will be able to start with this book and jumpstart their professions in options trading and take theirs.

CHAPTER ONE

Understanding Stock Options

Trading on the stock exchange can be a complex organization with as much potential for loss as gain. Options are no exception and hence are most practical in the hands of a practiced and achieved trader.

Nevertheless, the financier who learns to use stock options to his or her benefit will be in a well-placed position when they sustain what is called risk capital. Which is the security that is a danger but may likewise yield vast amounts of revenue? This can be achieved by utilizing stock options to acquire an underlying asset.

So what precisely are stock options? The financial investment education website Investopedia defines it best as, "An option is a contract that gives the purchaser the right, but not the commitment, to buy or sell a hidden asset at a specific price on or before a certain date. Options similar to a stock or bond is security. Despite its many terms, options trading is much simpler than its definition. In other words, options trading is not just what the name recommends: it provides the trader options so that he or she can potentially sustain a minimal loss if an investment does not prove rewarding.

Here is an excellent example of options trading: Assume a trader chooses to acquire the stock for a new phone application that will allow users to purchase groceries while in transit. The trader may speculate that the worth of the security will increase due to the current shutdown of comparable applications and their business. The buyer and seller approach one another, who informs the financier that the security costs $2000.

However, the financier isn't sure of his forecast, and so he decides to buy the possession as an option for the cost of $400. From here, there are two possible outcomes. Firstly, the security may indeed increase as predicted and wished for that the trader being put in a commanding position because the individual who offered it to him is under the commitment to sell it to the buyer for $2000. Despite the truth that the security is now valued at a much higher rate; because the purchaser currently purchased the $400 option.

Nevertheless, the trader may have speculated improperly, which would cause the second potential results. If the rate of the security decreases, then the trader is under no commitment to buy the security but will lose the preliminary $400 premium. While that does not sound much of a loss like in this particular example, the numbers can change dramatically, relying on the property. The potential loss might be higher either since the options to purchase the property is very expensive (more top threat and cost regularly accompany the most appealing potential profit) or because the worth of the asset has dropped at a disconcerting rate. Also, things get more complicated when taking into account that the security might potentially rally. If the price does decline, it depends on the trader whether or not to go through with the agreement, which would usually be inadvisable, with the hope that the asset will reverse. The buyer can then offer it and earn a profit, or to enable the agreement to end and call the option premium loss at the end.

As implied, for instance, options are derivatives. They are called such because they originate from an underlying asset, which in this case, is the phone application stock. In reality, there is a range of underlying financial investments from which to select, such as stocks, equity, government securities, or indices.

It is essential to bear in mind though that options trading can also be used to offer securities. Also, in the manner of the same as the example above, if the trader thinks the price of security already in their ownership is going to decrease, they can sell it for what is hopefully an attractive option if they are not able to offer it outright.

However, as indicated by the meaning, there are options trading requirements that might either hinder the trader or be helpful. The buyer is never bound to buy the security if the worth of the security is not increasing as hoped.

If the security is increasing, the buyer always has the right to buy the guard at the cost guaranteed by the seller. This is something that ought to be taken into the mind to consider whenever selling options, as it can result in a high loss, considering that the seller is continuously bound to sell the options to the purchaser within the parameters of the agreement Options trading includes due dates. The purchaser can buy the security before or on the date of expiration, which is agreed upon by the purchaser and seller when the contract is developed. If the expiration date passes, the purchaser will lose the initial investment. When it comes to a specific selling the option, they would get just the initial investment from the buyer and then be free to offer the security at another price ultimately.

Essentially, trading options is just an agreement. The function of the contract is to purchase or offer an underlying asset, which, in the example, is the phone application security. If the expiration date for the options passes, the seller is free to produce a brand-new one with a brand-new buyer.

Thus, options trading provides a way for purchasers to hedge their bets on the planet of investments. While the risks might race high, an accomplished trader might have the ability to use options trading to decrease potential losses, as opposed to trading just using methods that have countless dangers. Just like many other aspects of life, education is essential to end up being a wise and rewarding financier.

Protecting financial investment profits is accomplished by hedging investments, a fantastic ability that will permit the knowledgeable trader to reduce losses while enjoying the full advantages of gratitude. The downfall in hedging is that it costs money; there is no method to protect properties versus losses without paying some type of premium. This ends up being complicated extremely quickly because hedging an investment requires making an extra, adversely associating investment. Despite this, hedging remains a prevalent strategy amongst financiers, which is since options are a notoriously severe danger. Hedging does not assist in increasing possible earnings, only to reduce risk; therefore, it is best used with the high risk/high return securities previously pointed out.

Having the ability to manage underlying possessions utilizing options is likewise described as leveraging. Also, to hedging, it is one of the primary draws to options trading, as leveraging allows the trader to manage a large amount of cash with extremely little financial investment. Further speculation of that financial investment can then lead the trader to either let the options agreement end and therefore only lose the initial option premium or force the seller to cost the full strike cost As discussed before though, leveraging can work as a double-edged sword if preventative measures are not taken, whether they are hedging, picking suitable strategies to increase the investment, or having a precise exit technique.

When trading, options may be positioned into particular classifications. This is because options are defined by five key components, a few of which have already been mentioned; they are the underlying security, kind of possibilities, strike rate, expiration date, and system of trade. The components that are yet detailed are easily specified. There are two kinds of options called puts and calls, which will be discussed in the next chapter. The strike cost is merely the price agreed upon by the purchaser and seller at which to sell the hidden security. In the example, the strike rate was $2000. The unit of trade represents several shares, which is a portion of ownership by an individual in a corporation or other monetary investment that entitles the investor to a relative quantity of the profits. One must bear in mind that a person option agreement represents 100 shares.

CHAPTER TWO

Categories of options

In this chapter, we will check out the numerous kinds of options that are offered and how they work. By the end of the episode, we will present some various types of options that are available, consisting of business provided options and index options and how they vary from exchange-traded stock options summary of call options and put options.

The two primary types of options are call options and put options. A call option is the right to buy 100 shares of the underlying stock, and a put option is the right to sell 100 shares of an underlying stock.

Market value intrinsic value of options decreases as the marketplace worth of stock of the underlying stock decreases. If the marketplace worth of the underlying stock is below the strike cost, exercising your option would result in purchasing the underlying stock at a price more significant than the present market worth. Therefore, the opportunity has no intrinsic value, and modifications in the options price will represent a fall in time worth just.

Revenue is figured out by the increase in the market value of the underlying stock, less the premium paid, and loss of time value.

Income is restricted to the premium got. Losses are possibly unlimited; however, just happen if the option is cost a loss or worked out against the seller. They were speculating that the market worth of the underlying stock will increase.

It was knowing that the market worth of the underlying stock will stay stable or fall.

Option buyers (takers).

An investor or trader who wishes to buy options is generally anticipating a considerable movement in the rate of the underlying security before the expiry date of the options. Options supply the buyer with the chance to benefit from this expected rate motion, without needing to offer capital to cover the complete expense of the hidden security. However, this takes advantage of does come with a cost inherent in the time worth of the options.

Options likewise supply option purchasers with minimal risk. Their maximum loss on any options trade will be the amount they pay for the option (plus deal costs). For instance, let's assume you acquire a call option on CBA for $1, and over the next couple of weeks, the price of CBA falls by $2. If you had acquired the CBA shares, you would have lost $2 per share. Nevertheless, by purchasing the options, your loss is always limited to the options premium you paid, which, in this case, is $1 per share.

Tip.

The buyer of options pays a premium to obtain the right to purchase or offer the underlying securities. This premium represents both the expense of the optimum and the right possible loss on this deal. No matter the motion in the market value of the underlying security, the options purchaser's maximum failure on taking an option is the premium they spent for the options.

It is imperative to bear in mind that option purchasers have the right; however, not the obligation to exercise their options. If the option holder does not want to work out the options and effect a transfer to the underlying stock, they can liquidate their position (effectively sell their options).

According to the ASX, as of November 2010, usually, just 15 percent of all options traded on the exchange are worked out. Of the staying 85 percent, 60 percent of.

These are closed out, and 25 percent end useless. A significant number of options were bought and offered by financiers and traders for functions other than getting the underlying stock.

Options sellers.

Option authors charge a premium for offering options. Numerous options authors provide options to produce earnings from the option premiums. As an outcome, these options authors usually are anticipating that the price of the underlying security will remain flat or stable. This will result in the option of losing worth as the time worth of the option decreases.

Option authors may also be aiming to create a more significant benefit from the movement in the underlying security. The author of call options will be speculating on a fall in the cost of the hidden safe, and the author of put options will be thinking on the increase in the value of the underlying security.

As the options to work out rests with the buyer, option authors can have their options worked out at any time before expiration. They will not know if or when their choices may be exercised. They are more most likely to be applied when the options are 'in-the-money' and close to expiry. An OPTION is in-the-money when it includes intrinsic value. That is, for a call options, the marketplace worth is above the strike cost of the option, and for a put options, the marketplace worth is listed below the strike price of the opportunity.

Option authors also bring a much higher level of risk compared to options purchasers. Whereas the maximum chance for the buyer of the option is restricted to the option premium, the situation is quite different for options authors. An author of exposed call options is, in theory, exposed to unrestricted threat as they are exposed to boosts in the worth of the underlying stock. As the marketplace worth of the underlying stock boosts, the option author has the threat of needing to buy the underlying stock at its market worth, nevertheless high that might be.

A put options author is exposed to the worth of the underlying stock at the strike rate. If it is worked out at the strike price, the author of the option has the responsibility to purchase this stock from the option holder. If the market worth of the stock falls to absolutely no and the option is worked out, the holder of the options is required to buy the useless stock from the option holder at the strike rate.

Call options.

A call option is the right to buy 100 shares of the underlying stock at the strike cost. When they acquire the option until the expiration date of options, this right can be exercised by the taker (purchaser) of options at any time.

Buyer of call options.

By purchasing a call option, you will produce a profit on your options if the market worth of the underlying stock increases by sufficient to cover the premium you spent for the call option and any decrease in time worth that happens while you hold the option. This boost in market value must happen before the expiry date of your options, the purchaser of a call option deals with a time deadline in which to produce a benefit from the transaction. If you chose to purchase the underlying stock straight, you could wait for your forecasted increase in market price to understand a revenue on your financial investment. However, by buying call options over the same stock, you do not have this advantage. You will stop working to generate earnings on your call options if the market value of the underlying stock does not increase by an adequate quantity before the expiry date of the call options.

Tip.

Time is a crucial aspect in identifying if an option purchaser generates make money from their call option. The market worth of the underlying stock must increase by an adequate.

Quantity before the expiry date for the buyer of a call Options, to realize revenue on their financial investment.

The purchaser of a call option is speculating (and hoping!) that the marketplace value of the underlying stock will increase in worth before the expiration date of the option. If the worth of the market underlying stock increases and the strike cost is less than the market value of the underlying stock, the quality of the option will also increase. This implies that the purchaser of the call option can either offer the call at a profit, or get the stock below the price of the present market worth.

Sellers of options call.

The call option sellers are maybe hoping that the market value of the underlying stock will fall or remain flat, as this will result in a decrease in the worth of the call option. The seller can then redeem the options at a lower cost and understand a profit. If the underlying stock is valued and listed below the strike rate of the options, it is extremely not likely that the options will be worked out. The purchaser of the call options is not going to buy the stock at a price higher than the current market price! On this occasion, the seller will merely wait up until the expiry date, at which time the options will end worthless. For this instance, the seller could retain the premium they got on the initial sale of the option as a revenue.

Comprehending call options from a seller's point of view is a bit harder to begin with. As a purchaser of a call option, you are following a buy-hold-sell pattern, which is much the same as buying the stock directly. The main distinctions are the ability to expose yourself to the stock at a fraction of the cost of the capital, and you have a restricted time duration to sell or exercise your option.

When offering a call option, you are reversing this pattern and following a sequence of sell-hold-buy, or simply sell-hold. You are providing your options first, expecting the price of your option to fall and then repurchasing it at a lower rate.

Or even much better still, you sell-hold, and if the option has no intrinsic worth at expiry, you have no need to redeem at all.

Put options

A put option offers the option buyer the right to sell 100 shares of the underlying stock at the strike cost. When they buy the options until the expiration date of options, this right can be exercised by the taker (purchaser) of the options at any time.

Buyers of put options

The worth of a put option will increase as the market value of the hidden security reduces listed below the strike cost of the option. The option holder has the right to offer their stock at a set rate, even though the market worth of the stock is falling. If the underlying stock market value of the falls by enough to cover the premium you paid for the, by buying put options, you will create revenue on your option put option. This fall in market value with all option, needs to happen before the expiration date of your option.

Put options supply the option purchaser with an opportunity to speculate on falls in the market's worth of stock. Thinking on falls in-stock rates straight in the stock exchange is described as trading short or short selling. Short selling of shares straight can be pricey and tough. Put options can effectively provide the means for buying quick. As soon as again, time is an aspect to think about when trading or investing in options. To produce earnings on your put option, the marketplace worth of the underlying stock should decrease by a sufficient amount before the expiry date of the put option.

Tip

Put options can be useful to protect earnings on your existing stock holdings. The premium can be thought about to be like paying for insurance against losses a fall in the marketplace value of your shares.

The put option buyer is speculating that the marketplace worth of the underlying stock will reduce in quality before the expiration date of the options. If the underlying stock market value decreases, the variety of the option will increase (if the options are in-the-money). This means that the put option buyer can either sell the put options at earnings or, if they hold the underlying security, sell this stock at a price above the present market worth.

Instead of speculating, the buyer of a put option may purely also be taking the option position to secure profits on existing shareholdings. If shares they hold have experienced a current increase in price and they think that the stock worth will fall in the brief term, rather than offering their stock, they could buy a put option that would secure their revenue. The fall in the value of their stock holding would be balanced out in part by the gain on their put options if the market worth of the underlying stock did fall.

Put options sellers

The put option seller hopes that the market value of the underlying stock will increase or stay flat, as this will lead to a decrease in the value of the put options. The seller can then redeem the options at a lower cost and understand a revenue. Additionally, if the value of the underlying stock is above the strike rate of the option, it is highly not likely that the option will be exercised. The purchaser of the put option is not going to offer their stock at a price lower than the present market cost! On this occasion, the seller will just wait until the expiry date, at which time the option will expire uselessly. The seller would keep the premium they received on the preliminary sale of the option as a profit.

When offering put options, as merely selling call options, you are following a series of sell-hold-buy or just sell-hold. You are providing your options initially, hoping for the price of the option to fall and then repurchasing it at a lower rate. Or, still better, you sell-hold, and if the market worth of the hidden security is above the strike rate, the option has no intrinsic value, and you have no need to purchase back at all.

Company issued options

The business released options are options that are issued straight by a business. The company sets the conditions and terms of the options, and they are not noted on an exchange. Usually, these options are issued to existing shareholders or crucial workers for the functions of raising additional capital. These options offer the shareholders the right to buy new shares at a set cost (workout rate) before a set date. In these circumstances, the business is the author of the options. And an obligation to fulfill any options that are exercised.

As the private companies provide these options for particular purposes, the terms and conditions of these options are figured out by the company issuing the options. Therefore, the conditions and terms, including the expiration date, workout rate, and several shares covered per option, will vary. You require to read the paperwork thoroughly to determine the terms and conditions and the treatments needed to work out the option if you are released these types of options.

Index Options

Options over a share price is called Index options. An index price is shared in a group of noted shares. Each share in the index is provided a calculation, and weighting is done using their weighting and current market cost to identify the index value. This index value is revealed in points.

Index options offer you direct exposure to a group of securities that consist of the share market index. This enables you to trade a position on the market as a whole, or the marketplace sector or business that make up the index you wish to purchase.

The Australia options, which is ASX options over the S&P/ ASX 200 index. This is an index that is computed based upon the top 200 companies noted on the ASX—trading these options successfully exposes you to movements in the total Australian stock exchange.

The worth of your index options will differ with motions in the quality of the index, which is reflective of the total value of the group of securities it represents. Moves in the S&P/ ASX 200 index are viewed as reflective of the movement in the overall sharemarket, as this index covers the most prominent 200 stocks noted on the ASX.

There are a few distinctions to keep in mind between index options and stock options, which we will now go over.

Index options are European design options. This implies that index options can not be worked out before the settlement date. You can, nevertheless, purchase and sell them before the workout date. Being European design options likewise suggests that there is no threat of new exercise for the seller. The sellers of index options do not require to fret about their options being exercised before the expiration date.

Index options are cash-settled. This suggests that the value of the index options is determined on the settlement date, and upon exercise, all options are closed out with the pertinent cash value. You will be paid the worth if your index option agreement is worth something. If your index option has no quality on the expiry date, it merely ends uselessly. The money quantity you receive on expiry is the distinction between the settlement worth of the exercise and the index worth of the index. If your index options are in-the-money, you will only receive a cash worth settlement value on expiry that is computed utilizing opening rates.

The settlement amount is computed using the initial rate of each stock in the underlying index on the expiry date early morning. For every stock in the index, the first traded cost or opening price is taped for each stock in the index. The value of the index is then determined to use these initial values.

The premium and standard index options prices in points are expressed. The index itself is a pointedly expressed, so it follows that the premium and strike rate of index options is also revealed in positions. Each index has multiplier in an index, which converts these indicate a dollar worth estimated at a premium of 20 points would cost you $500 to buy (20 points × the index multiplier of $25 = $500). Likewise, the value of an index option agreement is calculated as the strike price of the option increased by the index multiplier.

Advantages of index options

There are a variety of crucial advantages in purchasing index options. The same benefits of investing in share options that we talked about in chapter 1 also apply to index options. They are risk management, speculation, income, diversity, and leverage generation.

There are likewise some extra advantages you can achieve from trading or capitalizing options in index.

Broader market exposure

We are representing an index of a large parcel of stocks. Therefore, the index is frequently representative of the market as a whole or an essential sector of the market. Investing in index options enables you to purchase an option that tracks a specific index successfully.

This will approximate an investment because of a specific parcel of stocks, providing you direct exposure to a broader market. In this instance, you have the advantage of diversification as your investment does not bring risk connected to a particular business. This may be offset by the primary market motion of all the other companies in the index if one company in the index does not carry out well. You may benefit from being exposed to the broad market represented by the index, without needing to purchase each of the individual stocks that make up that particular index.

Portfolio Defense

Investors who hold shares of a portfolio may wish to combat the effect of a market recession without having to offer their shares. Taxation on the realization of the financial investment gain, plus deal expenses, are two reasons why a financier may consider using options, and in specific index options, to protect their share portfolio.

If the market portfolio does not fall in worth declines as an outcome, buying index put options can provide the financier with some settlement. The increase in the worth of their put options will balance out the fall in the value of their portfolio.

As alluded to in the past, there are numerous kinds of options from which a trader can take advantage that will then allow him or her to sell or purchase options. Also, there are subcategories of options with various stipulations and benefits. It is crucial to examine and be familiar with these to use options for optimum profit.

Traders keep in mind would do well to that options trading does take a lot of practice and just those who are well versed in options trading and mindful of the motion and trends of business and monetary institutions succeed in this specific sect of trading. Being said that, here are the various categories and subcategories of options trading. Every two items listed are combined with one another. The call option opposite is a put options, and the opposite of the American options is European options.

Calls: This is a type of options used in the example in the previous chapter. Calls are used by buyers, implying that if a trader has a call option, they have the right, however, are not bound to purchase an underlying property at the strike cost before a formerly agreed-upon the date expiration.

The trader always wants the buyer to value of the hidden asset to appreciate exponentially so that they can purchase the underlying possession at a strike cost that is much cheaper than the value of the security and, after that, offer the hidden ownership for enormous revenue. In-, at-, and out-of-the-money is another term for this. When the value of the hidden possession is higher than the strike price, the purchaser is in-the-money. When the worth is the same as the strike cost, the buyer is at-the-money, and they are out-of-the-money when the value is listed below the strike price.

Puts: Puts are the opposite of calls. Having put options implies the trader is a seller. In this case, the seller will expect the rate of the hidden possession dropping and will sell it at a high price before the cost drops, therefore gaining a profit. The price will require to drop before the expiration date and is the catch for the seller.

If this happens, then the buyer will likely have paid the seller the full strike rate, which will be more than the worth of the property.

The initial seller gain will be options premium used to secure the contract if the cost drops after the expiration date, nevertheless. This likewise means the seller is probably losing money on the underlying property, which they still own. There are two more catches to offering puts, and they both come down to the purchasers right, however not the responsibility, to bring out the options contract. If the rate plummets excessive before the option contract's expiration date, the purchaser may choose to give up purchasing the hidden security, and the seller will be entrusted just the premium as a reward. However, if the seller composes a put as part of a strategy, they will need to remember that the put can invariably be designated, and the investor will be required to offer. In concerns to the-- in, -at, and-- out-of-the-cash terms, the precise opposite of calls is exact of puts.

Before proceeding to the other kinds of options, here is a quick note concerning some short information relating to those who take part in options trading. There are four positions that can be held that fall into two categories. The very first category is made up of the "holders" and consists of those who buy calls and puts. The 2nd consists of "writers" who offer calls and puts. This is similar to what is referred to as long and short positions within the stock exchange, respectively. As specified in the past, the most crucial differentiation between the holders and writers (buyers and sellers) is those holders always buy but are never obliged to do so. In contrast, the obligated writers to buy or sell, which tends to make the writing position a hazardous one. This is less confusing as is it becomes these principles are talked about even more in later chapters of this book.

American Options: The very first thing to keep in mind when thinking about European and American options is that the kind of options bears no relation to geographical areas. The titles differentiate merely are the two types of options. Having specified this, American options are the most typically traded one, since they can be redeemed at any time during the life of the option, even up to maturity, likewise called the expiration date. This flexibility allows buyers to acquire the options when the worth is above the strike cost well before the expiration date, removing the chances that the worth will drop and the buyer will lose on the original amount they paid to buy the option. American options typically reach their expiration date on the 3rd Friday of the month.

European Options: options European differentiate from their American equivalents because the buyer or seller may exercise their rights only at the option's maturity. This enables far less flexibility and requires the trader to be incredibly positive of their position before participating in the acquired options contract. A crucial point of European options is that unlike American options, the expiration date is always on the last Thursday of the month.

Index Options: Index options follow the very same general principle meaning as stock options, with one significant difference: traded on indices options are. Popular options index to trade on are the S&P 500 Index, the Russell 2000 Index, the NASDAQ-100 Index, and on perhaps the most well-known index, the Dow Jones Industrial Average. The premium is usually settled in money. Also, index options are not consistently available. For instance, European-style index options are typically traded, however only minimal indices, such as the S&P 500, will use American-style options.

Equity Options: Equity in itself, usually speaking, is the value of the property minus the worth of that property's liabilities. In this case, aptly defines Investopedia equity options, also understood as equity derivative, as "an acquired instrument with underlying possessions based upon equity securities. An equity derivative's worth will fluctuate with changes in its underlying possession's equity, which is usually measured by share cost" (Investopedia, Equity Derivative). This can also be believed of as purchasing or offering options for a corporation's stock.

Short-Term Options: This is the kind of option that was used in the example. With short options, the expiration date for the option can be anywhere from a couple of minutes to a few days into the future. This all depends upon the agreement concurred upon in between the buyer and seller. Success in short-term options trading is dependent upon the instinct of the trader and his/her knowledge of the marketplace and underlying properties. For example, a trader who is well notified relating to only technology would not wish to buy a short-term option for a share of a growing art repair company. Instead, the trader should either adhere to what she or he knows or end up being informed about locations which the investor is interested in pursuing. Education is recommended, given that it expands the scope for success.

LEAP: For the functions of education, it may be practical for starting stock option traders to believe in LEAPs as long-lasting options. LEAP, which is mainly for Long-term Equity Anticipation Securities, stands advantageous for long-term investors because the expiration date maybe 39 months. With an extreme such length of time, there is an opportunity for higher fluidity and flexibility, permitting the worth of the asset to grow or perhaps recuperate if it diminishes throughout the life of the agreement.

Everyday Vanilla Options: This name is a fundamental description for an option with no included benefits or terms. When the options are offered, the kind of options (call or put), expiration date, strike price, and single hidden asset are currently figured out. Furthermore, "the options are effective at the existing date, and when exercised, its payoff equates to the difference in between the worth of the underlying possession and the strike cost" (Financial Dictionary). This is an appealing option due to its pure nature and is generally found as an exchange-traded option. As the most common and necessary options available, it is a popular and sensible starting place for newbie options traders.

Unique Options: A popular over-the-counter option, exotic options offer buyers and sellers the chance to include and customize acquired contracts on any extra stipulations at their discretion. With so many more balls to juggle, traders must be familiar with the market before venturing into exotic options. Different from European and American options, this kind of agreement can vary in terms of the hidden asset, expiration date, and strike cost.

For instance, if a buyer telephones for an option in which he pays the seller $400 for the option and agrees with the seller that the strike price is $2000 at an expiration date of 3 days from when the option was purchased, they can include another stipulation to it. In this case, state that the terms are that the agreement does not enter into effect until the value of the stock reaches a certain rate point. The buyer would not deserve to acquire the options until the worth of the stock reached the formerly concurred upon the mark. This is just one of the numerous variations of exotic options, all of which require to be studied meticulously before being put into usage.

Exchange-Traded Options: The options are majorly traded through an exchange, such as the Chicago Stock Exchange, therefore exchange-traded options, also called noted stock options, fall under this classification. The merits of an exchange-traded option is that the hidden possession, strike rate, expiration date, and quantity can be viewed in advance because they belong to a standardized agreement. This is also a feasible options because taking part in a contract using an established exchange guarantees that the individuals can use the clearinghouse. As a clearinghouse member, the trader is accountable for reporting positions at the end of the day and also keeping an adequate quantity of money. That shows the trader's place in a debit account. While this may sound extraneous and confusing, the settle is that the clearinghouse is responsible for agreements being satisfied, and thus the trader getting paid. Essentially, a clearinghouse is an intermediary between sellers and purchasers.

Over-the-Counter Options: These are options contracts that are created beyond an established trading group, thus the name. Also called OTC options,

non-prescription option "has a direct link in between the purchaser and seller, has no secondary market, and has no standardization of striking prices and expiration dates" (Nasdaq, Over-the-Counter Option). The downside here is that the buyer or seller would require to actively look for potential organization partners with whom to make a transaction instead of just choosing options to buy from a currently available list. The benefit of OTC options lies in the ability to tailor the crucial components. Therefore a buyer and seller might work out long positions for later expiration dates or perhaps swap the strike cost. Nevertheless, the contract requires to be taped in a dependable method since OTC options do not use the thanks to a clearinghouse to assist settle debts; the purchaser and seller must exchange funds themselves.

CHAPTER THREE

ImportancesOf Options Trading

In this chapter, we will outline a few of the primary benefits of trading in options and why you may consider purchasing or offering options as a part of your total trading method. We will also discuss the significant dangers in buying and providing options, remembering that the threats included in options are substantially various for buyers of options compared with the risks for sellers of options.

Benefits of option trading

When purchasing options, you are investing in an asset with no real worth, with a minimal life, and which may be worthless within a few months. As you will quickly find, there are numerous benefits of trading options that can be used in a wide variety of methods.

We will now describe a few of the main advantages of options. These are extended attributes that apply to options. As we talk about the types of options in more detail and the methods that can be used for each kind of options, you will see the benefits (and drawbacks) of trading options.

It is likewise fascinating to keep in mind that a benefit to a seller will typically equate as a downside to the buyer and vice versa. The factor this operates in the marketplace is, the reason or strategy used by the seller is different from the idea the purchaser has participated in the agreement.

Tips

When evaluating the benefits of using options, you likewise need to think about the risks associated with your particular options method.

The benefits we will talk about are:

- Danger management
- Speculation
- Leverage
- Diversification
- Income Generation.

Danger Management

Options provide financiers with the ability to manage danger within their portfolio. Options can provide a financier with a hedge versus falls in the price of their present stock holdings. It can effectively allow a financier to lock in some profits on their holding, without needing to sell their shares physically.

This can be useful when an investor wishes to maintain their shares for a longer-term or does not want to understand a capital gain by offering their investment at the current time.

Purchasing a put option allows you to buy the right to sell your present shares at an advantageous price if you are anticipating a fall in the cost of those shares before the expiry date of the option. The investors are allowed to make a gain on the put options that will offset a loss on the physical shares, on the occasion that the stocks do fall in value.

You own 3000 shares in a stock presently trading at $10.50. You want to secure some revenue at this price as you feel that the price is most likely to fall in the brief term. To use this strategy, you purchase 30 put option agreements with a strike cost of $10.50. This costs you to buy $0.20 per share contained in each agreement (with 100 shares in each transaction).

This purchase provides you the right to offer 3000 shares at $10.50 whenever before the options expiry date. Your put option value will increase by a similar quantity (less any ended time worth) if the stock rate subsequently falls. Thus you are safeguarding yourself against a fall in the price of your stock. A fall in worth of your stock will be balanced by a rise in the value of your options.

If the stock cost stays at or above $10.50, then you would either not exercise your options or sell your option close to the expiration date (although it would deserve very little).

If the stock rate does fall to, state, $9.50, then the worth of your put options would increase by $1.00 (less any expired time worth). You could then offer these options for approximately $1.00 and realize earnings of $3000.00. This will balance out the fall in worth of your shareholding of a similar amount. Effectively, you have paid $600.00 for your options to Defend you against the fall in the price of stock position.

Speculation

The capability to trade online and the listing of options on the ASX make it very simple to purchase and offer options. The options trading makes it possible for traders at ease to buy an option contract with the intent of selling the options before the expiration date for a revenue. The traders may have expectations of an increase in the rate of the option (due to a change in the cost of the underlying security). And no objective of ever exercising the option if your option has intrinsic value, the value of your options will change much in line with the change in worth of the underlying stock. You will also see a fall in quality that is unrelated to any change in worth of the hidden security but is due to a fall in the time value of the option as it nears expiry.

How option move with changes in the value of the underlying stock?. These movements are for options that have an intrinsic worth in their premium.

As a speculator, you can acquire call options if you are expecting the rate of the underlying security to increase. As the underlying price of security rises, the intrinsic value of your options will increase by a similar amount if you are anticipating the rate of the underlying security to fall, your method may be to buy put options as the price of the underlying security drops. The intrinsic options value will increase by a similar amount. To produce a profit, you need the worth of the underlying security to move in your favor before the expiry date, and you would need to offer your option on or before the expiration date.

When purchasing and after offering American style stock options as a method to generate short-term revenue, you need to ensure you sell your options before the expiry date. This requires the cost of the underlying stock to move in your favor before the expiry date.

Leverage

Leverage is the ability to produce the same level of return from a prospective financial investment; however, utilizing a smaller sized initial expense. If you owned the real shares, Purchasing a call option with intrinsic value exposes you to a comparable gain or loss that you would attain. The cost of a fraction of the price options of the underlying stock. This permits you to benefit from changes in the value of the stock without paying the full fee of the capital.

Leverage does come with a new threat; the gains are amplified through the usage, so too are any losses. Some examples show how force can create a more significant portion return than can direct financial investment.

Your returned percentage can be magnified as a result of the leverage achieved through the usage of options. It is necessary to note that your losses can be equally magnified in some circumstances. Nevertheless, when purchasing options, your loss will always be limited to the premium you spent on the opportunity.

Idea

When speculating using options, you need to represent the fall in time worth of your option and your deal costs when assessing your trading opportunity.

Diversification

The use of options can offer you the opportunity to benefit from the motion in the rate of a stock at a portion of the stock price. This permits you to construct a varied portfolio for a lower preliminary expense. This comes at a cost as your options include a value for the time of expiry, which will decrease to no over the life of the option.

Income generation

When selling an option, you get an advance premium from the purchaser of your option. The premium kept, whether or not the option has worked out. This premium can produce an income stream if carefully selected options are sold on a systematic basis. The seller maintains the premium and has no further commitment if the options are not exercised.

There are several methods based on offering options to generate premium income. The goal is to sell options that are not likely to be worked out, or purchase back (closeout) your options before the expiration date if there is a danger they will be exercised.

CHAPTER FOUR

Risks of Option Trading

Although there are various advantages to options, like all monetary investments, there are also risks related to trading in options. The threats differ, relying on the type of option and are somewhat different for the seller and the purchaser.

Similar to any financial investment, you should just trade options if you comprehend how they work and how they fit with your overall trading or investment technique. Besides, there are a variety of threats that specify options that you must know and prepared to manage.

The dangers we will talk about are:

- Market danger
- Risk of expiring useless
- Threat due to leverage
- Potential for limitless losses (as a seller of options).
- Danger of margin calls (as a seller of options).
- Liquidity danger.

Market danger.

For the buyer of an options, market risk is the threat that the marketplace value of your options will decrease, therefore stagnating in line with your expectation or speculation. The market value of your options is mainly impacted by the market price of the underlying security but is likewise affected by the time of expiration—the volatility of the cost of the hidden security and even motions in the rate of interest.

The market threat for the option author is the risk that the marketplace value of the underlying shares will transfer to develop or increase the intrinsic worth of the option. This will increase the opportunity of the option being worked out or create a loss for the seller in closing their position.

You require to ensure you have a plan to manage your market threat and have a method if the value of your options does stagnate in your direction. Option pricing is gone over in more information in the danger of expiring worthless.

The expiration date is the day on which you need to either sell the option, or exercise the to expire uselessly. If an option is without intrinsic value, the worth of the option will reduce as you approach the expiration date, and your time value deteriorates (this is referred to as time decay).

The intrinsic worth will just exist in an option in the following circumstances:

For call options, the intrinsic worth will be inherent when the strike price of the option is lower than the market worth of the underlying stock. The value intrinsic will then equal to the difference in these two amounts. This develops because you have the option to purchase the underlying stock at a rate listed below the current market price.

For put options, the scenario is the reverse. Your option will have value intrinsic when the market worth of the underlying stock is listed below the strike price of the option.

The risk of an expiring option worthless is a threat that the buyer of an option needs to bear. This is an advantage for the seller, as they profit from the option premium they gather when an option expires useless.

Risk due to use.

Simply as leverage has the prospective to amplify your earnings on a trade, use equally can magnify your losses. A reasonably small change in the value of the underlying security can lead to a significant portion change in the value of the option. When purchasing an option, the option rate is only a portion of the price of the underlying stock; nevertheless, your revenue or loss on the option is close to the quantity you would make if you had traded the underlying stock at its full value.

Tip.

Although leverage can amplify your revenue or loss on an option contract, when purchasing options, your damage is always limited to the premium you spent for the option.

Possible for endless losses (as a seller of options).

Sellers of options take the responsibility to offer (call options) or buy (put options) the underlying stock at the strike cost if the option is worked out by the buyer of the options. If you have offered call options, you commit to providing the underlying stock at the strike cost if your choice is worked out by the buyer. You are losing the value between the present market cost of the strike and the stock price if you currently own the stock. You have offered an exposed option if you do not own the underlying stock. You will need to purchase the stock on the market at the current market value and deliver it to the option buyer who has worked out the option. As the marketplace value of the underlying stock has no theoretical limit, your losses on selling exposed call options are potentially endless.

As a put options seller, you have the responsibility to purchase the underlying stock at the strike rate if the purchaser exercises your option. If the marketplace worth of the underlying stock was up to or near absolutely no, you are still obliged to buy the stock, which is nearly useless at the strike cost. As the underlying stock cost can just fall to absolutely no, your losses as a seller of put options are only limited to the value of the underlying stock at the strike cost.

Risk of margin calls (as an option seller).

When you offer an option, you are required to provide security (referred to as a margin) to show that you can fulfill your responsibilities if the option is exercised. This margin can be in the type of the security underlying (if a call option), other collateral or cash value. If option increases in value, thus breaking you as a seller, you may be required to offer additional margin to cover the boost in your responsibility.

Typically, margins are needed to be paid within 24 hours, but your broker sets this time frame. If you fail to supply an additional margin upon demand within the required amount of time, your broker will have the ability to close out your option position or liquidate some or all of your existing shareholdings to satisfy your margin requirements.

Liquidity risk.

Market makers are the firms that offer quote prices (cost you get on selling an option) and deal costs (cost you pay on buying an option) for an option in a range. They will provide an options market for the most part; nevertheless, they do have the scope in terms of the rates, number of options, and times that they need to price estimate a bid and ask the cost for an option.

Tip.

In times of high volatility, the cost of your options might not move as you expect. The value of the underlying security might relocate your instructions; nevertheless, the option value may be adjusted for the threat of significant movement in the underlying security (the high volatility), suggesting that your option position does not reflect any earnings on the transaction.

CHAPTER FIVE

Option Pricing

The marketplace forces affecting the worth of stocks will, later on, impact the marketplace worth of the options attached to those stocks. The option itself has no underlying quality-- its value is obtained from the worth of the capital and your capability to buy or offer that stock.

In this chapter, explore we shall on the two components of an option rate. These parts are intrinsic worth and time value. We will look at the areas that impact the price of options, and how these areas vary from the aspects which affect the cost of a stock.

Stock rates versus option prices

Stocks provided by a company are limited in number, and as a result, their price is influenced by the forces of demand and supply. Like any limited product, if more individuals desire to buy a stock than individuals willing to sell, the rate will naturally increase. Likewise, if more people want to offer their stocks, and there are few buyers, the stock price will fall. The most extreme example of this is during a stock exchange crash, or correction, where sellers are flooding the market and, in the lack of any substantial purchasers, the rate falls dramatically.

Broadly, influence in the stock price by the performance (both actual and expected) of the company and all the industrial and financial elements that affect that real and anticipated performance.

With exchange-traded options, the exchange will permit investors to sell any number and buy options. They are not constrained by the variety of shares released of the underlying stock. Therefore, the price of options is impacted only indirectly by the forces of supply and need as they are not a restricted product.

The option value is mainly affected by the movement in the rate of the stock underlying, and by the time of passage. These factors are known as intrinsic value and time worth. To add further intricacy on various factors will affect the intrinsic value and the time value of any option price.

Option premium = intrinsic value + time worth

Intrinsic worth

Intrinsic value is the difference between the marketplace worth of the underlying stock and the strike value of the option. This is the most quickly understood element of an option cost as it represents a specified advantage that can be easily measured.

Intrinsic worth represents the ability to offer an underlying share above the marketplace cost (put option) or to purchase the underlying stock below the current market value (call option).

In-the-money options

Options that have intrinsic value in their rates are referred to as being 'in-the-money.' For call options, this suggests that the strike price of the option is listed below the current market price of the hidden share; therefore, there is value in working out the option. The value intrinsic is present as the option holder can exercise their option and buy the hidden shares for a rate lower than they might on the marketplace.

Out-of-the-money options.

Options that have no intrinsic worth in their pricing are described as being 'out-of-the-money.' For call options, this implies that the strike rate is above the current market value; therefore, there is no value in working out the option. There is no merit to buy shares at a price more significant than you might pay on the free market.

Call options offer the purchaser the right; however, not the responsibility to buy the hidden shares. It is better to purchase the shares on the share market directly if your options are out-of-the-money, and you wish to acquire the secret shares.

Option rates Suggestion.

Put options offer the buyer with the right; however, not the obligation to sell the hidden shares. If your options are out-of-the-money and wish you to sell your shares, it is much better to sell them on the sharemarket straight.

At-the-money options.

As suggests the name, an at-the-money option is an option where the strike rate of the option is equal to the current market price of the underlying shares. Let's consider this, as an example:

You are considering buying a $35.50 CSL call option as you think the market cost of CSL will rise significantly in the next two months. The current market rate of CSL is likewise $35.50.

These options are at-the-money; the option premium includes time worth just. There is no intrinsic worth in at-the-money options.

Time value.

Time value is a little bit harder to understand than intrinsic worth. Time value is the quantity you are prepared to spend on the possibility that the market will move in your favor throughout the life of an option so that you will profit on your purchase.

Time value in options will differ with in-the-money, out-of-the-money, and at-the-money options since each situation provides different opportunities and possibilities of a boost in the intrinsic value of choice. This is typical, the time value is most significant on at-the-money options, as this presents a chance for constructing inherent value into the option if the market relocates the ideal direction.

The further the strike cost is from the market value of the underlying stock; the following elements influence the less time worth the option will have time value:

- Time to expiry
- Volatility
- Rates of interest
- Dividend payments

- Market expectations.
- Time to expiry

The most apparent aspect impacting the time worth of an option is time itself. As valued time represents the possibility of a market motion in your favor, it follows that the more time you have in which to attain this market motion, the higher the chance is of it occurring. Hence, the longer the period left on an option contract, the higher the time worth will be. As the time draws close to the expiry date on your option, the chance for the option to increase in value minimizes. Hence, the valued time of your option reduces. This decrease in time value over the life of an option is called time decay.

Time decay is not a direct variable. That is, the time worth consisted of within an option cost does not minimize at a constant rate. Time worth lowers at a faster rate as you get closer to the expiration date.

When picking the expiration month of your option, you need to weigh up the cost of the option (which will be higher with more time to expiration) with the time required for your technique to work in your favor.

Volatility is the variety and speed in which a rate relocations. When a rate relocations by a large quantity within a short area of time, said it is to volatility high.

A buyer is looking for an option the price of the hidden share to move by an enough quantity to make a revenue on the option. For that reason, it follows that the volatility, or the range and speed in which the underlying stock relocations, will impact the price of the option.

The higher the volatility of the hidden share, the greater the time value of the option. Consider an option that is currently out-of-the-money. If the hidden share cost usually relocates a large variety within a brief space of time, it is more likely that the option will move into the cash and develop a value for the purchaser. As valued time represents the possibility of the marketplace relocating your instructions, it follows that options over show greater volatility will consist of a higher time value.

Rates of interest

When you purchase a call option, you have the benefit of taking advantage of as you just require to pay a fraction of the cost of the underlying stock to be exposed to movements in the price of that stock. For this factor, when interest rates increase, call option premiums will also increase in value.

You are successfully delaying the sale of your underlying stock up until you exercise the option when you purchase a put option. Put another way; you are postponing the time at which you receive payment for the sale of your stock up until you exercise your option. You would have those funds to invest in other places if you sold your stock right away. When interest rates increase, put option premiums fall as this delay in getting funds now carries a higher chance expense.

A rise in interest rates will trigger the premium of call options to trigger the bonus and increase on put options to fall.

Dividend payments

When a business states a dividend payable to shareholders, both it announces dividend payment date and an ex-dividend date. When trading options, it is the date that the ex-dividend is very important. The day that ex-dividend date on which all investors who own the appropriate class of shares at the end of trade on that day will be entitled to the dividend payment. The next day, the share price falls typically by an amount similar to the dividend amount, as anybody who purchases shares on that day dividend will not be entitled. The dividend will be paid to the owner of the shares on the ex-dividend date, despite whether they still own the shares on the payment date.

A lot of significant businesses reveal and pay dividends at a comparable time each year and frequently at relative quantities. They will likewise provide income updates and other details to permit financiers to approximate the timing and amount of prospective dividends.

When selecting and pricing options, it is, therefore, crucial to consider any upcoming dividend announcements or ex-dividend dates. If the shares underlying has an ex-dividend date throughout the life of an option, this will affect the intrinsic worth of the option, without the option holder has any rights to any dividends. For this factor, any anticipated dividend announcements will be constructed into the option premium.

Market expectations

Ultimately, it is the expectations of purchasers and sellers that figure out the marketplace value of options. This will be constructed into the rate of any option premiums if the sellers and purchasers have an expectation of a particular movement in the market rate of the hidden shares

Pricing models

As we have already detailed in this chapter, numerous factors will affect the premium price of an option. You need to consider the strike rate, the cost and volatility of the underlying stock, the time delegated expiry, anticipated dividends, and rates of interest in determining the reasonable worth of an option. An option model pricing is a formula that combines all of these factors to compute a fair value for you.

If options are priced at a reasonable value in the market, option prices models are used by financiers and traders to help them to identify. It is essential to note that the 'reasonable value' calculated by a rates model might not be the current market cost or the price quoted on the market by market makers. You still require to match a ready seller and a willing purchaser to sell an option and buy.

You do not need to be a specialist on option pricing designs to use one. An understanding of how they work suffices to be able to use an option pricing model to estimate the fair value of an option.

The ASX offers a theoretical option cost calculator on its site that you can use to compute a reasonable value for an option.

The calculator provide you also with estimates for all of the variables, including dividend and volatility, which you can change.

Some of the factors that affect an option cost are understood, consisting of the strike price, market value of the underlying stock, and the time to expiry. Other aspects, such as anticipated dividends, interest rate changes in specific the volatility of the underlying stock, require to be estimated to calculate a fair worth. The two financiers utilizing the same rates design might still compute a different reasonable value for the very same option if their assumptions about volatility and dividends are various.

Volatility Approximating

In estimating the underlying stock volatility, you require to consider both the historical volatility and the suggested volatility. Historical volatility uses the rate range of the underlying stock over a recent duration and measures the actual fluctuations over this period. If you are utilizing historical volatility, you are assuming that the underlying stock will continue to behave comparably over the life of the option. The current market value of options has been based on the marketplace, view of the anticipated volatility of an underlying stock over the life of options. This likely most will be based on historical volatility; other expectations will be built into this estimation. The worth intrinsic in the present market rate of the option is called suggested volatility.

Fair worth versus market worth

Based on your estimates of dividends, projection rate of interest, and volatility, you are able to use an option price calculator to determine what you feel is the reasonable worth for an option. You then require to choose if you wish to participate in an option deal at the current market value. You can execute a trading strategy to profit from this chance if you feel that an option is mispriced in the market.

In basic terms, if you examine that an option is misestimated (generally as the indicated volatility is too high), then techniques involving writing options may fit as you have evaluated that the option premiums are currently too high. Additionally, if you assess that an option is underestimated (the suggested volatility is too low), then strategies involving purchasing options will permit you to buy options you consider are priced listed below their reasonable value.

CHAPTER SIX

Ways to Buy, Sell Or Options Exercise

This chapter, we shall look at the mechanics of options trading, how to open a position, and how you can then close your employment opportunity if you want to. We will also look at how you sell options and the margin requirements that are connected to offering options.

Towards the end of this chapter, we go over the new documents requirements you require to finish to trade options with your broker and how this may impact the option strategies your broker will permit you to carry out with them. Our last subject is the makers of the market. We discuss what they do and who they are.

Opening a position

As we discussed in chapter 1, you need to define or select the four essential regards to your option before you can sell an option or buy. The four basic terms (strike rate, the expiration date, the underlying stock, and if you are trading a put option or a call option) is set by the exchange. For underlying each commodity, there will be a series of a variety of put and call options offered that have numerous strike costs and expiration dates. A list of the complete options is provided from the exchange and also from many brokers.

It is referred to as trade opening. Whenever you enter an options trade by either purchasing or selling an option. If you offered an option, it is a first sale, and if you bought an option, it is an opening purchase. Your option position, either as a seller or a purchaser, is described as an employment opportunity.

The overall variety of open contracts in a specific type of option is described as the interest open. The options by their code are listed, with a bid rate and an asking price. The bid cost is the cost at which someone wants to purchase this specific option, and the asking price is the cost at which somebody is willing to offer the option.

If you wish to purchase an option, you will put your order through your broker, just as you would buy a share. If you want to sell an option, you would likewise place your sale order through your broker.

You are able to place market and limit orders both for options. A market order is an order to sell or purchase at the best cost currently readily available on the market. A limit order is an order to sell or buy at a specific price only.

You might wish to continue to hold that position if you currently have an open area that is nearing its expiry date. It is possible to use a mix order to execute both of these trades in a single order. You can define the net cost at which you want to roll over your position, but you do not require to determine a cost for the leg of each trade. If the order goes through, the close of both the preliminary position and the opening of a new location will be carried out at the same time.

It is vital to note options orders all on the ASX are suitable for day orders. This means that any requests that have not been filled at the end of the trading day will be erased. If you still want to put your order the next day, you will require to place a new order in the early morning.

Closing a position

To close your option position, you just place an order to cancel out your employment opportunity. To narrow your option position, you would put an order to sell the same type and amount of the option contract if you had acquired an option.

Clearing Options

The clearing and settlement functions for the options market are entirely various from the market share. On the market share, all the trades are executed between a specific buyer and seller, and settlement of the business takes place three trading days later on. In Australia, the ASX does the functions of both solutions and trades.

Trading of Options on the ASX; however, a separate organization, ASX Clear, is accountable for the settlement function. This needs ASX Clear to both clear all options that are traded on the ASX and ensure that all contractual responsibilities associating with options are met. If an option holder wants to exercise their option, ASX Clear is accountable for ensuring that they designate this to an option seller and that the seller satisfies this obligation.

When you position an option order through your broker, your broker becomes your trading participant and is accountable for registering your trade with the ASX. When the trade is carried out, a contract is produced between your broker and the other celebration's broker. This contract is called the marketplace contract. At this point, a procedure of novation occurs in which the market agreement is changed by two separate agreements are as followed:

Between the broker and ASX contract Clear

A contract between the other celebration's broker and ASX Clear.

Under this procedure of novation, ASX Clear becomes the counterparty to all open option positions. As an option buyer, you do not require to evaluate the credit danger of the seller and their capability to satisfy their commitments if you decide to work out or sell your option.

Purchasing or selling an option develops an agreement between parties. Unlike when you are buying or offer shares, there is no transfer of ownership or title to the underlying shares.

Option settlement

As we have simply described, ASX Clear is accountable for the settlement of all OPTION contracts. Solution for options agreements occurs one service day after the trade date. This is typically described as T +1 (where T stands for transaction day). This is different from share deals, which pick the 3rd service day after the agreement and are referred to as T +3.

You need to pay your premium one service day after you purchase it if you buy an options contract. You will receive the incentive of one business day after you have sold it if you offer an option.

Exercise options

If you exercise or wish to buy your option, you require to notify your broker who is required to send a workout notice to ASX Clear. When ASX Clear receives a workout notice, it will arbitrarily choose an author who has sold the same type of OPTION and will designate the workout to the writer. It is far too late to liquidate your position as soon as ASX Clear has assigned a workout notice to an option you have offered.

When an option is worked out, the transaction is settled within three working days after the option is exercised; that is, T +3. This is in line with the stocks of settlement. This is a reason that the option's writer can purchase the underlying stock from the marketplace (which settles T 3) if they require to adhere to the workout of a call option, and they do not presently hold that stock. You will receive and pay for the underlying shares three service days after exercise if you exercise your call option. If you have offered a call option that is applied, you will receive payment for the shares at the strike rate and need to deliver the shares three service days after the exercise. Option agreements are settled T +1.

The workout of options are settled T +3. If you exercise or do not an in-the-money OPTION before the expiry date, it will end worthless, despite just how much intrinsic value might be attached to that options. To prevent this, you need to guarantee that you monitor your option positions and either offer or exercise your options before the date of expiry.

It is possible to set account for trading to auto-exercise so that your options will automatically be exercised if they are in-the-money at expiry. This is particularly helpful for cash-settled index options, as the workout of the options continually leads to a cash payment rather than the delivery of an underlying share.

Trading expenses

Payable Brokerage will be on any OPTION orders that are carried out. Brokerage rates will differ in between brokers and might be payable at a flat rate or as a percentage based upon the option premium, or a mix of both a flat rate and a portion. You will need to consult private brokers to identify the brokerage rates and structure that will best suit you. ASX Clear likewise charges a cost per contract, which may be included in your brokerage or may be charged to you separately by your broker. Youwill also pay an exercise fee if you want to exercise your OPTION.

Limits

When you write a contract of an OPTION, you have a prospective obligation to deliver the underlying shares if that OPTION is worked out. As an OPTION author, you may likewise have potentially limitless danger if the market moves versus your position. To ensure you can fulfill this obligation, ASX Clear requires all options writers to provide a margin.

Tip

If you offer an options agreement, you only need to supply a margin. Option buyers need not provide any margin for their employment opportunities.

ASX Clear determines the quantity of a security that it deems needed to ensure that the option's writer can meet their obligations under the options contract. As the options agreement worth is impacted by the market price of the underlying stock, the value of any margin requirement will also change as the market price of the underlying stock changes.

ASX Clear computes the margin requirements utilizing a system referred to as the ASX Margining DERIVATIVE System (ADMS). This marginal calculation of requirement using a set formula that considers the current option premium and the volatility of the hidden security.

The margin needed for options consists of two parts:

- **A margin premium**

The margin is the premium value of the premium connected to your OPTION at the close of every day. This is generally the quantity you would need to close out your option position by buying the same type of options.

The risk margin is developed to cover the possible motion in the premium margin on any given day. This is determined by the recommendation to the intraday movement of the price of the hidden share, and this movement is referred to as the daily volatility. This volatility is expressed as a portion and understood as the margin period. The ASX publishes and updates the margin for all OPTION classes each week.

Tip

Your margin requirement will be computed on your whole portfolio of open options agreements so that some positions might offset the margin requirements of other positions every day.

As you understand, because of the procedure of novation. ASX Clear has a broker contract with your option agreement, instead of with you straight. ASX Clear will enforce the margin on your broker, who will, in turn, require you to offer them with a margin for your option contract. You must know that your broker might examine your margin threat differently to ASX

Clear and need a more significant margin than that calculated under ADMS.

How to pay your margin

As an OPTION seller, you will need to provide either cash or other security to cover your margin. The additional collateral generally includes shares you own or bank assurances. If you are offering shares as collateral, your broker might need more than your margin to guarantee versus any harmful falls in those share values.

Usually, your broker will establish a separate options account where they will hold your margin, including the premium you got on offering the options agreement. They will then move shares or money between your trading account, and your options account as required to cover your margin. When you close your options contract, and it has been settled, they will transfer the value of your options account back to your trading account.

When your margin boosts and you do not have the readily available funds in your trading account, you will get a margin call from your broker. This will need you to deposit extra funds or security to cover the margin within a set amount of time, usually 24 hours. If you are unable to or stop working to meet a margin call, your broker might close out your OPTION positions without further reference to you.

Opening an options account.

To purchase or write an option, you will need to open an account of an option with your broker. You will sign an Options if need Client Agreement, which remains in addition to the brokerage contract you require for a share trading account with your broker. As part of the processes of setting up an options trading, your broker needs to identify your suitability for this type of trading technique. It is most likely they will ask you to finish a questionnaire to assess whether options are an appropriate investment for you. You might be requested details about your financial investment experience, financial position, danger tolerance understanding of options, and your business goals in trading options. Your broker might limit the techniques you can trade through them based on your responses to those questions.

Market makers

The ASX will establish many original series of options that are available for traders and financiers to sell and purchase. However, there may not always be providing retail traders a bid and ask rate for every single individual option. Market makers are the banks that can provide quotes and offers on the market so that financiers and traders can purchase and sell options for which there is not a retail counterparty. Having market makers offer these bids and ask likewise helps with valuing an options position.

There not be a difference for you if you purchase from or sell to a market maker than if you are buying from or sell to a retail investor. In truth, you will not understand if your option trade is with a market maker or a retail investor.

Market makers are financial organizations that run as professional traders and generally trade a wide variety of monetary instruments. They get a cost from the ASX to provide the quote and ask rates for options. Required to meet the requirements on the variety of agreements provided, the spread between the bid and ask price, and the duration over which they offer these contracts. The range is the distinction between the quoted rate (price at which the market maker is ready to buy an option) and the asking cost (price at which the market maker wants to offer an option).

You need to think about the spread as an expense of your options method. Throughout this book, we describe options examples with the market value of the options being a particular cost. In reality, there will be a cost to buy the options and a rate to sell the options. The range between these rates will add to the price of any options method.

Tip: The spread is tight (less difference between the ask and bid prices), the better for you as a financier. A big spread means that it will cost you more to leave your position.

Market makers are not required to offer a market all day every day. There is no warranty that the option you want to trade will have a price and amount available to trade. Specific occasions, such as company statements, high volatility in the underlying stock, or low liquidity in the underlying stock, will affect when market makers supply their bid and ask quotes. If a quote is not readily available for the options you wish to trade, you can request a quote from the market maker through your broker. Even still, it is sensible to have a plan if the marketplace maker does not offer a quote for your option, especially if you require to close an open option position.

CHAPTER SEVEN

How To Pick Option Strategy

When selecting an option technique, in this chapter, we will look at the essential factors you require to consider. When share trading, you have chance to purchase the option , then sell or hold your position. With options, there are many more options, each with various risks and chances.

No matter the method you pick, your objective will be to either earn a profit or restrict a prospective loss. In pursuit of these objectives, as a buyer of options you seek to purchase your OPTION at the most affordable price possible, and after that offer it (or exercise it) at the highest price reasonable. As an options writer, you work directly against the buyers in seeking to offer your options at the highest cost possible, and after that, close them out at the most affordable price possible or see them end useless.

For any options trade, the motion in the OPTION premium while you hold it will identify if you earn a profit or loss. You, for that reason, should think about all the elements that will trigger a modification in your OPTION premium. These aspects include: Movement in the rate of the underlying stock (and all the factors that might affect this).

Time to expiration and time decay

Modifications in volatility.

This is share trading in contrast, where you only require to consider the motion in the cost of the stock. Time decay and modifications in volatility are distinct to trading options. Although the motion in the price of the underlying stock is the most significant element affecting most options, it is essential to consider the impact of time decay and any modifications in the volatility of the underlying stock cost when crafting your option trading strategy.

Pointer.

Even if the underlying stock price is in relocations in your direction, you can still make a loss due to the impact of time decay or an unforeseen modification in volatility.

Movement in price.

The most significant factor affecting the cost of your option is motions in the cost of the underlying stock. You need the view of formed how the market cost of the underlying stock move is going. Since the time limitations in trading options, you likewise need to form a view of the cost motion of the underlying stock over a particular time duration and match your options expiration to this frame time.

You can determine your view on the movement price of the underlying stock using fundamental analysis, technical analysis, or a mix of both. The technique used to form your opinion is not appropriate to choose your options technique, as long as you can hypothesize about the movement of rate within the restricted life of an OPTION.

The following general guidelines can be used about picking an OPTIONS method based on your view of the cost motion in the underlying stock:

If you are anticipating significant movement in the market cost of the underlying stock, purchasing options might be a suitable technique. If you are not expecting a substantial motion in the market rate of the underlying stock, writing options may be an ideal strategy.

The impact of time decay is the reason. For an option buyer, any favorable movement in the market price of the underlying stock needs to be large enough to offset the time decay experienced while holding the option. The change in the market price of the underlying stock requirements to be significant enough to put the option in-the-money (if it is not there already), and boost intrinsic value sufficient to offset the reduction in time worth.

You might consider composing options as a method if you are expecting that the rate of the underlying stock will stay within a limited cost range. Once again, time decay, the reason for this is. If the underlying stock rate remains reasonably static, there will be little change in the intrinsic worth and a decline in time value, triggering the cost of the options to fall. The revenue capacity for an option writer is always the premium got, so big price motions in their favor are not beneficial to OPTION authors as they do not affect the revenue made.

Tip.

Option writers are typically looking for time decay to minimize the value of the options they compose so that their options expire worthlessly. The options author then keeps the option premium as a revenue.

Time decay.

All options have a minimal life that is specified by the option expiry date. All options will go through time decay over the life of the opportunity, and this reduction in time value will increase as the OPTION approaches the expiry date.

Time works against options buyers as they are speculating on a considerable cost movement in the underlying stock to happen before the expiration date. Not just do option purchasers require to hypothesize on a price motion, this motion should take place before the expiration date.

Tip.

Your view on the timing of cost movement in the underlying stock will affect your option of the expiry month.

Time decay likewise works against OPTION buyers, as it lowers the value of an OPTION regardless of any other favorable movements in the price of the underlying stock. Any increase in the intrinsic worth of options will consistently be minimized by the time decay of the OPTION.

As an OPTION purchaser choosing an expiry month, you need to balance versus having sufficient time for the stock price to relocate your favor and the cost of this time. Longer-dated options have a more significant time worth and, as a result, will likewise have a more significant premium. The OPTION strategy success will be extremely reliant upon the time that you have to the options expiration date, and the quantity you spent for that time.

As an OPTION seller, you need to stabilize the additional premium you get for longer-dated options versus the increased possibility that the underlying stock price will move against you in this time, and you will incur losses over and above your option premium.

Volatility.

Volatility is the cost variety in which the underlying stock to move is expected. As discussed earlier in chapter 4 on pricing, the volatility of the underlying stock is an essential element determining the time value of an option. This will impact the time value and, therefore, the premium rate of an option if there is a significant change in volatility in the underlying stock.

If the volatility of the underlying stock lowers, this suggests that the price range in which the stock will move has been decreased.

It then follows that the value of time of the option will drop as the stock is less likely to attain a rate motion that will lead to a profit for the buyer of an option.

Therefore, if you have an unforeseen increase in the volatility of the underlying stock rate, this will increase the time worth of the options.

You have been enjoying the price of a mining stock for a long time. It has been moving within a minimal range in the last couple of months and has been experiencing decreased volatility recently. You feel the stock is going to break out into a trending upward relocation, which will develop a significant increase in the volatility of the stock rate.

In thinking about buying options over this stock, you require to consider your view of a boost in the rate of the capital, and an increase in the volatility of the stock rate. The motion in the stock price will impact the cost of the option the impact of this motion on your option price will depend on the kind of OPTION you purchase and the present market value of the stock concerning the strike rate of the options (that is, in-the-money it is).

The volatility in a change of the underlying stock cost will cause an increase to the options premium if this change has not been prepared for by the market and priced into the options already.

If you determine that a stock rate will experience a boost in cost volatility, a strategy involving buying options is likely to be beneficial as this will lead to an increase in time worth of your OPTION. If the stock price determined will experience a reduction in volatility, this will benefit an option writer by reducing the worth of the OPTIONs.

CHAPTER EIGHT

Techniques For Buying Call Options

In this chapter, we will talk about some general qualities, risks, and advantages included explicitly in techniques for purchasing call options. Usually, buyers of call options have a bullish view about the marketplace cost of a specific stock and are looking to benefit from this predicted increase in market price.

The most well-known technique for buying call options is speculating on a boost in the market worth of the underlying stock. It is an essential strategy that is more popular than purchasing put options, as it is more easily comprehended. In this chapter, we take a look at the thoughtful approach along with a variety of other less popular techniques, including purchasing call options.

Purchasing call options.

When buying call options, you are hypothesizing that the rate of the underlying stock will increase by a substantial amount within the restricted time duration to produce a revenue. The percentage returns on your trade if you are proven proper are enormous. If you are incorrect, you can lose some or all of the premium initial you paid.

Buying the right to you are to purchase 100 shares of the underlying stock at the strike cost at any time before the expiry date. You pay a premium for this right. Once you have bought your OPTION, you have three options:

- Sell your Options before expiry.

- Exercise your options before expiration.

- Allow the option to expire worthlessly.

As outlined earlier in chapter 6, the action you take will rely on the movement in the market rate of the hidden share, your expectation of any future motion before expiry, your factors for purchasing the call, and your danger tolerance.

Time is a substantial aspect of figuring out how you manage your options trade. Everyday options that you hold, the value time of your option will decrease. And it will reduce at an increasing rate as you approach the expiration date. In truth, even if the market price of the underlying stock increases before expiry, you might still lose cash on your OPTION due to the impact of time decay, counteracting any increase in intrinsic value.

Tip: The most significant problem for call option buyers is the lack of time and declining time worth in their options. Typically the market value of the underlying stock will increase over the life of the OPTION; however, it may not increase by enough to offset the decline in time worth. As a result, the buyer of the call option does not earn earnings on their investment.

Methods for purchasing call options

When the price of the WPL market was $40.00, you chose to buy a $40.00 WPL call option for $3.50. By the expiration date, the cost of WPL risen had to $42.00; however, your call option was now only worth $2.00.

How can you have money lost on your OPTION when the market cost of the underlying stock has risen?

When you bought your OPTION, it was at-the-money. As a result, the overall option premium of $3.50 consisted of time worth. Even though the stock cost increased by $2.00 and the intrinsic worth of your option increased by $2.00, this was offset by time decay of $3.50.

- Increase in intrinsic value$ 2.00.

- Decline in time value($ 3.50).
- Your net loss on the options *($ 1.50).

This estimation does not consist of deal costs. The above example shows that to earn a profit on buying a call OPTION, the marketplace worth of the underlying stock requirements to increase by enough to both:

- Balanced out the time decay.
- Create development in the intrinsic value of the OPTION.

There are several factors why you may think about buying call options as your trading technique. These include the following:

- Gain use
- Limitation your threat
- Hold-up a stock purchase
- Hypothesize for revenue.

Method 1: gain use.

Purchasing call options supply you with the benefit of taking advantage of. You need only to provide a fraction of the capital to purchase call options compared to buying the stock outright. This allows you to magnify your portion returns if you are proven proper.

Method 2: limit your danger.

Getting call options, instead of acquiring the stock directly, also allows you to limit your losses if the stock cost falls. You might wish to speculate on a boost in the market worth of a specific stock; however, you might also not want to be exposed to prospective losses if the marketplace value falls considerably. If the stock you purchase, you are exposed to the full quantity of any fall in the stock cost. With call options, nevertheless, you can just ever lose the premium you paid, despite how far the stock rate might fall.

Method 3: postpone a stock purchase.

When you purchase a call option, you are purchasing the right to buy 100 shares of the underlying stock at the strike price anytime on or before the expiry date. Therefore, you are securing the rate you will pay for the shares if you decide to work out the OPTION and buy the stock before the expiry date of the options.

You may want to invest long term in a specific stock as you feel it will increase in worth; nevertheless, for some factor, you wish to delay your purchase. Or perhaps you want to buy the stock however wishes to see it increase in worth first to confirm your analysis of an anticipated price boost. Buying a call option permits you to postpone your purchase but still lock in the price at which you will acquire the stock. The marketplace has experienced some substantial falls in value recently, and you wish to take advantage of the price depressed. There is a stock single you have been watching that, before the fall, was trading over $30 per share and is now trading at merely $18 per share. You think that the cost will rebound; however, you do not have the funds offered at this time.

You choose to buy a $19 call OPTION that has five months to expiry. The premium is $1. This purchase provides you the option to acquire the stock at $19 per share whenever in the next five months. You have five months to raise funds to purchase the shares and still purchase them at $19. Based upon what the stock rate does over this time, you can choose to offer your call options or exercise your call options and buy the stock at $19.

Method 4: hypothesize for profit.

A significant factor for buying call options is hypothesizing to generate short-term revenue. You are just speculating on the cost of the underlying stock rising by enough total up to make earnings on your options. You are not acquiring the call options with any intent to exercise them.

Time decay will trigger the worth of the call option to fall as long as you are holding the Option. For this factor, you need to be mindful of how you select the call options you wish to trade. You will require to stabilize the time you need for the stock to move in your instructions against the time value (expense) in the options premium.

You likewise require to consider the strike price concerning the current market price of the stock underlying. You need options to be in-the-money to produce a boost in intrinsic worth. Call options will be more affordable when they are out-of-the-money, as more extensive price motion is needed to generate inherent value in the option.

Conditions you should search for in selecting a call OPTION for speculation consist of:

The strike price need to be close to the current market value of the stock. When they are in-the-money options, this will ensure that the boost in the underlying stock cost will be shown in the price of your option.

The expiry time must be extended enough for your stock cost to increase adequately to balance out the time decay and create a profit on your call options.

Options with a low time value in the premium will lower.

The time decay, your options will sustain. As value time is the worth of the possibility of your options producing a revenue, call options will have a low time value if the market perception is that the underlying stock cost will remain steady or reduction.

You have been watching a mining stock just recently whose share price has been quite flat for a long time at around $25.00. Based upon your analysis, you believe the stock price will break out of its existing price range and move considerably upward by a minimum of $4.00 within a few weeks.

You choose to purchase 40 $26.00 call options for $0.10. These call options are low-cost as they are out-of-the-money, and the marketplace expectation for the stock is to remain flat. You only wish to run the risk of a little quantity to have the ability to take advantage of this possible relocation.

You will have a premium of the loss you paid of $400.00 if the stock does not increase above $26.10. If the stock cost does increase to $29.00, as you expect, you will make a profit of $15600.00.

Risks and drawbacks of buying call options

There are some risks and downsides to acquiring call options that you require to be familiar with. Three primary dangers you need to consider are the time to expiration, time decay, and a fall in the volatility of the underlying stock cost.

Time to expiry

You are playing versus time, the value of the underlying stock requirements to increase by an adequate amount before the expiry date for you to earn a profit on buying options call. Your risk is that the stock underlying will stagnate in your favor before the expiry date, and you will lose some or all of your option premium.

Time decay

You likewise lose time worth on your options for each day that you hold them. The rate at which you lose time worth also increases the closer you move towards the expiration date. So you need a more significant rise in the price of the underlying stock to offset the time decay the closer you get to the expiration date. This requires to be factored into any options to continue holding your options as you approach the expiry date.

Idea: You may be appropriate in hypothesizing on a price rise; however, you may not earn a profit on your options if this rise is not big sufficient or doesn't occur before the expiry date of your options.

You must comprehend the pricing of the underlying stock and how this will impact the worth of your option at expiry. In particular, you require to be knowledgeable about the strike price and when your option will be in-the-money so that it has some intrinsic value. You should likewise understand the rate that the underlying stock needs to grab you to recuperate the option premium you paid and recover the cost on your trade. This will allow you to analyze the cost movement required before expiration for any call options you are considering to buy. You can then identify which strike cost and the expiration date is most proper for your call option method.

Idea: A pay-off diagram is an excellent tool for you to easily see the rate that the underlying stock should reach for you to offset the time decay over the life of the option.

Fall in the volatility of the underlying stock rate

As we went over in chapter 4, the time worth of your call option is based upon the implied volatility of the underlying stock cost. If the underlying stock rate experiences a decline in volatility, this will lead to a reduction in the value of your options. The factor for this is that when the underlying stock cost is experiencing a smaller sized variety of movement, the potential to profit on your call options is lowered.

You need to choose which call option you wish to purchase as soon as you have decided on your call options technique and the underlying stock. There will be options of a variety available with different strike costs, different premiums, and various expiration dates.

So how do you choose which are the most beautiful call options to purchase? The factors you need to consider in choosing your option consist of the:

- Strike rate concerning the current market value expiry date
- The volatility of the underlying stock cost
- Options premium.

Strike cost about the present market worth

Where the price strike is in relation to the market's current worth of the underlying stock will determine how far the underlying stock. Cost requires to increase to produce some intrinsic value (be at-the-money) and then how far above this rate you will recover cost and begin to earn a profit.

Depending on your view upon the stock underlying, you need to pick a call option with a strike rate that satisfies three conditions. You believe that the marketplace worth of the underlying stock will:

Methods for purchasing call options

Increase above the strike rate so that your options have intrinsic worth (unless you purchase in-the-money options).

Boost sufficiently above the at-the-money worth to balance out the premium you spent for the OPTION. Increase even further to develop an adequate return on your investment.

Expiration date.

The expiry date determinant is a key to whether your option method achieves success. You need the market worth of the stock to satisfy the above three conditions before they expire option. Assessing the frame time in which a stock will move needs to be based upon your analysis of the stock and is typically a harsh assessment.

If the cost of this stock will move adequately within your time frame to create earnings on your call options, the volatility of the underlying stock price will figure out. A stock with low volatility experiences just a small modification in cost and will not be likely to produce earnings for a call options buyer unless the volatility increases.

OPTION premium.

The cost of your options, or the option premium, will straight affect the earnings or loss you make on your option trade. Some basic standards selecting your OPTION you can use the following:

- A call option will strike lower the price:
- Require a smaller increase in the share rate to create revenue.
- Be more expensive than a similar outdated OPTION with a higher strike cost.

A call OPTION with a more extended expiry date will:

Give you a higher possibility of achieving earnings on your call OPTION as you have more time for the underlying stock price to move adequately in your favor.

Be expensive more than a call option with a much expiry date shorter.

Buying an out-of-the-money consistent call option is with a bullish view of the underlying stock as you require a significant increase in price to generate revenue on your call options.

Buying an in-the-money call option or an at-the-money is a less bullish view; however, it still requires an increase in the value of the underlying stock cost above the time value in the call OPTION.

Your challenge in choosing a call OPTION is to:

- Determine how far you think the underlying stock price will increase.
- Identify how long you think it will require to increase to that cost.
- Find call options that have a price strike and date expiry that fit with your analysis.
- Calculate your break-even point based upon premiums offered.
- Find the least expensive options that satisfy your requirements above and will produce a sufficient ROI.

CHAPTER NINE

Strategies For Buying Put Options

In this chapter, we are to move from a bullish market view to a bearish outlook and will concentrate on how you can use put options to make money from a falling stock rate. Provided as you are buying put options gives the right to sell your stock at a set price, you can lock in a selling cost in a falling market to either make money from this move or secure existing positions.

The standard method for investing in the stock exchange is to buy in a rising market and to remain out of a falling market. Put options, however, provide you a chance to benefit from a falling market. The value of an in-the-money put options increases as the price of the underlying stock falls. The more the fall in the market, the more your put option increases in value.

Purchasing put options can also assist you in securing earnings in your stock existing holdings. You can lock in a selling price (price strike on your put options) so that if the worth of your stock falls, it will be balanced out by a boost in the value of your put options. This resembles buying insurance for your stocks against a rate drop. All you lose is the premium put option you paid if the cost doesn't fall.

Buying put options

Buying a put option provides you the right to offer a stock at the strike cost at any time before it ends. Even if the market rate of the underlying stock has fallen below the strike rate, if you exercise your put option, you can offer your inventory at the higher strike rate.

Buying put options is a method you can use if you are expecting a fall in market value. As with all options, you pay for your premium put options. You may lose some or all of the premium you paid for the put options if the underlying stock rate does not fall.

It is not required for you to own the underlying stock to buy put options. You are still able to make money from a falling market by merely buying and selling the put options. Remember, as a buyer, you can offer the underlying stock, not the responsibility to sell. There are 3 OPTION strategies you can take after purchasing put options.

- Sell your option before it ends.
- Exercise your OPTION before it ends.
- Allow the options to end useless.

As we talked about in chapter 6, the strategy you take will rely on the factors you acquired the put options, the motion in the price of the underlying stock, your expectations of any more movements in this price, and your risk tolerance. Your options are limited to offering your OPTION or permitting it to expire worthless if you do not own the underlying stock.

You do not require to own the underlying stock to purchase put options. Time is a substantial aspect when buying put options, only as it is when purchasing call options. When buying a put OPTION to generate revenue, you require to think about the limitations of time to expiration and time decay.

Even if the marketplace worth of the underlying stock tips over the life of put options, if this fall is not substantial enough to cover the loss of time value, you will not benefit from your financial investment.

There are four main reasons for purchasing put options:

- Gain take advantage of
- Limitation your threat
- Safeguard your current long position
- Hypothesize for revenue.

These strategies operate in the very same way for call options other than that the value of your put options increases as the market worth of the underlying stock falls below the strike price of the option. In this chapter, we will cover only the points that are particularly pertinent for put options under each method.

Strategy 1: gain use

Buying put options to benefit from a falling share price is as essential as buying call options. You have a restricted threat and have the advantage of taking advantage of compared with short selling the stock.

Short selling is an approach of selling a stock on the marketplace and then repurchasing it later on. This is a strategy used to make money from a falling market as you sell now at the current market value, with the expectation of purchasing the stock back later at a lower rate. There are considerable limitations on brief selling shares enforced by both the stock market and brokers, plus not all brokers offer this service to all financiers.

Short selling is the opposite deal to buying shares straight as you offer the shares initially and then repurchase them at a later date. Your goal is to benefit from a fall in the share rate.

Offer stock Expectation Buy stock:

- At the current future
- Market value will fall

Buy stock Expectation Sell stock

- At current At future
- Market value will rise

In the very same method, as you have the advantage of leverage when buying call options, you likewise get the benefits of taking advantage of purchasing put options. You can acquire a reasonably sizeable direct exposure to the share rate movement for only a fraction of the expense. The percentage fall in the stock underlying will result in a considerably more massive percentage boost in your put OPTION value if your put option is in-the-money.

Strategy 2: limit your risk.

Utilizing put options enables you to speculate on a fall in the marketplace rate with restricted danger. When purchasing put options, the most you can ever lose on your deal is the overall premium you spent on the options. On the other hand, if you were to brief offer a share, your losses would amount to the value of any increase in the price of that share up until you close your position, despite how much the share rate might increase.

Strategy 3: safeguard your current long position.

There will be times when you think these shares may fall in worth if you hold shares. Many financiers react to this circumstance is one of 2 way:

The shares sell.

I hope the price and ride out the fall recuperates.

The smart investor has a third option. Buying put options provide you the capability to safeguard the overall value of your shares without the requirement to sell them.

There may be several factors you do not want to sell your shares, although you think that there is going to be a correction in the market cost of those shares. These reasons may include the following:

- You might not want to sustain the transaction costs of selling and later on buying the shares.
- You might not wish to lose your privilege to the dividend earnings shares on those.
- You may not wish a tax liability to incur on the sale.

Like all other traders, you can not be 100 percent sure that there will be a fall or be precisely sure when it will take place.

Purchasing put options conquers a lot of these issues. When purchasing put options, you do not need to sell your shares, so you keep your entitlement to any dividends that might be stated. You do not sustain a tax liability on sale, and if the share price goes up, you will still gain from this price increase.

Buying put options to secure an existing position is a hedging technique and a bit like buying insurance for your shares. You are securing an asking price for your shares. Any falls in the marketplace worth of your shares will be offset versus a boost in the value of your put options. No matter how far the share rate drops, your shareholding is safeguarded at the strike rate.

If the price of the hidden shares falls, you still have three OPTION courses of action offered to you.

You can keep your shares, offer your options, and understand a profit to offset the fall in your worth shares.

You can exercise options and sell your shares at the exercise price.

You can wait up until closer to the expiry date to determine your course of action.

Your hedging technique is guaranteeing versus a possible risk. Nevertheless, if this threat does not eventuate and your shares increase in worth, you benefit still from this increase. This would not be the case if you sold your stocks buying instead of options put.

You need now to assessing if you continue to wish to hedge against a prospective fall in the share price by rolling over your put options into another put option position, or you might have.

Modified your analysis and no longer want to enter into another hedging technique. For example, 10.4, we use the very same scenario as in the previous case but take a look at the benefit of this method when the share rate increases.

You presently hold 2000 NAB shares. You feel that the market stock is bearishly looking and desire to secure your NAB holding against an anticipated fall in value. NAB is presently trading at $25.00 per share.

You are prepared to fall covered in NAB of $1.00 to minimize the cost of protecting an even higher fall. So you decide to buy 20 $24.00 NAB put options for $0.70 so that you can safeguard the value of your NAB shares if the rate falls listed below $24.00. These options have three months to expiry. Three months later, the share price of NAB has, in truth, continued to rise and is now $26.00. Your put options are still worthless are out-of-the-money.

- Preliminary investment 20 options
- 2 000 shares.
- The system costs $ 0.70$ 25.00
- Expense$ 1 400.00$ 50 000.00.
- Current cost$ 0.00$ 26.00.
- Current worth$ 0.00$ 52 000.00.

Net revenue/(loss) *($ 1 400.00)$ 2 000.00.

* Net profit does not account for deal expenses.

If you decide to sell your NAB shares in anticipation of a fall in worth, instead of purchasing the put options as insurance coverage, you would not have gained from the increase in value of your NAB shares.

For example, your put options you have cost $1400; however, your shares have increased in value by $2000, so even though you were hedging against a potential fall in the market value of NAB, you were still able to gain from the resulting boost.

Once again, you now require to assess if you wish to continue to hedge against a prospective fall in the share price by rolling over your put OPTION into another put options position. Perhaps you still feel that the marketplace will fall, and you were too early, or possibly you have modified your analysis and no longer want to enter into another hedging strategy.

When picking a put OPTION to safeguard your present position, the options will come down to just how much you are ready to pay for the options and for how long you want the security for. Options that offer a greater level of protection (a higher strike price) over a longer duration (later expiration date) will have higher premiums.

Strategy 4: hypothesize for earnings.

Purchasing put options is a popular trading technique for creating a benefit from a falling stock cost. You are hypothesizing on the price of the underlying stock falling by enough amount to cover your OPTION premium and generate a boost in the intrinsic worth of the put options. In this strategy, you need not to hold the stock underlying as you have no intention of working out the OPTION. Your method is to buy the put OPTION and sell it for revenue before it ends.

The conditions you must try to find in picking put options for short-term revenue are the same that we looked at for choosing a call OPTION for short-term earnings.

The strike price ought to be close to the current market price of the stock.

The time to expiry must suffice.

Options with low time worth in the premium will have less time decay; however, they are also less most likely to produce earnings. The risks and disadvantages of buying put options resemble purchase call options.

- Danger always limited to the premium you paid
- Minimal time to expiry
- Time decay.
- Fall in volatility.

Other techniques for benefiting from a falling stock cost consist of short selling and selling call options. However, the risk profile for these methods is hugely different. Short selling and selling call options expose you to endless danger.

Pick your put option.

In choosing your put OPTION, it is insufficient to correctly forecast that the marketplace value of the underlying stock will fall. You are hypothesizing on a significant sufficient motion to happen within the life-limited of your OPTION. Even if correctly you pick the downward movement within your amount of time, this will be offset by the reduction in time worth of your options.

Low options priced that are out-of-the-money have a lower danger and time value and will need a much bigger movement in the cost of the underlying stock to produce any amount intrinsically. The efficient market is in re-pricing options to represent market expectations, time to expiry, and the movement in the price of the underlying stock. Low priced options are low-cost for a factor. There is little time value in the options as there is only a small opportunity that the options will produce any intrinsic worth before they end. If you purchase an in-the-money put option, any movement in the underlying stock rate to the disadvantage will develop a dollar for dollar revenue in your put OPTION (less time decay). However, any boost in the market value of the underlying stock will likewise directly minimize the worth of your put options as long as it remains in-the-money.

It is erroneous to think that inexpensive options are always deals. Cheap options are out-of-the-money and most likely to expire worthlessly.

You require to think about the very same factors in selecting your put options as you consider when choosing a call option. These elements include the following:

- Strike price with the present market worth
- Expiration date.
- The volatility of the underlying stock price
- Option premium.

Some general standards you can use in picking your put option are as follows:

Put options with a higher strike cost will need a smaller sized fall in the share rate to produce a profit be more costly than a similar dated option with a lower strike price.

A put OPTION with a more extended expiry date will provide you a higher opportunity of attaining earnings on your put option as you have more time for the underlying stock rate to move adequately in your favor.

Be expensive more than a put OPTION with a much shorter expiration date as it has a higher time value.

Buying an out-of-the-money put option consistent is with a bearish view of the underlying stock as you need a substantial reduction in cost to produce a profit on your put options.

In-the-money put option Buying, or an at-the-money is a less bearish view, but still requires a fall in worth of the underlying stock cost over and above the time worth in the put options.

Your challenge selecting in a put option is to determine how far you believe the underlying stock cost will fall.

Figure out the length of time you think it will require to fall to that cost.

Discover put options that have a strike rate and expiration date that fit with your analysis. Compute your break-even point based upon premiums offered. Discover the least expensive options that meet the requirements laid out above and will create enough return on investment.

CHAPTER TEN

Strategies for selling covered call options

Selling call options can be a high threat or quite conservative, depending upon whether you own the underlying stock or not and how you structure your trade. If you offer call options and you own the underlying stock, you are offering covered call options. This is a conservative method with a limited threat. If you call prospects to sell and you own not the underlying stock, you are selling exposed or naked call options. This is a high danger strategy with potentially unlimited risk.

In this chapter, we will go over the general qualities, advantages, and drawbacks of offering covered call options. We will also talk about several techniques that can be used and the threats attached to these strategies.

Offering covered call options is a technique in which you can earn an income in the kind of option premiums got. This is especially effective as a technique when stock rates stay flat or within a narrow trading range. This method allows you to generate extra earnings from your stock position without relying on capital growth.

It is crucial to evaluate if this method is suitable for you and your investment goals if thinking about offering covered call options. This includes establishing an understanding of how to carry out a call selling strategy and the risks involved and having a proper level of experience in the stock exchange.

Offering call options

When offering call options, you reverse the order of a typical investment or trading deal. You open your position by providing the opportunities first, and then one of the three strategies will take place:

- You can purchase the option back later on to close your area.
- The option expires useless so that you do not require to purchase it back at all.
- The options are worked out versus you.
- Buyback call options
- Offer call options end useless options
- Options are exercised versus the seller

Time is an advantage significant to call OPTION sellers. Just as time works against the buyer of an option, it works for the options

Techniques for offering covered call options seller:

For an OPTIONS seller to lose money through the sale of a call OPTION, the marketplace value of the underlying stock price should increase by an adequate total up to balance out both the time decay and produce a boost in the intrinsic value of the options. And this must be achieved within the minimal life of the OPTION before it expires.

Time on your side works well as a call options writer (seller).

An OPTION which contains a higher time value in the OPTION premium has higher potential earnings for the option seller.

The higher the time decay in options, the much better it is for the OPTION seller.

As an author (seller) of covered call options for income, you are hoping that the worth of the underlying stock will stay constant and below the strike price of the options. In this circumstance, the option will have no intrinsic value and will not be exercised. The worth of your underlying stock will likewise stay steady and not lose value. If the marketplace worth of the underlying stock remains below the strike cost to expiration, the options will end useless, and you, the writer, will retain the OPTION premium as revenue.

As an options writer, your earnings are mostly the decreasing time value that the purchaser experiences over the life of the options.

When you call the option to sell, you are approving the purchaser of the option the right to purchase 100 shares of the underlying stock at the strike price at any time before the option expires. This implies that you are handling this responsibility, and assume the danger of being needed to provide those 100 shares in the event that your OPTION is exercised.

As an OPTIONS writer, you have no control over if or when your options may be worked out. This is the purchaser; if your call is out-of-the-money so that the market worth of the shares is below the strike price, then your request will not be exercised. Your danger ends up being evident when the market worth of the underlying stock moves above the strike cost of the OPTION.

It is essential to note that as a call options author, you do not commit to keeping your option position open to expiry. You can close your options position at any time before expiration by buying back the same option.

There are several possible results for an OPTIONS writer. The actions you might take as an options author will depend upon how the worth of your OPTION changes and what your expectations are for the time staying on the options.

If your call options out-of-the-money, you can remain either:

Hold to your expiry call options, at which time they will expire uselessly, and you will keep the OPTION premium as an earnings

Close your option position at a time by purchasing back the options at their current market price.

If the marketplace value of the underlying stock relocations above the strike rate and your call options move into the cash, you are at risk of having your options worked out at any time. At this moment, the following options are readily available: You can continue to hold the open options position.

You may enjoy selling your stock at the strike rate, or you may feel the price will fall, and you choose to run the risk of the options being exercised to see the possibilities return out-of-the-money.

Your OPTION position can be closed at any time by redeeming the options at their current market price.

Your position can be rolled to a new OPTION with a higher strike cost and later expiry date. This includes the time buying back your employment opportunity and selling a new one.

They will most likely be worked out, and you will be obliged to deliver the underlying stock at the strike price if your options are in-the-money at expiration. When selling call options, it is crucial to understand the threats and prospects for loss to handle your position effectively.

Selling covered call options

As a stock financier, you will experience the number of times throughout which the price of your shares remains flat, or within a narrow trading variety. This time, you will experience not any growth on your financial investment, and the only gains you will get will be from any dividends paid during that time. If you think that your shares are not likely to move significantly, the majority of investors would simply examine one of two options:

- Hold your stocks to get any dividends to be paid and hope that the shares will ultimately increase in worth.
- Invest your capital and sell shares in other shares or financial investments that are likely to produce a much better return.

However, selling covered call options offers you the third course of action that will enable you to earn earnings from your financial investment even when the worth of your shares is not increasing.

When composing covered call options, your options are 'covered' by the underlying stock that you currently hold. In producing hidden call options, you are approving the right to the purchaser to purchase your underlying stock at the strike price. To guarantee that you satisfy this obligation in the occasion of your options being worked out, required are lodge your stock to ASX Clear. (Your broker on your behalf will do this.) If your choices are worked out, ASX Clear will provide the shares to the counterparty that worked out the options and forward it into account at the purchased rate.

While your lodged shares are as security for your covered calls, you are unable to sell them. You do, however, still maintain ownership of the stock (unless your option is worked out) and will receive any dividend privileges that develop during that time.

If you are thinking about selling covered calls, you need to think about the following:

You ought to expect that the market rate of your underlying shares will stay flat or may fall.

A decrease in the volatility of the marketplace cost of the underlying stock will be advantageous to you.

If the market rate of the underlying shares boosts above the strike rate, you may be bound to offer your shares at the strike price, which would be below the current market value.

If your shares increase significantly in worth, your profit potential is restricted even.

Following are three essential techniques when writing covered calls you can use:

- Provide income as a source from the premium OPTION.
- If your view is that the marketplace rate of your stock is most likely to stay flat or within a consistent trading range.
- Selling call options over this stock can offer you with income from the option premium when your shares are not producing any capital gains.

Methods for selling covered call options

Provide some protection from a fall in worth stock of you.

If you are concerned that the value of the shares might fall, however, do not wish to sell them at present.

Writing covered calls over those shares will supply earnings that can be offset versus the fall in worth, thus providing you with some downside security and limiting your total loss.

Potentially sell your shares above the marketplace worth. You can write a call option to offer your shares at the strike cost you are pleased to get. You get both the OPTION premium and the strike cost for your stocks if the market value of the underlying shares relocations above this price, and your options are exercised.

Technique 1: offer an income from the OPTION premium

To produce an income stream from selling covered calls, you must have the view that the market price of your underlying shares will stay flat, or at least listed below the strike rate of your options. This will permit you to keep the options premium as earnings when the options end useless, and the value of your underlying shares will stay stable.

The very best possible outcome when selling covered call options is when the market worth of the underlying stock is at or just listed below the strike rate of your call options. When this takes place, you will have two favorable results:

- Your shares have not fallen in worth.
- You keep the full OPTION premium.

Technique 2: supply some defense from a fall in the value of your stock.

When the market worth of your underlying stock is falling, will provide you with premium income that, selling covered calls, you can use to balance out the fall in the value of your stock.

You need to determine that the technique for holding your shares, even though you are anticipating them to fall, stands. This is frequently the case for a long term financial investment method and an expected short-term retracement in price.

Next, you need to identify just how much defense you wish to have and select your OPTION accordingly.

You own shares of 4000 WBC that are currently trading at $21.30. You are worried that the market is weak, and your shares are going to fall in worth; however, you desire to hold them for the longer term.

To acquire a higher level of security, you would need to offer a more top-priced call option. This an option would be that had a more extended expiry date (therefore a more significant time value) or a lower strike price.

Technique 3: potentially offer your shares above the market value.

To achieve a better price from offering covered calls, instead of selling your shares at your target rate, you provide a hidden call option that has a strike cost equal to your target price. Instead of getting your target rate on sale, you sell your shares at your target price and get your call option premium.

In this method, the most you will ever get for your shares is the strike cost plus the premium. You require to account for both the options and the hidden shares Whenever you determine your profit or loss on composing covered call options.

Dangers and disadvantages of offering covered call options:

There are a few dangers and disadvantages to selling covered call options that you require to be mindful of. The most considerable threat is that there may be a significant fall in the rate of your stock underlying. This loss will result in value on this stock that will only be partially balanced out by the OPTION premium you received.

As the stock holds as collateral for your call options, you are unable to sell this stock up until you close your option position or the option expires.

Another drawback of offering covered call options is that they restrict the revenue you can make on your underlying shares. If your analysis is inaccurate and the market cost of the underlying stock has a big unexpected boost putting your options in-the-money, your options may be exercised.

Upon workout, you would be required to offer your underlying shares at the strike price of the option, missing out on the increased value above the strike rate. This is referred to as a chance expense. It is not an understood loss that you incur, however a revenue (or chance) that you miss out on out on.

CHAPTER ELEVEN

Strategies For Selling Naked Call Options.

You are taking a guaranteed premium income now to forgo a potential gain throughout the life of the options.

You are not obliged to hold your covered call options to expiry. If the marketplace rate of the underlying stock boosts towards the strike cost or relocations above the strike price, you may think about purchasing back your options at a loss. If you did not want this to happen, this would get rid of the danger that your options will be worked out.

Although it is most likely that your options will be exercised near to the expiry date, this is not always the case. You require to accept that it may be applied at any time if your option is in-the-money. You likewise need to be conscious of any ex-dividend dates, as your options will be most likely to be worked out if the underlying stock is about to go ex-dividend.

Suggestion: When your options move into the cash, you require to either accept the threat of exercise or redeem options to close your position.

Select your covered call options.

You need to choose on which call OPTION to write as soon as you have determined upon your covered call option technique and comprehend the risks included. For any stock, you will have a variety of exercise prices and expiration dates to select from.

The lower the strike price, the bigger the premium you will receive. This will offer you with higher earnings and more protection versus a downside relocation in the underlying stock. The lower strike rate also suggests that you will receive a lower price for your shares if the market value increases and your options are exercised.

Your option of strike price will depend on your view of the market worth of your underlying shares and your reasons for writing the covered calls. If you have an outlook bearish and are concerned about safeguarding your downside risk, a lower strike rate fits with this view. If your picture is more neutral and you wish to hold your stock, you will need to select a strike price that you think will keep your options out-of-the-money for the life of the option.

Techniques for offering covered call options:

Longer-dated options will have higher premiums, but they also increase the time over which the options may move into the cash and be exercised. Your danger here is that the underlying stock has a longer time in which to break out of its present trading range before the expiration date of your options. This will work versus your covered call technique if the stock cost moves unexpectedly either up or down.

You require to be prepared to have the options exercised Whenever you write a covered call option. There is always the threat of your option being used if the call is in-the-money. Up previously, all of our examples have involved selling calls covered that are out-of-the-money. However, this does preclude you not from selling calls in-the-money for short-term revenue. You do, however, comfortable need to be with the threat that your options might be worked out at any time that they remain in-the-money.

Your decision to offer your options has netted you a tidy short-term revenue in addition to offsetting the fall in the value of your underlying stock.

Following conditions are some for you to be aware of when picking your covered call OPTION:

The strike rate of the OPTION is higher than the original expense of your underlying shares. If the OPTION is exercised, this will ensure you make earnings on both your option and your shares.

The call is in-the-money, but not deep-in-the-money. This will mean that the options have intrinsic value that will move one to one with motions in the underlying stock price. This provides a chance to close your option position for short-term revenue.

The call is not deep but out-of-the-money out-of-the-money. This will indicate that the overall options premium is the time value, and the time value will be higher than if the option was deep out-of-the-money. As long as the underlying stock rate remains listed below the strike cost until expiry, you will keep the complete OPTION premium as revenue.

The time to expiry. The time to expiry requirements to be enough time to create time value in your option when you sell it, but not too long to decrease the threat of the options moving into the money.

The options premium. The premium you get for your OPTION needs to be large enough to compensate you for handling the risks of an option writer. When choosing your covered call option, you need to consider all of the lists below elements:

- Your technique for offering the call OPTION Ã the premium you will receive
- The mix of time worth and intrinsic value in the premium Ã time delegated expiry

Your expectation of motion in the price of the underlying stock in the time delegated expiry, the gap between the current market cost of the underlying stock, and the strike price of the options.

In managing your covered call position, you likewise require to consider your goals in holding the underlying stock in addition to your call options strategy. This will influence your options to close out an options position or to continue to keep it when it is approaching or is currently in-the-money

Techniques for offering naked call options

Selling naked call options, or exposed calls is a strategy where you offer call options but do not own the underlying stock. This is a high threat technique, as your losses are possibly unrestricted. Since of the high danger profile of offering naked call options, this technique is just recommended for traders who have enough experience and ability in the market to handle such a position.

In this chapter, we will discuss the benefits and disadvantages of offering naked call options and a few of the strategies that can be used.

Selling naked call options

When selling a naked call OPTION, you are giving the right to the purchaser to buy 100 shares of the underlying stock at the strike price. What occurs if your options move into the cash and are exercised?

Theoretically, you are needed to provide the stock to the option holder. You would need to purchase the stock at the dominating market price, and after that, offer it to the holder of the option at the price strike. This may result in a loss to the options seller, as the options will only be worked out if the market cost of the underlying stock is higher than the strike rate of the option. And this is where the limitless danger can be found in. As there is no theoretical limitation on how high the speed of the underlying stock can rise, there is no limitation on the losses you might incur.

The settlement time for working out an OPTION is T +3 (three days after a workout). This is to enable time for the purchase of the stock underlying(all stock settlements are T +3) if required.

This is the settlement contrast to period for buying and offering options, which is only T +1.

In practice, nevertheless, it is the settlement house, ASX Clear, that delivers the underlying stock on the exercise of options. You will remember from chapter 11 that when you offer covered call options, ASX Clear holds your stock to 'cover' your OPTION position. If the option is worked out, ASX Clear collects the sale follows the holder of the option and provides the shares to them. ASX Clear passes then on the proceeds to sell the OPTION writer.

For naked options call, upon exercise ASX Clear will buy the stock at the current market value to provide to the holder of the option who exercised the OPTION. ASX Clear would also gather the earnings on the sale of the stock at the strike cost As an options seller, and your account would be debited with the difference between the expense to acquire at the market worth and the sale proceeds at the strike cost.

When offering naked calls, you are needed to supply a margin that is held by ASX Clear. This margin is determined as the amount of security that ASX Clear deems required to guarantee that you can meet your responsibilities under the option agreement. This margin quantity will differ with the marketplace cost and volatility of price motions of the stock underlying. ASX takes the funds clear they require on the workout of an OPTION from your margin. Describe chapter 5 for more detail on margins.

The losses from selling the naked option call can be significant if there is a substantial boost in the market value of the underlying stock above the strike cost.

As talked about in chapter 11, essential attributes of offering either covered call options or naked call options are:

Time.

When selling option calls due to time decay, Time is a substantial benefit.

Control.

As the seller of options, you have no control over when or if your options will be exercised. This is the right of the OPTION purchaser. You do, nevertheless, have the option of closing your options position at any time before it is worked out and before expiration.

Option worth.

The most substantial elements that will affect the value of your OPTION are:

- Modifications in the market cost of the underlying stock.
- Modifications in the volatility of the market rate of the underlying stock

Time staying to expiry.

The most considerable difference between selling covered call options and offering naked call options is a threat. When selling covered call options and the marketplace moves versus your option position, you only sustain the opportunity expense of selling below market price. When selling a naked option call and the market moves versus you, your possible losses can be unrestricted and substantial.

Due to the involved risks, brokers will have specific requirements that you should satisfy to sell naked call options. These will consist of the level of equity in your account, and your experience in trading both options and equities.

Generally, you will be appointed an options trading level based on your experience, which will determine what types of methods you can use. Offering naked call options (and offering put options) will require a higher options trading level than buying options or offering covered call options.

When selling options call is when the market worth of the underlying stock is equivalent to the strike price of the options plus the OPTION premium, the break-even point. Therefore, it is still possible for an options writer to earn a profit on the sale of naked call options when they are exercised, as long as the marketplace worth of the underlying stock is less than the break-even price.

Workout of your option does not necessarily imply you lose on your OPTION trade. You just understand a loss if the market worth of the underlying stock is above your break-even point.

Naked call OPTION strategies.

When offering naked call options is to make earnings from your trade, your goal. To benefit from offering naked call options, you need among the following occasions to occur:

The underlying stock cost stays below the strike rate so that the OPTION wastes time to value and ends worthless. The underlying stock price falls so that the worth of the option reduces, and you can close your position at a profit. The underlying stock price increases, however, by a small adequate quantity so that the time decay on your option offsets any other increase in time or intrinsic worth.

When handling your naked call option position, you can either:

- Close your positioned option at any time before it is worked out and before it expires
- Hold your option position.
- To close your option position, you merely redeem the option at its current market value.

The method which you handle your open naked call option position will depend upon the movement in the price of the underlying stock and the subsequent effect on the market worth of your option.

There are four ways at which the market worth of the underlying stock can move:

- The value of the underlying stock falls
- The worth of the underlying stock stays constant.
- The worth of the underlying stock increases but remains below the strike rate of the option—the value of the underlying stock increases above the strike price of the options.
- The worth of the underlying stock falls.

When the market worth of the underlying stock falls, this is a piece of excellent news to the seller of a naked call option. The quality of the option will decrease due to time decay, and the possibility that the prospect will move into the cash is reduced.

You may want to close your option position at this time if you wish to realize revenue on your trade by purchasing back the option at a lower rate. You do this only if you would felt that the market worth of the stock underlying will reverse and might above move the price strike of the option. Now deep as the option is out-of-the-money, it is more likely that you would merely hold the option to expiry and see it end useless.

The value of the underlying stock remains constant when the marketplace worth of the underlying stock stays constant; the quality of the option will decrease due to time decay.

You may close or wish your option position at this time if you want to understand a profit on your trade by redeeming the option at a lower rate. As soon as once again, you would do this if you felt that the market value of the underlying stock might rebound.--and move above the strike rate of the options.

The worth of the underlying stock boosts but stays below the strike rate of the option when the market value of the underlying stock increases towards the strike cost of the option, the value of the option will alter in 2 aspects:

- It will increase due to a higher possibility of the option moving into the cash.
- It will reduce due to time decay.

The real modification in the worth of the option will rely on the interaction of these elements and might produce an increase, reduction, or no change in the value of the option.

You might want to close your option position at this time if you wish to avoid workout and are concerned about the increased danger of the market worth of the underlying stock continues to grow.

The worth of the underlying stock boosts above the strike price of the option

When the marketplace value of the underlying stock increases above the strike cost of the option, the option will be in-the-money, and workout is likely. The amount of the option will probably boost due to an increase in intrinsic worth.

You may want to close your option position at this time to prevent workout or additional losses due to the possibility of more considerable boosts in the value of the underlying stock rate.

As a seller of an option, you open your option position with a sale and close your option position with a purchase.

When selling naked call options, we will now consider a couple of strategies that you can use When handling any of these option techniques. You have the opportunity to close the position at any time (as we have merely detailed) based on the movement in the market value of the underlying stock.

Method 1: offering out-of-the-money naked call options.

When offering out-of-the-money naked call options, you are hypothesizing that the worth of the underlying stock will remain at or below the strike price of your option. If this happens, your call option will expire uselessly, and you will keep the option premium. This technique is described in WBC shares are trading currently at $21.30. You feel the price market is going to remain relatively constant and will not move over $22.50 in the next three months.

You choose to offer 40 covered call options for $0.50 with a strike cost of $22.50 and three months to expiry.

Over the next three months, the market value of WBC traded between $21.00 and $22.00 and was trading at $21.80 on the expiry date. The options expire worthlessly

- Option list price$ 0.50.
- Overall earnings on sale$ 2 000.00
- Option worth on expiry$ 0.00.
- Earnings on offering covered call options *$ 2 000.00.

Profit does not include deal expenses.

If, nevertheless, the market worth of the underlying stock boosts or you feel that the likelihood of an increase has become considerable, you can close your option position before expiry to understand a profit on your trade and prevent possible loss or workout.

Method 2: selling in-the-money naked call options.

Offering in-the-money naked call options is a risky and highly speculative strategy trading. As the options are in-the-money, they can be exercised at any time. You likewise face a one-to-one correlation between an increase in the market value of the stock and a boost in the intrinsic worth of your options.

This technique should be used only by traders experienced. When you believe it can be used, there will be an abrupt fall in the market worth of the share underlying. Any result that show fall is in an equivalent fall in the value of the options, which can then be closed at a revenue, or potentially expire useless if the market worth of the underlying stock falls.

Threats and disadvantages of offering naked call options:

The most substantial danger in selling naked call options is the capacity for endless losses if the marketplace value of the underlying stock boosts above the strike rate throughout the life of your option.

There are two other disadvantages to be mindful of: The requirement to offer a margin versus your open position is a significant downside associated with selling naked call options. If the market moves versus your call option and you will be needed to provide extra margin in the form of cash or securities, this margin will increase. Typically, you will be required to supply this within 24 hours.

Another essential drawback is that if you do suffer a loss on your option position and are unable to contribute extra funds to your account to cover the required margin, your broker might sell your securities existing to cover this loss. The sale of these securities may be poorly timed and not in line with your financial investment technique.

Due to the significant risk of possibly unrestricted loss from composing naked call options, it is essential to examine if this strategy is suitable for you. As we have stated, writing naked call options is a hazardous method, and you must consider the list below to consider identifying if it is a proper strategy for you.

Your danger profile. If the level of threat involved in selling naked call options is suitable for you, you require to assess. This needs to be examined because of your capability to manage a position with the potential for substantial losses, plus your financial capacity to sustain a worst-case circumstance. You do not want to erase your trading account from only one naked call option that moved all of a sudden.

Your understanding of the danger and of options:

It is imperative that you fully understand the risks involved and the specifications of the options you are considering composing.

It is simple to end up being ecstatic about the potential for profit and downplay the prospective risks.

Your trading experience knowledge of a specific trading strategy is necessary; however, it does not change trading experience. Getting in such a high threat strategy, such as selling naked calls, needs you to have a reasonable level of expertise in the market. Your experience in the market will assist you in choosing appropriate call options, handling the inherent risk, and figuring out what level of threat you can handle, both emotionally and economically.

Your capital. When writing naked call options, you are needed to provide a margin to cover your position. Therefore the size of your trading account will determine the number and size of naked calls you can compose. You need to allow also additional capital in case of a margin call or adverse motion in the market worth of the hidden shares.

Your trading and financial investment objectives:

In crafting your total trading and investment goals, you will have broad goals about the types of trades you wish to get in, the level of threat you want to take, and the returns you want to produce. Composing naked call options may, if you are looking for high-risk, high yields, be appropriate for a portion of your overall portfolio. If you are looking for long-lasting, steady development, then other methods might be more suitable.

CHAPTER TWELVE

Strategies for offering put options

When you expect the worth of a hidden share to remain flat or increase a little, offering put options is a method you can use to benefit. Selling put options has the very same relationship to the worth of the hidden share as buying call options. The value of the invisible stock boosts, and so the earnings on your option position increases. The threat profile is different in this chapter, and we will take a look at the benefits and drawbacks of offering put options and likewise explore a few of the methods you can use when offering put options.

Selling put options.

When selling a put option, you are giving the purchaser the right to offer you 100 shares of the underlying stock at the strike rate. You receive a premium for accepting the threat that the option might be worked out, and you will be needed to buy the underlying stock at the strike cost.

As with selling a call option, when offering put options, your profit is restricted to the premium you get. If the market worth of the underlying stock is below the strike price of the option, the option will only be worked out by the purchaser. If your options are worked out, you are required to purchase the underlying stock at the strike rate, which will be higher than the present market worth of the capital. As a put option seller, you have control over not if or when your options might be worked out. You can, however, close your position option at any time before the option is exercised or expires.

The possible outcomes that you might deal with as a writer of put options are:

- Your option remains out-of-the-money and expires useless.
- You choose to close your option position before expiration.
- Your option moves into the cash and is worked out before expiration. This will need you to buy the underlying stock at the strike price.

Usually, the very best result for a put option seller is if the marketplace worth of the underlying stock stays above the strike cost of the option. This will lead to the option ending worthless, and, as the options seller, you keep the option premium as earnings.

You feel that the price of CBA hold is going above $50 over the next two months, so you decide to sell 10 $50 CBA put options for $1 when the marketplace price of CBA is $51.

By the expiration date, the price of CBA performed stay above $50. As the market worth of CBA never fell below $50, your put option was never in-the-money, so never at danger of being worked out.

At expiration, the put option is still out-of-the-money and expires useless. You maintain the $1000 premium as earnings on your option trade. This calculation does not include transaction expenses.

For example, the cost of the underlying stock moved in line with your expectations, and the option expired useless. In case 13.2, let's think about the scenario if the price of the underlying stock fell, contrary to your expectations.

Example.

You feel that the rate of CBA is going to hold above $50.00 over the next two months, so you decide to sell 10 $50.00 CBA put options for $1.00 when the market rate of CBA is $51.00.

In the next month, the cost of the CBA $48.50 is up. Your now options in-the-money and are priced at $2.00. What should you do?

For example, above, the marketplace worth of CBA has not moved in line with your expectations, and your options are now in-the-money. You have two options.

If the market worth of CBA continues to fall, Ö You can close your option position to mitigate the risk of the options being exercised or sustaining further losses. To narrow your position option, you would need to acquire the put options for $2, realizing a loss of $1000 on your trade (before deal costs).

Your other OPTION is to hold your option position. You would do this for one of 2 reasons. You might feel that the cost of CBA will rebound above $50 very quickly, and you are prepared to run the risk of workout in the short term to recoup the loss on your option position, possibly. The other factor is that you may feel that $50 is a fair cost for CBA, and you are happy to purchase the stock at this price. Your premium will offset the above market value you are paying so that the net cost of buying the shares is efficient $49.

Threats and downsides of selling put options

Selling put options brings the risk of considerable losses. Nevertheless, these losses do have a limitation, unlike offering naked call options. The worth of a put option increases as the worth of the underlying stock decreases. The maximum loss you can sustain is restricted to the strike cost of the option. If the market worth of the underlying stock fell to absolutely no, then your loss on the option would be the worth of the hidden shares at the strike cost, less the premium you got on selling the put option. Although it is unlikely to occur, this is your optimum risk exposure when selling put options.

You can alleviate the risk of loss through cautious options of stocks. It is not likely that a stock will trade below the company's net concrete possessions over the longer term (although it might fall below this in the short-term). When selling put options, referring to the net tangible ownership of the underlying stock gives you a reasonable basis in which to assess your threat.

Another element to consider requirements margins. When you sell options put, you are required to offer a margin to make sure that you can satisfy your responsibilities under the put option. This margin will increase considerably if your put option moves into the cash and is a threat of workout. You, therefore, require to have all set funds readily available to fulfill any margin calls.

The third threat you face is a workout.

You have the need to full capital required to acquire the underlying stock at the strike cost and commit this capital to purchase those shares if your put option is exercised. This can tie up your money in stocks which you now need to handle.

When selling naked call options, examining the risks of offering put options is a little various from your threat. With naked call options, you will realize a money loss if your options are worked out. When selling options put, you need to be prepared to purchase the stock underlying if your options are exercised. Although you can resell these shares on the marketplace right away, or whenever you pick, you need to be still prepared and able to acquire them entirely in case of exercise of your options.

There are methods in varieties you can apply when selling put options. The arrangements all depend on the expectation that the value of the underlying stock will remain consistent or boost in worth. We will talk about the following methods:

Supply an income source from the option premium utilizes your capital additional.

Shares purchase at a discount to your target rate.

Technique 1: supply an income source from the option premium

Hypothesizing on the rate of the underlying stock to create a short-term profit is the most popular reason for offering put options. To an income stream generated from selling put options, you should have the view that the marketplace price of the underlying shares will remain flat, and above the strike cost, you pick for your option. If the marketplace worth of the underlying shares does stay above the strike cost of your options, they will end useless, and you will retain the option premium as earnings. Consider this technique in WBC shares are currently trading at $21.80, and you are hypothesizing that the marketplace rate is going to stay reasonably constant and will not move below $21.00 in the next three months.

You choose to offer 40 put options for $0.50 with a strike cost of $20.50 and 3 months to expiry.

Over the next three months, the market worth of WBC traded between $21.00 and $22.00 and was trading at $21.50 on the expiry date.

The options expire uselessly

Option sale rate$ 0.50.

As your options were never in-the-money, (the marketplace worth of WBC never fell listed below the price strike of $20.50). For example, 13.3, there was never any possibility of your options being exercised. Your options ended useless, so as the option writer, you maintain the option premium of $2000.00.

The circumstance would be various if the market value of the underlying stock fell.

Example

WBC trading shares are currently at $21.80, and you are speculating that the market price is going to stay relatively constant and will not move below $21.00 in the next three months.

You decide to offer 40 put options for $0.50 with a strike cost of $20.50 and 3 months to expiry.

Over the next month, the marketplace worth of WBC fell to $20.00, and the put options are now worth $0.90. You choose to close your option position.

It is imperative whenever offering put options that you are prepared to purchase the underlying stock at the strike rate. For that reason, when selecting your put options, it is smart to choose stocks that you are comfortable owning at strike costs you feel represent reasonable value for those stocks. You can then manage your stock position appropriately.

This does not suggest that you want the options to be exercised, and might well select to close any open put option positions that are at threat of being worked out. It does indicate that you acknowledge that work out of your options is a threat of selling, and you are prepared to accept this threat and have a technique if the risk eventuates.

You have had success selling put options recent with no being exercised. You are feeling positive and have simply sold put options on five various securities to generate a considerable option premium.

In the area of a few days, an international occasion has caused a remarkable drop across the whole stock market, and all your put options fell under the cash and were exercised.

You now have to offer the capital to acquire all five stocks at prices above their existing market worth. You have to sell a few of your current stocks at a depressed value to satisfy your obligations under the put options.

Certainly, example 13.5 is a worst-case scenario. It is crucial to consider this result as a possible threat. In this example, you would have shares sold that you wished to keep at a reduced cost, to purchase stocks below their current market values. Your portfolio would be carry-ing a considerable unrealised loss, and you would have no free capital.

Method 2: utilise your extra capital.

This technique is based on your speculation that the market is misestimated and you do not wish to invest at present costs. Selling put options will enable you to create superior income, using your extra capital to fulfill the put options margins.

You will profit from the premium option if the stock rate continues to increase or stays above the strike rate. If the value of the stock underlying falls towards the strike price, you can either close your position or let the option relocation into the cash and buy the stock at the strike cost. In any case, you keep the option premium as a return on the capital you provided as a margin to sell your put options.

This technique operates in the same manner as method 1. The distinction is that this might be used as a short-term strategy for investors with spare capital who think the marketplace is overvalued, instead of an ongoing method of speculation for earnings.

Method 3: purchase shares at a discount rate to your target rate.

The 3rd technique in selling put options is to set your strike price at a target purchase rate to purchase the underlying stock at this cost. This is a method you can use if you wish to buy the underlying stock at a set cost that is listed below the current market price. The benefit of offering put options is that in addition to purchasing the stock at your target cost, you also get the option premium. Let's consider this, in example 13.6

You would like to purchase 500 WBC shares at $20.00. They are currently trading at $21.80. You decide to offer five put options for $1.80 with a strike rate of $20.00 and six months to expiry.

Over the next couple of months, the marketplace value of WBC is up to $19.50, and you get a notice that your options have been worked out.

Option price$ 1.80, Proceeds on sale$ 900.00 overall—purchase WBC at the 20.00 10 000.00 cost.

The net qualified expense to purchase WBC *$ 9 200.00. The current market price of WBC at 19.50 9 750.00

When the cost hit $20.00, for example, 13.6, you desired to buy WBC. So putting rather than in a limit order to purchase the shares directly, you sold a put option. This achieved your preferred result to buy the stock at your target rate and earned you an extra $900.00 in option premium. When utilizing this technique, there is the risk that your options may not be exercised. This risk is highlighted in the example below:

You wish to purchase 500 WBC shares at $20.00. They are presently trading at $21.80.

You choose to sell five put options for $1.80 with a strike cost of $20.00 and six months to expiry.

Over the next few months, the market worth of WBC fell to $20.10 to $22.00 increased.

Example: the disadvantage illustrates a bit of this technique. If the stock rate does not fall low enough for your options to be worked out, you might miss out on out on acquiring the stock. In selling your options put, you are required to supply capital as margin, so even if you chose to purchase the stock at above $20.00, you might not have the complimentary to do so in the capital. In that event, you would need to close your option position.

As a put seller option, you risk losing future revenues in the following two ways.

If the cost of the underlying stock increases, you lose the profits you might have gotten if you had merely directly bought the stock.

If the price of the stocks underlying falls drastically, If the option is exercised, are still needed to purchase the stock at the strike rate. You will be paying the market price above, and the sharp fall may alter your stock on this position.

In both cases these, you still retain the premium option as revenue. If your expectation is for the worth of an underlying share to remain steady or to rise somewhat, selling put options is a technique to generate a profit.

When selling option put, you are granting the purchaser the right to purchase the underlying stock at the strike cost any time before expiry.

If you are offering put options, you should be prepared to acquire the underlying stock at the strike price. This will guide you in your options of options.

Generally, the very best outcome for a put option seller is that the rate of the underlying stock stays above the strike price of your option so that your options end useless, and you keep the option premium.

Selling put options carries the danger of significant losses. Your losses limited only are to the value of the hidden shares at the strike cost. This will take place if the value of the underlying stock is up to zero.

When selling options put into ensuring you can fulfill your obligations on the occasion of workout, you are needed to supply a margin.

You are in danger of exercise at any time; the option is in-the-money. You should only offer put options over stocks that you would be comfy buying at the strike cost.

The three primary strategies for selling put options are:

- Provide an income source from the option premium use your extra capital

- Purchase shares at a discount rate to your target price.

The most popular strategy for offering put options is to produce an income from the option premium. This involves speculating on the marketplace value of the stock underlying remaining above the price strike of the option.

You can always close your option position before a workout and before expiration if you want to avoid the danger of your exercised option being.

You can use capital spare as margin when selling put options as a short-term measure to earn additional income. You can offer put options as a method to buy stocks at your target cost. You choose the options based upon the stock you wish to purchase and the strike cost at your target purchase cost. You accomplish your objective in buying the stock and maintain the option premium if your options are worked out.

There are two risks in utilizing put options to acquire stocks at your target rate. The stock price might rise, and you miss out on getting in, or the stock rate may fall significantly, and you are required to purchase the stock well above the market rate.

CHAPTER THIRTEEN

Options Trading Frames Time

Time frames are an integral part of options trading and require to be given mindful factors to consider when initiating any investment. Timespan is represented with charts such as those that will be laid out in the next chapter. There is a countless amount of time, as they can range from as brief as one hour to several months long. It depends on the investor to analyze the time frames to forecast how the market will move and hence if the financier requires to offer or purchase options.

What precisely requires to be examined? That the trendline would be, which is detailed in the time frame chart. By looking at the table, a financier will have the ability to inform if it is bearish or bullish and, using the trade signals discussed in the next chapter, when the marketplace is going to continue or reverse its pattern. There is not just one pattern that investors need to be worried with. There are three trends: primary, intermediate, and term in brief.

Every security underlying can be represented with these patterns, which are reputable depending upon the length of their time frame, Having a longer time frame.

It allows investors to track the pattern of a hidden stock more precisely. Consider example a 3-month very long time frame versus a 5-minute timespan. The 5-minute frame would reveal a tiny portion of the possession's pattern, which may be an abnormality when taking a longer timespan trend into account or perhaps might appear incorrect, depending on just how much noise is happening in regards to that specific possession. Therefore, considering that a long-term pattern is more reputable, it is the most accurate for locating the primary trend.

The main pattern ought to always be the financier's central issue. This is not since it is the just one worth focusing on. On the contrary, various trends will be used by different kinds of investors, such as a day trader versus a position trader. When it comes to the position trader, it would be smart to make the primary trend a priority since it focuses on long-lasting time frames and, after that, make smaller sized earnings using the intermediate-and short-term frames. To this in juxtaposition, a day trader would mainly use the main pattern as an umbrella for the short amount of time she or he would mostly deal with as calls and puts are quickly traded. It is, therefore, best for a starting investor to focus on the work she or he would most like to do and then find the suitable timespan for it, continually basing calculations off of the primary trend. This can be achieved by utilizing the short-term pattern in connection with the faster amount of time and the investor's preferred time frame for the intermediate-trend, all while tracking the primary trend in the long period frame.

In line with the concept of tailoring timespan and securities to a financier's options, the two timespans passed by as the investor's primary issue ought to be used to match the principal amount of time. Depending upon how the investor selects to use the time frames, the financier could gain benefits on three separate levels, enacting a lot of the strategies talked about in the previous chapter. For instance, a financier might hold a long position on a stock using the primary trend to forecast movements within the market for that particular underlying financial investment, likewise referred to as the underlying pattern. As soon as this has been identified, the investor uses whatever amount of time is most suited to his/her style of trading (brief for day trading, long for position trading, etc.) to figure out the intermediate trend pattern. The financier then generates a short-term model to implement strategies that may satisfy any variety of functions. These might include utilizing the short-term trend and time frame to develop insurance for the extended position, to enjoy benefits with calls or puts as the pattern varies, or any other of the numerous usages of short-term trends and time frames. How the time frames are made use of is entirely up to the individual financier and therefore is a versatile method to increase and create earnings utilizing the investor's natural trading strengths.

One word of caution must be kept in mind relating to the short-term trends. Frequently, since they are so little, short-term charts can end up being overcrowded with a high volume of financiers and trigger the table to appear very volatile when, in fact, it is not. Financiers should beware not to over-analyze the chart and regularly compare it with the main pattern in words of Investopedia author Joey Fundora, "Short-term charts are typically used to validate or dispel a hypothesis from the primary chart" (Fundora, Multiple Time Frames). It is those hypotheses drawn from the contrast of the first and short-term charts that lead investors to make reasonable forecasts relating to the market and implementing options trading methods from there.

Since there is timespan consisting of trends that represent all underlying properties, neophyte options traders can typically become puzzled by the inconsistent details. State, for example, the main pattern for the stock of business XYZ in a very long time frame shows the stock is bullish. Nevertheless, when the investor looks at a short-term trend on two days, the stock appears to be entirely bearish without any apparent signs of a rally. The investor must not worry and begin to offer all of his/her shares; instead, the financier should realize that the short-term pattern is merely a little of the primary trend portion. Which, if it is a pattern continuation, will keep its bullish outlook and continue to climb up the chart. To see from this example is easy to see why the company and a clear understanding of options trading before entering the service are invaluable tools.

Among the keys to growing a portfolio is to concentrate on the future patterns of the marketplace rather than the past. Many financiers who are either novices or extremely frightened of losing cash rely purely on past information given by extended period frames, rather than focusing on how the trend might be the future act. This is where signals in trading, detailed in the next chapter, end up being extremely beneficial. The factor they are being discussed here is since it is essential for financiers always to be looking towards the future. While seasoned financiers might do their best to show the truth to the contrary, the marketplace is a fickle animal, and not every relocation can be predicted and upon acted. If that were so, no one would lose ever, which would naturally result in a complete market crash. Trends do reverse and change; it depends on the investor to understand the patterns and make informed decisions as to how to act upon the direction.

CHAPTER FOURTEEN

Trading Signals and Trading Signal Providers

Trading on the stock exchange can be overwhelming. With many prospective contracts out there, it's tough for traders to understand which ones they need to sell or buy and which ones they must release by. In times of trade increase and volatility within the marketplace, traders count on trade signals to help identify their next relocation. Trade signals mainly originate from technical signs, which are "any class of metrics whose value is derived from generic rate activity in a stock or possession ... Technical indications are used most extensively by active traders in the market, as they are developed primarily for analyzing short-term cost movements" (Investopedia, Technical Indicator). These might be available in the type of various charts that develop different shapes, such as a wedge, rectangular shape, or triangle, which will suggest to the trader what movement will happen in the market for a specific underlying security. Also, charts might form bullish or bearish pennants, which further enables traders to figure out the worth of options and predict motions within the marketplace. In this chapter, various signals will be analyzed, and descriptions will be offered to demonstrate how investors may use signs to their advantage. The half of the first chapter will be devoted to kinds of signals, while the latter half will focus on trading signal service providers. If this sounds a bit like a hokey fortune-teller reading tarot cards, do not stress; similar to all things in the market, it's quite technical. The last recommendation is to look at the old main trendlines on very long time frames to get a concept of where trade signals turn up and how the market reacts to them. With practice, investors will be able to spot the chart signs easily.

Flag

This very first example of a trading signal is relatively easy to comprehend. A flag sign is a boxy fit, concise, and generally inclines in the opposite direction of the market pattern. It represents a moment briefly when the market breathes and stays relatively neutral before continuing the trend it had been going on previous to the flag. This moment of calm before continuing the pattern is called the combination period. After spotting the banner on a bullish continuation pattern, investors may decide to start purchasing calls, given that the trade rate is low and financiers expect it to increase per the trend. Identify a flag on a trendline by trying to find anywhere two parallel lines completely frame the visual market pattern.

Pennant

This chart is a short-term chart extension pattern. With a pennant pattern, asymmetrical triangle points its peak at the market pattern increase or reduction, depending on whether the trend is bullish or bearish, respectively. In basic, a pennant is formed just after a flag symbol, and subsequently, it is, in some cases, referred to as a flag pennant. Because the objective of a trading signal is to forecast when it is a great time to buy or offer, utilizing a bearish or bullish pennant pattern to predict market trends can, even more, notify which techniques to use to maintain or appreciate possessions.

Rectangular shape

The rectangular shape trade signals are incredibly similar to a flag with one exception: unlike the flag, the rectangular shape signal has a lot longer and more resistant consolidation period. This essentially suggests that during the combination period, financiers might have a hesitant mindset towards the marketplace. The trend will measure the state of mind of participants (a.k.a. willingness to sell and buy), which results in a regular horizontal pattern firmly compacted in between the sharp market trends. When looking at a trendline, investors will quickly have the ability to see where long rectangular shape boxes in the lines and will use it to make market predictions.

Triangle

There are three types of triangle patterns: rising, symmetrical, and descending. These correlate to a neutral, bullish trend and bearish, respectively. According to authors Chad Langager and Casey Murphy at Investopedia, "The basic construct of this chart pattern is the convergence of two trendlines-flat, rising or descending-with the cost of the security moving in between the two trendlines" (Langager, Murphy, Analyzing Chart Patterns). [9] Depending upon the nature of the trendline, in addition to the resistance and support

(meaning whether financiers feel the trading cost will move down or up) happening within the triangle, investors may pick to hold long or brief positions upon the breakout, which is when the trendline abandons the triangle pattern.

Wedge

Wedges fall under two classifications: falling and rising. These appearances in a bullish or bearish can then make a pattern. The tricky element of the wedge is that for a newbie, it will look like the market cost will continue to increase in the beginning glance. Once the trendline outbreaks of the wedge, it will maybe moving in direction opposite as when the wedge it was. This means that investors, generally speaking, spotting upon a wedge, know that the market is going to begin moving in the other instructions. That is the minute lots of financiers will begin starting new methods to make the most of the market change.

Head-and-Shoulder This signal is used to figure out when a trend is going to become tired and reverse itself. It portrays a precise balance within the market as sellers bring the trendline down, and purchasers press it back up once again. This signal indicative can be of an upward or downward pattern, depending upon the current market climate. Usually, the market will rally three times; after the last shoulder (or third peak), the trend will reverse its bullish or bearish position. Like other signals, financiers can use this info to purchase or offer calls and puts as essential.

Some beginning investors who are daunted by trade indications elect to enter of online signal providers whom financiers can pay to look out of any possible significant shifts in the market, which an investor can then use to his or her benefit. As the saying goes, absolutely nothing in this world comes for totally free. Trade signal companies can cost a hefty amount of cash since the best trade signal providers take risk management into account. And offer clients a selection of packages that will arrange each person's needs in terms of trade interests, investments, and beginning capital.

Investors must always be wary when signing up for services from signal companies. The Internet is cluttered with frauds, and generally, an allegedly relied on signal supplier appears as mere false months after being touted as one of the most excellent signal companies available. When a supplier provides services complimentary of charge, a clear caution indication that a financier is stepping into a fraud is.

Furthermore, fraudulent websites will need the trader to invest a specific quantity of capital, which the trader is then sure to lose. Even if the financier thinks he or she has found a protected site, in-depth research must be carried out before buying a membership to any signal provider website. The dangers are far too excellent to stroll into a contract blindly and are comparable to trading options before reading a book about it.

CHAPTER FIFTEEN

An Options Guild To Success

This chapter will take account of all of the information currently discussed and put it in a step-by-step guide for novice financiers in options trading. Naturally, individuals might originate from the strategy; however, they want; this is merely an example of actions to take that describes the options open to investors. Amateur yet well-informed traders will have the ability to contend in options trading in no time if this fundamental summary is followed. Additional ideas are listed at the end of the chapter to assist financiers in preventing the mistakes of options trading, therefore leading them to portfolio gratitude.

Selecting a Security can be done by investigating the financing areas of significant news corporations. A basic search will show up outcomes such as CNN's Money section, which notes the most active companies according to the S&P 500. It would be wise to look for out the guidance of a buddy or mentor if the investor is already partly immersed in the financing world. New options traders, and especially those who are new to trading in basic, should approach options trading cautiously. Rather than diving right in, investors must get their feet wet by exploring a limited variety of securities and options so that they can monitor gains and losses and prevent errors for future investments.

Pick OTC or Regulated Trading while this can be decided at a later stage, it is suggested here so that new financiers can describe the boards of a controlled exchange such as the New York Exchange stock. When choosing a call or put that is well matched to their tastes, practiced traders can pick up an OTC option later on if wanted, such as a call to cover the expense of insurance put, likewise referred to as a married put.

Select Strategies Before starting trading, financiers will require to be sure they recognize with a few basic strategies that can be implemented with a stock. Without these strategies, options will simply sit with the financier being none the wiser or well equipped to get profit. Recommended techniques are the long call, bull call spread, and bear put spread, short straddle, and long straddle. A lot of other strategies are built on the base of these 5; subsequently, mastering them will enable the investor to become more advanced in his or her approach and, therefore, trades. There is one method that needs to be settled at the beginning of the organization endeavor, and that is the exit strategy.

Financiers need to decide ahead of time what they can manage to lose, which will be determined by their net capital upon entering the trade, and if they are willing to lose it. The reason this is so essential is since if the stock price drops below the strike cost for an investor's put, they could incur unlimited debt.

If this halfway happens through the life of the option contract, the investor will require to decide if they wish to ride the stock cost out or instantly acquire a call to help offset the put.

Whatever the financier chooses to do, it is essential not to panic ought to trade not work out, and even if it is working out, the trader needs to have an exit strategy continually. In the words of the senior analyst in options Brian Overby, "You need to choose in advance your upside exit point and your disadvantage exit point, along with the timeframes for each exit" (Overby, How to Avoid the Top 10 Mistakes New Options Traders Make).

Continuously have a strategy, stick to it, and ideally, losses will not ever be too considerable.

Analyze the Market Investors will require to study the time frame charts connected with their underlying security options. Consider all three patterns in concerns to the time frame and note how the security is moving within each. Investors must attempt to make a forecast relating to how the design will run in the future utilizing the trade signals gone over in the previous chapter. These investors will be lead to the next step.

Purchase Options and Trade Finally, the minute investors have been waiting for. Based upon conclusions drawn from studying timespan charts, financiers will require to purchase the suitable calls or puts. At the very same time, financiers must choose one or two of the strategies which they are currently familiar with that they think will work well in today market environment.

If trading via a controlled exchange, options for the methods might be picked from a list published by the transfer, the investor will not just need to choose a call versus put. However, likewise, if American vs. Europeans want to trade options, long vs. short, and plain vanilla vs. exotic. For a new options trader, Plain and American vanilla options are strongly advised as the previous is quicker available, and the recent deals fewer complications. The combination of the 2 is most likely to gain rewards for somebody brand-new to options trading. Once the suitable options have been chosen for the excellent method, investors will be able to execute their preparation for options trading success by buying or offering their possibilities. From there, it's all as much as the marketplace!

5 Mistakes to Avoid in Options Trading

Using a strategy called"One Size Fits All," This is never, ever real. Since the marketplace is continuously changing, techniques should continuously alter. A married put going to work not at every time frame, if just for the fact that it gains such minimal revenue. When selecting methods for particular underlying properties and time frames, financiers require to be sensible.

Doubling Risk to Cover Loss Taking this method is comparable to a gambler getting in a poker game with an all-or-nothing state of mind after having just lost everything in his wallet. Methods can either fail or acquire capital, and financiers require to be sure they are not attempting to overcompensate for the loss by investing in a bad trade. If a specific strategy is not working, the investor would be best off deserting it all together as quickly as he or she is able, utilizing the financier's individualized exit technique.

Greed Though it's to be exciting on the uptrend and gaining financial benefits through options trading, it's critical for investors to realize when they require to go back. This is where having an exit technique on the uptrend comes in since; eventually, the market will reverse itself, and investors do not want to be captured losing all of their robust generated income on the downswing just because they got a little greedy.

This can be partially offset by continually analyzing the time frame charts and searching for trade signals. When doing so, financiers must not just search for new opportunities, however likewise end up being conscious of prospective fiscally damaging scenarios.

Concentrating On One Asset Once the investor has gotten his/her "sea legs" in concerns to options trading, it is essential to diversify those options.

A portfolio needs to include numerous properties, and while managing multiple options and strategies simultaneously may be daunting to newbie investors, it is imperative not to put all of the eggs in one basket. As quickly as the financier feels comfy, they must take on brand-new underlying possessions and develop their portfolio.

Neglecting Future Trends A typical mistake amongst brand-new financiers is to confuse historical patterns with future ones. Past models are only a sign of future trends in that their shapes can be used to predict a change in the model, which is what the pennant, flag, rectangular shape, triangle, wedge, and head-and-shoulders signals are used for. Puzzling the two will lead financiers to make unreliable predictions and hence lose money on faulty techniques. Instead, investors should practice finding future chances by examining old timespan charts, which will hone their skills and acquire them future incomes.

Options trading is a fantastic method to construct a portfolio and earn capital. With time, brand-new investors will find out and make mistakes to correct them. Ideally, with this step-by-step guide and ideas for errors to avoid, investors will feel great entering the world of options trading and taking on the market.

Conclusion.

Trading options do not need to be complicated; in truth, it can be as complicated or straightforward as the specific trader wants it to be. Similar to any other investment tool, options trading ought to be in every investor's tool kit. Having the ability to use such versatile methods and options opens up doors to higher financial chance, which is the principle that the entire investment industry rests on. So, either the trader is brand new to the world of investment or a skilled expert looking to broaden their horizons. Options trading must consistently be considered as a premier financial investment tool that can be used to shape an investor's future into one filled with chance, convenience, and monetary stability.

OPTIONS TRADING STRATEGIES

How To Build A Six-Figure Income With Options
Trading Using The Best-proven Strategies For
Intermediate and Advanced

Nathan Bell

INTRODUCTION

Options are among the most potent money-making asset classes ever devised. They were not designed as a money-making tool. Instead, their primary purpose for existing is to limit risks associated with the portfolio. Whether you are considering a portfolio of one stock, a hundred stocks, stocks mixed with some commodities, or other related combinations, options can be used to either improve your portfolio's return on capital, take advantage of the opportunity to improve yield, or limit your investment risks by exchanging a little revenue capacity for the "insurance coverage" a long option offers. If you are looking to buy an option with the aim of limiting your risk, somebody has to be on the other side of the trade.

In years past, the opposite of the trade was generally taken by professional options traders. The vocational options trader was a legendary creature who made thousands of dollars every day by "picking the pocket" of the corrupt specific financier. The professional options trader was simply someone who understands the fact that options trading is nothing more than an exercise in basic probability theory. And this possibility theory is easy enough to find out; with a little time and effort, many people can master it and use it for their advantage.

Today options markets are, for the many part, so efficient that you can trade either side of a narrowly estimated market. Thus, there is nobody out there picking anyone's pockets. Options provide the fairest, most equal-opportunity one can expect.

When most investors hear the words options trading, they believe "too much danger," they believe "calculus ...too complex," they think "too time-consuming," and they believe "the professionals will clean my clock." Nevertheless, none of these thoughts are accurate. This does not imply that options trading is elementary that anybody can do it. If you are a motivated student, trading options is not that difficult to learn. Though it is hard, practically anyone can learn how to trade options with a little effort. Let's illustrate this point by considering each of the other excuses separately.

If options trading has a bad rap, it got it as an outcome of the Crash of 1987. That single event has, to date, altered the way individuals price options. Throughout the crash, there were stories of some traders losing everything as a result of being brief "naked puts." Does that mean there is truth to the declaration that options are too dangerous?

Many people are comfortable owning stocks. Which trade brings higher risks?, owning 100 shares of XYZ stock or being short an XYZ put (which commands 100 shares of stock)? Would you be surprised to know that owning stock is, in fact, riskier? And would you be amazed to see that you have much better odds of earning money being short an out of the cash put than being long stock? The difference in the odds can be considerable and entirely unexpected to many people.

Perhaps you have taken time to do your homework and have discovered that option price models are typically based on either some form of the Black-Scholes model, which is a partial differential formula, or the binomial model, which is a decision tree-style design. As a retail options trader, you do not need to understand the calculus behind the designs. Your broker must supply you with all the calculus-induced models you require to trade effectively and successfully! And some do so at no charge to you!

For you to be effective at options trading, Instead of the calculus behind the price models, you need to understand the odds, or probability theory, behind options. You don't have to become a statistician. You simply need to understand a few fundamentals, which are dealt with in this book.

While it will require some time and effort to learn about trading options effectively, when you master the process, you can trade by committing about ten minutes each day to it.

I hope you will stick with me as we check out the world of options.

CHAPTER ONE

Why Trade Options?

Many people ask, "With lots of places to invest and with the complexity of the markets, would I not be better off, letting a professional manage my money rather than trying to trade options myself?" The reluctance to go into the world of self-directed investing is understandable. However, experiences in the world of investments have shown that no one takes care of your money like you do. Many money managers go through about three to six months training program, and they get off running and trading your hard-earned savings.

The next questions that come up are; "But options are so complex, am I not much better off just trading stocks?" and "How could I potentially contend with the options professionals?"

Being Strategic without Direction

If you put about three or more market experts or professionals in the room and ask, "Which of you can forecast market and specific stock direction the best?" you better be ready for the heated argument that will ensue. The economist will say she can because she understands the mechanisms that drive the market in the long term. The essential expert will tell you that everybody understands the market increases in the long run, but he can separate which stocks will go up one of the most. The technical expert will say, "Hey, people, the marketplace moves in two directions. And I can tell you when you will be near assistance or resistance levels, and when the Fibonaccis have retraced."

Often a hot topic of debate, research shows that market movement is mainly random in the long run. And this premise of random (Brownian) motion is, in fact, at the heart of every alternative pricing design.

If markets move arbitrarily, then how does anyone earn money in the markets? Well, markets move arbitrarily, but with a "favorable drift." This means that in the long run, nearly everyone who owns a diversified stock portfolio ought to generate income. Which quantity ought to be around what is understood as the "risk-free rate of return." Over the past 50 years, that has totaled up to a bit over 6.2 percent each year. Now, that's a fair little bit of modification so that you might do even worse with your cash. But you can likewise do better-- a lot better.

As the technical analyst said, the marketplace relocates two instructions. Over the past 50 years, the market (as represented by the S&P 500 index) has gone up on 52.89 percent of the days and down on 47.11 percent of the days. Why try to make money by guessing which stock will go up the most? Options permit you to benefit from movement in either direction or from no movement at all! To put it merely, options are strategic without being directional. You can earn money from virtually any situation if you craft your trade correctly.

A Word about Leverage

This is a concept that is often criticized. When leverage is used appropriately, it is one of the most effective methods of enhancing portfolio returns offered. Why are we talking about leverage, and how does it relate to options?

Leverage, simply put, is when you use borrowed money to enhance the return on your investment. It increases the risk of your portfolio. If you are to be effective at trading, you need to understand the fact that risk can be a definite idea. All monetary instruments are simply ways of moving risk. As long as you are "paid" more than you view your risk to be, risk-taking, therefore, becomes your means of making money. To put it simply, you need to stop thinking of risk as something to be avoided and start embracing risk as your process of generating income. It is half of the risk versus return trade-off that needs to play a part in every trade you make.

The types and amounts of risks you take on in your portfolio ought to depend on your specific circumstance. Inputs to this decision consist of how old you are, how capable you are at enduring drawdowns (and replacing those lost funds), how well you comprehend riskier trades, how many edges you view in the trade, and on and on. One compelling piece of information options gives you is how much risks the options market individuals as a whole perceive in a given trade. So, you have many investors' cumulative views at your disposal to help you.

Returning to leverage, you don't remember saying you wished to borrow any money, do you? Maybe your credit ranking is not up to snuff. Or possibly you simply do not want to make those monthly payments. No concerns! You have two means of accomplishing leverage with options without needing to submit yourself to a credit check each time you borrow and without receiving those big coupon books in the mail. When you open a margin portfolio margin account, you are, in reality, establishing a mechanism for borrowing money. You do not even need to ask to get from then on. Your broker will immediately provide you additional funds and charge your account only for interest on the quantity utilized if you go beyond the capital in the report.

More to the point is that options are levered instruments in and of themselves. If you wish to buy 100 shares of GOOGL (Google) stock ($ 590) in your IRA (no leverage), you would have to create around $59,000. However, for a mere $3,300, you could command the very same 100 shares for the next 189 days, by purchasing a Mar 15 600Call option. Sure, the option has a different risk profile as well as profit and loss profile, but above a specific cost ($ 633), you will fully take part in the stock's benefit. After 189 days, you will either require to cough up the rest of the money to hold the stock or sell out your options to secure your earnings without ever having to create the additional money. Now! Where else can you borrow that sort of money without a credit check?

Going a bit deeper into what options leverage implies to your returns, let's say GOOGL stock goes up to $650 at the expiration of the options. While it holds, you will make more cash with stock in this example, let's examine the ROC (return on capital) for each trade.

As you can see, the non-annualized ROCs for the two methods are10.17 percent for the stock purchase and 51.52 percent for the purchase of the call options. Rather a distinction! And one that may make a trade inGOOGL possible, thinking about not everyone has $59,000 to plunk down for 100 shares of stock! This is the power that options offer.

Multiply that power by the loan you automatically receive in your margin or portfolio margin account, and you have the structure for some returns!

Options Are a Decaying Asset.

You know the old saying that a new vehicle loses 30 percent of its value the second you drive it off the lot? That might be overemphasized a bit though, the principle is clear. Options are just like cars, though as an option's devaluation starts slow and speeds up, the more detailed it gets to completion of its "life." At least you can use vehicles while they diminish, but you can't drive your option to the shop with the aim of buying a gallon of milk or a cup of yogurt. So, what good are options? To the owner of an opportunity, its decay causes a little bit of impatience in the hope of seeing your option grow in price just before the collapse "gets you." To the seller of the option, who took on the risk of the brief option, decay is their friend. So why would you ever purchase an option if you know it will decay away in time and serve no practical purpose while doing so? Well, options are not quite that fundamental. There are two parts to the value of an option, and they are called intrinsic value and extrinsic value.

Another point needs to be made about the rotting nature of an option. When you acquire an option, you are paying more than the option is (inherently) worth at that time. To put it simply, you are spending some premium (typically called time premium or insurance premium) for the right such option offers. Let's take a look at an example. Let's say XYZ stock is trading for$ 48.50, and the $47 call is trading for $2.25. If you purchased the call, exercised it instantly, and sold the stock you received from the exercise, you would get $1.50 for your trouble, exclusive of fees. Let's walk through this. You get to buy the stock for $47 and offer it out at the market price of $48.50 when you exercise the $47 calls. That suggests you keep $1.50. This is your intrinsic value. However, you paid $2.25 for that call, so you are still out$0.75. This is the extrinsic value, or time premium, which you paid for. It is this quantity of $0.75 that will decay away unless the stock rallies. And if you purchase an out of the money option, it is all extrinsic value by meaning. This means that if you buy an option, your probability of making money from it is less than 50 percent. Why purchase it? A long option has limited loss (what you pay for it) and limitless revenue capacity.

CHAPTER TWO

Options Trading Strategy Tips to Earn Money

It's relatively simple for us to generate income by trading because 90%+ of our trades pay. It's crucial to restrict risks by trading a small number of contracts and liquidate your trades early. The trading option premium has a high statistical possibility of earnings. The following strategies will help you streamline your options trading career.

- **Limit Your Information Sources:** Do not check out a website like SeekingAlpha.com or see CNBC. Those are for home entertainment purposes and will not assist you in making money.

- **Create a Watch List**: Only trade a few stocks, and try to have positions on 4-5 underlying stocks at one time. Just keep things incredibly easy and neglect everything else. I hugely recommend that you narrow the number of stocks that you trade. If you have an account size of $20,000, you ought to just trade 1-2 stocks at one time.

- **Trade from Your Phone**: You can make all trades from your phone and not necessarily use any charting software application. Keep things easy because if you complicate matters, it'll negatively impact your returns.

- **Get Familiar with the Recent Trading Range**: Get comfortable with the new trading range on the stocks in your watch list. If the trades at the high end of the variety, sell a call. If it trades at the low end of the array, offer a put.

- **Trade Naked Options**: Contact your broker and demand the ability to trade naked options. It's a lot more secure and a lot easier to manage positions.
- **Sign up for Trade Alerts:** Receive real-time trade notifications so that you optimize your profits and lessen your mistakes.

Factors To Consider For Trading Options

1. High returns

With options, you can accomplish high returns. 100% to 400% is not unusual in a matter of weeks or perhaps days. With the higher rate of return, you likewise deal with higher risks.

2. You can earn money when the market is fluctuating up and down:

All you need is for the market to be moving. You pick either a Put or Call option based upon what you believe the marketplace is doing.

3. Options are inexpensive:

Options are indeed cheap. A couple of financial investments have this type of cost. You might restrict your losses by putting in a stop-loss order.

4. Leverage

When purchasing options, you make use of leverage. Generally, you acquire option contracts worth of 100. You are not the owner of the stock, and you own the right to buy or sell the stock at a given cost. You sell the option or purchase the option which serves as insurance coverage to the buyer or seller of stock. You use your 100 to 1.

If you wish to learn how to make money in options trading, the first step is to develop a strategy for options trading. Don't merely leap in blind, but take a while and think of your objectives and how you plan to attain them. Numerous portfolios don't consist of any options trading methods at all, but that's a mistake. There's a lot to get from this element of the market.

Limit your drawback and grow your potential for profit by approaching options without fear. Trading options does not need to be a complex process if you don't desire it to be. Buying options to keep up with the cost motions of future stocks enables you to reduce your threats while concurrently opening the door for endless revenues.

Options can likewise be used for hedging and giving your portfolio a little cushion. Think about it; you buy insurance when you buy new cars and truck or other essential items, why not consider protecting your portfolio with insurance? Hedging can function as the last hope if your portfolio gets to that point.

There are a couple of methods that financiers can approach options. Instead of just purchasing shares in stocks that you anticipate will rise in value, you can buy call options to increase your advantage.

CHAPTER THREE

What to Look for in a broker

Before you trade any financial instrument, you need to open a brokerage account. Indeed, that might require more paperwork! But for many, that is not the worst part. There are many terms and principles embedded in the documents that are foreign to a lot of new investors. And there are many warnings regarding the dangers of different types of investments. In reality, there are additional risk disclosures particular to options you need to check out and sign when you create an account that allows options trading. But what brokers do not alert you about are the risks that are inherent in selecting the right brokerage firm.

Banks Versus Brokerages

Many people are comfortable putting their money into banks. They ensure that when they drive to their local branch and ask for $300 to do some shopping, the bank will comply. They are also confident that when they decide to withdraw large portions of their accounts, the bank will not have an issue creating the funds. This is particularly true for bigger banks. In spite of some times of distress, such as the financial crisis of 2008-- 2009, the reality that the government-run FDIC (Federal Deposit Insurance Corporation) insures as much as an overall of $250,000 for each deposit category in each insured bank provides additional security to the depositor. But what do banks do with your cash when you transfer it? If you are to be truly comfortable, shouldn't you understand what happens with it when you drop it off? Well, soon after you drop your money off, the bank is out loaning it to somebody else or some other business.

So, why am I telling you of the safety of your bank account when we are speaking about brokerages? Well, in my opinion, if you choose the proper brokerage, your cash is even more secure there. When you deposit funds in a brokerage account, your financial organization has a legal commitment to segregate your funds into a separate account for your advantage. In other words, your funds will not be at risk if Tom or Fred loses his task and can not repay his loans. Though the FDIC does not cover your account, it is, in fact, covered by SIPC (Securities Investor Protection Corporation). And it is covered for $500,000, $250,000 of which can be in cash. In total, it is included for twice that of your account. Of course, this security does not encompass trading losses or fraud. Instead, it covers you against your brokerage company going insolvent due to less dubious reasons. SIPC is not a government-run corporation. It is funded by the member companies that are covered by SIPC. So, though SIPC exists to secure you, just as when you pick a bank, there is no reason to lure fate. You do not want to depend on the "safeguard" under your account. Let's look at more steps you should consider to secure your money.

Depth of a Broker's Pockets

Just as the small, local bank down the street is luring but fails to have as much "room for mistake" as the big bank in town, a big brokerage firm is usually a safer bet with less threat of losing your funds. Initially, large brokerages, by meaning, have deeper pockets. Hence, just as JP Morgan Chase was able to quickly hold up against losses from the "London Whale's" trading as a result of its deep pockets, a large brokerage can also stand up to damages triggered by errors. Even big brokerages do not start as large institutions. They have paid their dues and are usually run by experienced industry experts with knowledge far beyond those of most small firms. They have also "vetted" their policies to be sure they are safe and correct and operate in all (or virtually all) market conditions. More prominent companies also generally have instituted what we call "business risk management policies and procedures." These are created to add security against all recognized threats to the company.

Trading Risk Management

If you have been around floor traders for any length of time, one remark you may have heard is, "My cleaning company's risk managers are a pain in my ass!". This is one point in which it appears professional traders are misguided. A market breakdown could then put the firm at risk of losses beyond their ability to cover, thereby putting everyone's money at risk.

Account Types

There are numerous ways to categorize account types. This section of the book will focus on the three models that apply to options trading. For our purposes, we will categorize accounts as the following:

1. Cash

2. Reg-T Margin

3. Portfolio Margin

Cash Accounts

Perhaps the most common type of cash account is an IRA. You can get permission from your broker to trade options with the following restrictions:

- All option purchases must be paid completely.
- You can never be short stock or short naked calls.
- When you trade a covered call, your stock is restricted.
- All option sales must be backed in cash up to the maximum loss possible.

Since options are levered instruments in and of themselves, the ability to trade options in a cash account vaults your account type into the category of a "partial margin account." This is just semantics, so do not get puzzled. Your IRA is still tax-deferred

Reg-T Margin Accounts

Unlike a cash account, where all securities must be paid for, ultimately, a margin account enables an investor to borrow money from his broker to cover the expense of the security (for long options) or to cover the threat of the security (for short options). Regulation T limits the amount obtained toward the trade to no higher than 50 percent.

Some people would ask: "Doesn't that increase your risk?" Margin can increase your risk by allowing you to put on more trades than you would otherwise have the ability to make without a loan. If you diversify your portfolio correctly, it does not always have to increase your risk. The act of levering will increase your return on capital, as long as you pay.

Portfolio Margin Accounts

In April 2007, the SEC started permitting portfolio margining in retail accounts. For portfolio margin accounts, the margin is calculated based upon the total risk in the portfolio. This indicates if trades have offsetting risk, margin can really drop as you include trades. The margin is determined each night by the OCC (Options Clearing Corp.), using a system known as the "TheoreticalIntermarket Margining System" (TIMS). This system calculates the most significant potential loss for all positions (in aggregate) in an item class across a variety of underlying volatilities and rates. That margin amount usually is less than that calculated by the Reg-T margin system. And once again, position margin is not additive but rather determined as a total portfolio, thus offering the account type its name.

One point about portfolio margin accounts you must know. Many portfolio margin accounts have much higher minimum capital requirements than do margin accounts. At my broker, you can open a Reg-T margin account with as little as $2,000, while a portfolio margin account needs a minimum of $125,000. Some brokers will require you to pass an examination displaying your understanding of margining and trading before allowing you access to a portfolio margin account. Though there are advantages to a portfolio margin account, they are not for everyone and are controlled for the higher good of the broker's customers.

Overall, more recent options traders ought to be looking to open a margin account, while knowledgeable traders that qualify need to want to open a portfolio margin account. You do not always need to use the increased leverage offered, but it is good to have access to it when a situation for which it is helpful develops.

Commissions

Commissions of all kinds are the expense of working. Lots of traders will go shopping brokerages based upon fees alone. This is a bit short-sighted for some reason. Initially, we will go over the kinds of commissions that brokerages charge, and after that, we will discuss their ramifications for our trading and our choice of brokers.

Commissions are typically charged in three ways:

1. A per deal charge up to a certain number of agreements.

2. A ticket charge plus a per agreement charge.

3. Per agreement charge alone.

The very first type, a fixed price, per transaction charge, is uncommon in the options world. It is a lot more familiar with stocks where you may be able to trade approximately 1,000 shares of stock for a set charge, and even limitless shares per deal for a set fee. These kinds of setups may be excellent for someone who trades stock in big chunks. But for a more recent trader who is trading ina little account, I would highly recommend staying away from this kind of structure. Let's look at an example where you are charged $7 per deal, and you generally trade 100 shares of stock per trade. That would exercise to $.07 per share in and $.07 out, which means you need to make $.14 per trade just to break even.

Moving back to the options world, the equivalent of this type of structure is the "ticket charge plus deal cost" setup. Using an example, you may be provided a $7.95 ticket charge plus $0.75 per agreement cost. This indicates that for each option deal you make, you will be charged $7.95, plus $0.75 times the variety of contracts carried out in your order. If you trade one contract, your fee is $8.70 (($ 7.95 + (1 $0.75)). For 10 contracts, your commission would be $15.45 (($ 7.95 + (10 $0.75)), or $1.545

per agreement. If you trade 50 agreements in your order, your charge would be $45.45 (($ 7.95 + (50 0.75)), or $0.909 per agreement.

An alternative may be to sustain a per contract cost only. That fee, for new accounts, might be $1.50 per contract. As you can see, if you are trading one agreement per trade, you would be far better off with this structure as you will be paying $1.50 per trade instead of $8.70 per trade. As a 50-contract trader, you may be better off with the mixed structure, but my guess is that if your typical contract size is 50 contracts, you might get your per deal charge down low enough to wish still to avoid ticket charges.

Among the fascinating things to note is that brokerages will often attempt to force new traders to have a ticket charge. This ensures the brokerage will make cash on each deal, even if you do not! This is backward, as a new trader will cease to be an options trader at all with those types of fees. After all, if you are starting to trade and are selling a $1 enormous credit spread for $0.35, and your commissions are $8.70 to put it on and $8.70 to close the trade, your optimum revenue is now ($ 0.35-- (2 $8.70)) or$ 0.176, while your prospective loss is ($ 0.65 + (2 * $8.70)) or $0.824.

With your likelihood of profiting at around 65 percent, these trades are practically assurances; you will lose cash over time. I suggest not opening an account at a brokerage that insists on a ticket charge. The majority of brokerages, but not all, will negotiate this. If the one you are taking a look at will not, it is time to take a look at another company.

Presuming you have opened an account and picked a fixed commission schedule, I just want to put commissions in perspective. They are variable costs (i.e., expenses you sustain only when you make a trade) that can positively affect your success, there are other considerations that offset and, in my view, far surpass the commission schedule's value.

We will deal with a lot of them in more detail later in the book, however, for your factor to consider:

- Trading liquid options with tight bid/ask spreads have a much higher result on your profitability than commissions. Here is an example. Let's state you are trading a relatively illiquid stock called XYZ. The option you want to offer is priced estimate $3.40 bid at $3.70 deal. If you need to quit $0.30 getting in and out because of the bid/ask spread, you are genuinely getting $30 per contract, due to the options "100 share" multiplier. Contrast this with the distinction between a $1.50 and a $1.00 commission structure per share, and you will rapidly see the bid/ask spread in this example is 60 times larger.

- Of course, your option of which options you choose to trade, and therefore the width of the bid/ask spread, is relatively untouched by your option of brokers. However, your broker's ability to get your orders filled somewhere in the middle of the spread is of substantial importance.

- Back to that robust front-end system: Having a trading system that assists in finding and handling your trades is also of substantial importance. What good are cheap commissions if you can not discover a way to make money trading?

- Data feeds can be expensive. Brokers charge a monthly cost to their customers as a means of recovering their costs of information acquisition. Others will take in those costs as a cost of doing organization. Depending on how frequently you trade, this might be a significant consideration for you. If you get lower commissions, however, have to pay data-feed fees, you may be paying more in the long run. You are exchanging variable costs for fixed expenses.

- There is nothing more frustrating than trading in a slow market for several years, and then, when you eventually have an active market, your broker's systems can not maintain, and you fail to make the most of a golden opportunity. This reliability, when again, can be much more crucial than a 25 or 50-cent reduction in commissions.

CHAPTER FOUR

Phases of the Market

This chapter will check out the cost patterns that continuously come back in the market and talk about the participants that produce the models. It handles not only the designs themselves but the psychology of the marketplace participants and why the action of the traders exposes itself in the continuously duplicating patterns.

We understand mathematically that when a trade occurs, the marketplace needs to be in balance. When the trade occurs, the rate can go anywhere. This chapter is written to help explain the market in different phases. The terms used are not universal in any way but are vital to this study. Some people have different names used for them, but for this book, we will use the definitions as stated below;

■Congestion

I believe that all liquid markets have the same cycle. It does not matter what the hidden asset that is going to be traded; it will go through a period. I think that the preliminary phase of any market is congestion.

When the participants are confused by congestion is the section of the cycle, the current price action. The long and the brief traders will exchange positions as the steady hands continuously change. If you are a short-term trader, this can happen as numerous as five or six times throughout a session. Unless you are a countertrend trader (selling as rate advances and buying when it decreases, likewise called the weak hands), trading in this kind of market can be aggravating. You might purchase a number of tops and offer a variety of bottoms. This is known as getting whipsawed, and it is one of the problems of being a reactive trader. Another name for reactive traders is trend following. They search for the direction that cost is moving and then use technical analysis to" follow the pattern." I am not a stringent pattern trader; however, instead, react to the current market stage.

When the market starts to whipsaw, I continuously lose cash on the first set of trades. The congestion stage is marked initially by fictional limits called support and resistance. It might assist in believing in relief as the floor of the market, and that resistance is the ceiling.

Support is where the weak hands will balance down and buy additional shares of stock or agreements to reduce their average cost. It is also the position where traders who have been observing the existing market will make a buy. If the support holds, the long traders will become the steady hands, and the shorts (weak hands) will be required to either take profit or begin to cover their loss and look for a new area to get in. They will press the market to the other side, and it will start to find some resistance if the new purchasers are strong enough.

Resistance will bring sellers back to the market, countertrend traders will" average up," and the shorts offer additional shares or contracts to raise their typical sale. The resistance will also restore traders who have been observing, and they will start to provide. If the strongholds, the short traders will become the steady hands, and the marketplace will force the long traders (now the weak hands) either to take profit or lock in their loss. They will push the market back to test the support a 2nd time if the sellers are strong enough.

This test is understood as a double bottom. It is significant, as it will be among the most profitable trades that you make in weekly options. If the double bottom holds, it will bring more buyers into the market, and the sellers will begin to take profit or lock-in loss. The strong hands will now be the buyers, and they will take the cost back to the previous resistance. If that point holds, it will become a double top, and it is hugely significant as the blockage area will now be defined.

As long as the market remains in the congestion pattern, it will be traded the same way of buying the double bottoms and selling the double tops. Congestion can last for a very long time. If you purchase every day, it might last for months, even longer.

It might continue some days or weeks if you are a day trader or a swing trader. Many specialists believe that market is in congestion more than 60 percent of the time. They hit on the exact top and bottom. Fundamentalists state that this pattern is a self-fulfilling prophecy; professionals say that traders recognize this pattern and adapt their trading style to take advantage of it. Undoubtedly, I agree with the professionals. The breakout took place when the long traders from the 3rd double bottom (triple quadruple; I always use double) in a row held, and they forced the sellers out at the next double top.

■ Breakout to the Trend

When the previous support and resistance levels fail to hold, the breakout to the trend will start. The double top and double bottom sellers will begin to feel pressure when their standards are violated; they know that breakout and pattern traders will be entering into the market as new cash. This imbalance will begin to generate more buyers or sellers, forcing the countertrend traders to abandon positions. When the market makes its first more significant high or lower low, the culmination of the purchasing or swelling will occur. Profit takers will enter the market, and they might be signed up with a wave of countertrend traders that might force the cost below/above the old support or resistance levels. If that happens, it would be entitled to a false breakout. After the low is made, the marketplace made a series and reversed lower highs and higher lows. When the double leading failed to hold, the rate ultimately rallied back into the congestion phase and broke out to the pattern on the benefit.

When the profit taking subsides, if a more significant low or a lower high holds, the trend is confirmed. The market never goes in one direction permanently; even in a pattern, there will be some price motion to the opposite of the trending market as profit taking and countertrend traders will continue to try and move price in their favor—the upward or down angle at which the trend.

Most of trending markets can not sustain a price rise/fall on an angle of over 45 degrees. As you can observe, the price meanders around the mean as profit taking and countertrend traders take their piece out of the pie.

Eventually, the marketplace will make a high/low that has a lower high or more significant low follow it on the next cost swing. This is the first indication that the trend may be reversing. A market is pausing before it resumes its pattern, or the present trend may be ending. The strong hands that had been managing the market will become the weak hands, and when this occurs, it will reenter the congestion stage. The brand-new congestion might be a breather, and the fight between the steady hands and the weak hands may solve itself in a breakout back to the previous significant trend. If the market is making a rounding top or bottom, the new congestion stage will cause a breakout to the opposite side of the existing pattern, and a brand-new trending phase will begin to the reverse side of the current market.

■ Blowoff

If the current trend doesn't resolve itself in a rounding top/bottom and costs begin to accelerate at a much steeper angle than the sustainable 45-degree rate, the market will more than likely end in a blowoff. The blowoff phase of the marketplace is always the least quantity of time in any of the three steps; however, it might lead to the absolute rate movement. When the weak hands get squeezed to the limitation, the blowoff takes place. They can no longer fight the trend, and they are forced to cover, probably through the absence of capital or margin calls that should be satisfied. During the blowoff rate, phase and time may become infinite; meaning rate reaches a vertical relocation of 90 degrees. Every tick is either higher or lower, the weak hands end up being price-insensitive, and the only thing they show exciting is getting enough amount to end the discomfort. The degree of the blowoff draws in new cash to the old, weak hands' now-vacated position. The strong hands begin to take profit. They might also join the brand-new money in altering instructions. When this happens, the classic V pattern is formed in the market. Ultimately, the marketplace goes back to stability, and a new market pattern starts.

The vital principle provided is that in a liquid market, the significant rate patterns offered in this area can be depended on to repeat with regular frequency. They might have elements linked, as in the examples of a blowoff resulting in another blowoff, however, the one thing they share is that they are mathematically ensured to repeat.

CHAPTER FIVE

Call Options Versus Put Options

Put options

It's essential to understand the various kinds of options when trying to make money trading options. There are two primary kinds of options, call options and put options. Both are a kind of contract. These option contracts include two parties, the option holder and the option issuer. The option holder is conferred with the right to perform a specific transaction with the issuer, but the holder isn't required to carry out that deal.

Call options manage the right to buy and put options to afford the right to sell. The strike cost is the agreed-upon rate for the property under contract. In stock trading, the property is the share. A call option offers the option holder the right to buy a share or shares at a strike rate for an identified period. When the time is up, the contract hits its expiration date and becomes worthless. A put option offers the option holder the right to sell shares at a strike cost for a set amount of time.

If an investor believes the worth of shares will rise, they purchase call options. If they understand the value will fall, they buy put options. The ability to properly check out an options chain is essential to succeed in buying and selling options at earnings.

Benefits of Trading Call Options

In addition to making more money with options trading, you can also take advantage of the way they function when it comes to risks.

The majority of equity options and index option contracts in the United States benefit one month and end on the third Friday of that month. As the stock exchange continues to adjust to changes, more transactions are altering this rule and providing option contracts with weekly expiration dates for a quicker turn-around on more significant stocks and indices.

American call options offer a fair bit of versatility compared to European options. A trader can implement their call option agreements at any time before the deal expires with American style options. Still, European style options need the trader to wait until the expiration date to enforce the agreement.

Call options likewise offer limitless earning possible with minimal risk for loss.

If you acquire a call option contract for $1 per show, a strike cost of $10 per share, and the price rises to $1000; your call options would have an intrinsic worth of $900 per share, leaving you with huge earnings.

If they drop to $0 per share, you'll just lose what you spent on the contract. Say you buy an agreement for 100 shares. That's a loss capacity of $100 with a revenue potential of more than $90,000.

Five Reasons Why Options Trading Is Better Than Stock Trading

Options trading has been the center of much debate of current years. Is it dangerous? Can we declare bankruptcy? Indeed, options being a form of the derivative instrument are even more complex than the stocks that they are composed based upon and, like a wild stallion, can harm you if you do not know how it works and how to use it properly.

I will provide five reasons options trading is much better than stock trading to resolve the age-old misconceptions of how unsafe options trading is. Let's remember this: Options trading threatens just when you do not comprehend it.

1) Variable Leverage

The take advantage those options give you is possibly the primary reason that people gravitate to options trading in the first place. Trading options enables you to make a lot more earnings on the same carry on the underlying stock. You are merely making 1% revenue on a 1% relocation in your favor when you purchase the stock itself without margin. Nevertheless, in options trading, you could be making 10%

revenue on that same 1% relocation the stock made or even as much as 100% on that same 1% relocation!

Yes, the charm of leverage in options, unlike in futures trading, is that it is FLEXIBLE!

You could handle more leverage for more danger or lower take advantage for lower-danger by picking options of different strike costs and expiration month.

This explains why the beauty of leverage in options trading is that it permits you to make the same trades with much lesser cash; as such, you could simply use only cash you can pay for to and mean to lose in any unsuccessful business for each options trade. Hence, leverage helps you manage your losses significantly!

2) Low Capital Required

Apple Inc., AAPL, is trading at over $295.36 today, which implies it takes $29,536 to purchase 100 shares today. However, AAPL's at the cash call options cost something like $715 to control the earnings on that same 100 shares of Apple!

3) Bet Downwards Without Margin

You might only short the stock, which sustains margin. However, in trading options, all you need to do to bank on a stock moving downwards is to BUY its put options with no margin required at all. That's right; purchasing put options for earnings to drawback works the purchasing call options for revenue to upside precisely. There is no significant need to own the stock ahead of time, and there is no requirement for margin!

4) Multi-Directional Profits

In stock trading, you only make money when the stock goes in the directions you desire it to. There is no other way to benefit in both circumstances simultaneously, and there is no chance to make a profit if the price of the stock does not move. However, in options trading, such multi-directional earnings are possible! There are options methods that allow you to benefit no matter if the stock goes upwards or downwards quickly, and there are options strategies that profit even if the cost of the capital stays unchanged! Such is the real magic of options methods, which significantly increases your opportunities of winning in options trading versus stock trading!

5) Play Banker

Tired and ill of always being at the player's side of the table? In options trading, you could switch instead to the banker's side of the table and do what market makers do by offering options to individuals who are desires to take the bottom of the player! When the players lose, as they typically do, you get to keep the bet as earnings much like a real banker! Just options trading has the "bet," which you get to follow and it is known as "extrinsic worth."

CHAPTER SIX

Trade Probabilities: What to Look For

•Interest Rates

We spoke earlier about margin accounts. With those accounts, your broker will instantly loan you cash when you have surpassed the quantity of money available in your account. That advantage does not come free of charge. Your broker will have to charge you interest on the funds you borrow. Not all brokers reveal this to you; it appears to surprise many newer traders when they suddenly have an interest charge hit their accounts at the end of a month. And comparable to our conversation on commissions, the rates charged usually are less considerable than other issues.

Stock Borrow and Loan

Stock obtain and loan might not be a very crucial topic for you most of the time if you are continually trading extremely liquid stocks and options. Sometimes (like after specific corporate actions), a share in which you have a position might end up being hard, or impossible, to borrow. Let's talk about a couple of terms, and after that, examine how picking a great broker might make your life much more comfortable.

Shorting Stock

Individuals new to trading are typically confused and shocked by the principle of "shorting a stock." Shorting a stock is when you offer stock you do not presently own. How can you offer something you do not own? By obtaining it from someone else, naturally. It is not like you are borrowing your next-door neighbor's lawnmower and delivering it to a person across town. That may make your neighbor a bit upset. Stocks are more generic. That is, one share of XYZ stock is the same as any other share of XYZ stock (offered we are mentioning the very same class of stock). Your broker discovers someone to borrow the stock from on your behalf and permits you to provide it with. Why would you do that? You will do that if you think the price of the stock is too high and wish to benefit from its going back to a more "reasonable" cost. You "sell" it now, and you must repurchase it later in the day and time to "return" it to the lending institution of the stock. Once again, the borrowing and returning are all done by your broker and are transparent to you. What could go incorrect if this is all done behind the scenes? Why speak about it at all, aside from to say it is a normal part of stock trading? We are getting to that!

Easy to Borrow

In normal circumstances, everything goes efficiently with the stock obtain and loan activity. Every trading day, your broker finds every stock that you receive in anticipation, or another customer, may have the desire to do so. When the stock is readily available, that is easy to obtain. That indicates you can short the stock without any issues. Usually, this is reflected via your broker's trading software by a lack of any tagging. Some brokers might tell you it is easy to borrow (ETB), but typically it is an absence of notice that tells you all is well.

Hard to Borrow

There are times when lots of people, all viewing the very same image, come to the same conclusion. Individuals who are going long might offer their stock (and might even go short the stock) if that conclusion is that the stock is overpriced. By providing their stock, they no longer have stock to offer. Individuals who have no position might select to brief also. The schedule of stock to borrow begins to diminish, and the stock ends up being "hard to obtain." When a stock is tough to acquire, it will be assessed your trading software, and if you wish to short the stock, you will most likely require to have direct communication with your broker. The broker will search further for you to find the stock. At times, they might offer to lock up stock for you for a fee. This charge is reflected by an interest rate you should pay to hold the stock aside for you to obtain versus. Your trade now handles a new risk/return ratio for you to consider before moving forward.

- Impossible to Borrow

When there is no stock available to borrow at (virtually) any rate, we call this stock "impossible to obtain." You can not short this stock. Your trading software application will stop you. Your broker, somewhere on their website, releases a list of impossible-to-borrow stocks for your perusal every day.

- Buy-Ins

What happens if you short a stock when it is easy to obtain but later becomes impossible to achieve? By law, your broker can not allow you to remain brief the stock if the stock that your broker borrowed in your place gets pulled away (either offered or the owner simply refuses to lend any more). Your broker looks around for brand-new sources of stock to obtain and shows up empty. You are now based on what we call a "buy-in." This suggests that later in the trading day, the broker will buy some or all of your stock back on your behalf and location it in your account. Your short position will be decreased or end at the price your broker chooses to pay.

- Short Interest

One method to anticipate the problem you may have in borrowing stock is to track a stock's short interest. "Short interest" is specified as the difference of shares sold briefly and not yet repurchased. If you sell shares you own, this does not impact the short interest. If you sell shares you do not own (short the stock), this sale gets shown in the brief interest number. How can you interpret the short interest number? There are two methods, either of which can be utilized to raise a warning.

Let's say XXX stock has a short interest of 6 million shares, and ZZZ stock has a short interest of 24 million. Does this mean shorting ZZZ stock has more threat than shorting XXX stock? Not necessarily. There are two different aspects in which we can compare the short interest number to evaluate our risk.

Initially, we can compare this number to the stock's float. A stock's float describes the number of shares that are offered to be purchased and provided by the general investing public. By dividing the short interest into the raft, we get a reading as to the portion of offered shares that are presently provided short. We can get a stock's float from a variety of commercial sites (such as yahoo. finance.com), as it is an extensively recognized and distributed number.

Returning to our example, if XXX stock has a float of 24 million shares, its short interest is 25 percent. If ZZZ has a raft of 480 million shares, its short interest is 5 percent. So, XXX would have a more significant buy-in threat, all other things being equal.

We can also look up the stock's "days to cover" number. Days to cover describes the stock's short interest divided by the daily volume of the capital. This offers you an idea of how hard it might be for brief sellers to purchase back their stock. When the days to cover begins to approach near double digits, one gets worried and will frequently aim to start paring back the short position.

Where Your Broker Matters

Why go over all this in a section called "Stock Borrow and Loan"? As soon as you have gone through a buy-in, you will most likely say you would rather have a root canal. You will do everything you can to avoid another. A large, trusted broker will have a large stock, and many relationships forged that will give it much better access to stock availability for loaning. Size isn't the only factor to consider; size and credibility frequently play critical roles in your broker's capacity to borrow stock on your behalf.

Trading Platforms

Some brokers have numerous platforms, one for frequent traders (and experts) and another for the typical retail trader. If you do not fall into the first classification, I would be wary of accepting the "dumbed down" platform. Unless the broker can encourage you that they are streamlining your life by protecting you from unwanted information, it appears they are telling you you're a second-class resident who might not use and discover the tools other "smarter" traders use. An excellent front-end trading system should do this few things at a minimum:

1. Must be easy to use and provide excellent methods to learn the platform

2. Enable you to see historical options and stock data

3. Have a mobile platform offered

When shopping for a broker, you need to think about a lot more than merely commissions. Consider your broker as your partner in the organization. When searching for a partner, do you look for the cheapest option, or do you find the one who adds one of the most value? Defend the very best commission structure you can get, however, only after thinking about all the other worth propositions offered by each broker. In my opinion, 25 or 50 cents per agreement differential in commissions. As a number of the traders, state, "You do not understand what you don't know." Until you have dealt with many platforms, had to handle different firms on buy-ins, or had your trading platform shut down during busy market conditions, you have a little conceptual basis for these decisions. I hope you at least now have a better concept of the concerns you ought to ask and what value you need to get from your broker.

CHAPTER SEVEN

Making Profit From Trading Options

Different elements can affect an option's cost, so traders can't anticipate to start purchasing call options and making revenues simply. Only particular trades will end in a receipt for the buyer; others will cause a loss. A trader will just successfully benefit from trading call options when they buy options for a stock that is anticipated to increase at a decent rate over the following week or month.

Consider how much you anticipate the stock to rise. This is where excellent research enters play. Understanding a specific option's history and prepare for their future is vital to earning a profit.

Buying out-of-the-money call options for a $50 strike price isn't a great move if the cost is just most likely to increase 5 cents per day. However, if the stock is most likely to move as much as 50 cents per day, it has the potential to be a terrific play. The volatility also plays a significant role in whether it's an excellent concept to purchase its options. Some people take pleasure in the thrill, but a lucrative trader represents the market thoroughly and does not take numerous substantial threats.

Although lots of traders only purchase out-of-the-money options, like we said in the past, this isn't, in fact, a powerful technique. OTM options do use low costs, so they have the capacity for some severe turn-around. However, they're risky. Some traders much like the concept of owning several options, so they 'd instead buy a lot of more affordable OTM options than a couple of strong ones.

Think about whether you play the lottery. Possibly trading in OTM options is something you 'd delight in if you do. The options exchange shouldn't be performed like the lotto. The odds don't have to be wrong. Play it smart and offer yourself excellent odds.

Ways to Improve Your Options Trading

Here are actionable steps you can begin today to improve your options trading:

1. Find Out and Master Options Trading Fundamentals

You must understand the basics of options before you venture out option trades. It must be followed by orderly. It's the reason that we discover how to do basic math and subtraction before we go into the department and multiplication.

You require to know whatever about "puts" and "calls"-- from how they work and when it's finest to use them. This likewise consists of understanding everything related to them like expiration dates to where they are found on the first option tables. Skimming the essentials to enter into more innovative trading is just betting.

2. Read Books on Options Trading

Technically, they don't need to be everything about options trading, given that there is overlap in every investment book. The objective is to discover various methods of trading the market. You'll find out about things you have not understood about before, and you'll even be able to improve your initial trading method.

One excellent benefit derived from reading books is that you can also find out more about the covert trading elements you do not see daily like investor psychology or market psychology. Did you understand that these psychologies are the reason that technical analysis exist?

3. Streamline Your Technical Analysis

You're most likely doing yourself a disservice if you are looking at 6+ more technical indications and use multiple technical analyses concepts versus other technical analyses concepts.

Just learn and use the fundamentals like MACD, support/resistance, trending channels, divergence/convergence, and moving averages.

4. Continue to Paper Trade

Because you are trading genuine money, it doesn't suggest you require to stop learning and attempting out different techniques, just. You have to keep on playing the market from all angles. You can try a contrarian method if you are a market conformist (you tend to go with the trend) If you usually close out credit spreads, try keeping one open while legging in an OTM put option.

Experiment and continue to fine-tune out your strategy.

One excellent suggestion is to develop two similar trades—one in your routine account and the other in your paper trading account at the very same time. You can make experimental changes to your paper account over time and see how it fairs against the live account. This is a cool way you can test different techniques while having a baseline.

5. Select an Option Trade That You Love and Master It

A fantastic way to enhance your options trading is by mastering a support trade. Learn all the ins and outs of your practice by back-testing historical data, checking present conditions using paper trades, and checking out your favorite sell books.

When you understand the intricacies of your go-to trade, then you'll be able to better acknowledge scenarios and markets that your trade will thrive in. In turn, you'll receive a higher probability of success and earnings.

The secret is to stay with the first trade like an iron condor or credit spread—no innovative layered trades.

6. Adhere to Your Trading Plan

All successful traders have a trading plan. This suggests, they have a strategy to enter a trade, make changes, and exit positions based upon SPECIFIC occasions. Successful traders DO NOT make arbitrary decisions. Everything they do is determined, measured, and examined.

You can make an easy-to-follow trading formula based on technical analysis if you wish to as well.

7. Await Opportunities

This is a massive issue for newbie traders. It was even an issue for me when I started trading. I would have a couple of stocks on my watchlist that I wished to get into. However, I knew it wasn't the correct time. When I'm not looking, the stock takes off, and then. On a few celebrations, I have chased after stocks that ultimately turned against me.

These kinds of situations hurt in 2 methods: 1) damages your ego, and 2) dents your portfolio balance.

If you have the very same problems, don't worry. Luckily, it's been well recorded that reliable yearly portfolio efficiency is typically brought on by having a strong exit strategy.

8. File and Learn From Your Previous Trades

Every trade is a finding out experience. Do not focus solely on losing trades; however, also look at your winners. There is always something you can discover.

For losing trades, look into why the trade lost or possible ways you could have avoided it from happening. Examine your entry, the adjustments you made, the exit, and the total market behavior.

For winning trades, look into why the trade won, and possible methods you might have even benefited more. Evaluate your entry, the changes you made, the exit, and the total market habits.

It's the same analysis for both types of trades if you see. After a couple of trades, you'll begin to acknowledge crucial attributes to why some trades win and why some trades lose. From there, you can recognize what adjustments need to be made to mitigate a loss or increase revenue gain.

9. Continue to Learn From Successful Traders that STILL Trade

They will frequently look over your shoulder and guarantee that you are setting yourself up for the best trade possible for the existing market when you have a mentor. You'll understand that their guidance is sound when you see them trading their suggestions.

I find that it's entirely wrong to receive trading guidance from someone that doesn't trade themselves. If you don't think you need on-going options trading education and assistance, ask yourself these questions:

- Why do expert athletes have coaches?

- Why do Fortune 500 companies employ consultants?

- Why does the President have advisers?

The answer to all of these concerns is basic:

Coaches hold you accountable, assist you to specify & reach objectives, are on the outside looking in, and they can provide a wealth of understanding when dealing with the subject at hand. Basically, coaches assist you progress traders.

Profit By Keeping to Your Plan

Leaving money in options is a waste of your properties if the waiting isn't going to make you an earnings. The safest technique is to make your trade as quickly as revenue is available. Plenty fall into the temptation of greed by earning much, but waiting too long might soon result in you kicking yourself since you lost an opportunity.

Before purchasing an option, make a strategy. You must choose on a target earnings with your plan. As quickly as your option hits that target, make the trade. Stick to your guns. Even if the goal is struck early on in the contract period, make the trade

Earnings By Knowing the Factors

One of the key elements to profiting from options trading is having a mutual understanding of the stock market and its current trends. Individual stocks do not move entirely out of touch with the market.

Understanding every aspect that impacts a stock before you purchase its options is the very best way to manage your threat. Don't delve into any decisions blindly or ill-informed. Normally, more expensive options are less most likely to make you a profit, so beware when accepting your option contracts.

We desire you to succeed. A lot of new-to-the-scene traders jump into the game without cautioning or much understanding. The more you understand, the more active you are likely to be. Find out more about trading by joining our Free Bootcamp now! The specialists at RagingBull are here to inform and assist you in reaching your full trading potential

CHAPTER EIGHT

Choosing Your Trades

Now that we have considered the probability formulas and theoretical background, you may be questioning, "What good is all the details, and how can it help me to generate income?" I'm thankful you asked, as it's time to put this theoretical background to use. There is no guarantee that a provided trade will pay. If we can develop a methodology that takes advantage of what we know about an options trade, we can make money in the long run. Taking benefit of the probabilities is crucial to our success.

Selecting Your Underlying

Before you can search for trades, it is essential that you produce a list of underlying that you like to trade. This list needs to consist of liquid items that have adequate volume and open interest to make sure of an efficient market. If the quote/ ask spread is too broad, you might be quitting any edge you battled so tricky to accomplish. The list needs to be long enough to provide you sufficient underlying to trade, yet brief adequate to filter out any "sound" and provide you with only viable trading prospects. Additionally, I like to be familiar with every one of the underlying I trade. I advise you to begin with a much shorter list of core trading prospects and include new underlying as you are able.

The very first action in lining up a trade is to choose an underlying that you feel will provide you a probability edge. We now take a look at a variety of processes that will help us in this mission.

From a simplified viewpoint, if our objective is to buy low and offer high, or to provide high and then buy low, we need to determine which inputs of options rates have the most significant effect and are of the most considerable importance. Recalling at the data into the Black-Scholes design, we can rapidly dismiss rates of interest and dividend (both foundation of our standard calculation), as they are relatively static in nature days to expiration, but essential when we pick a technique, have little effect on our choice of underlying, as time passes equally for all. The same can be stated for strike cost, as that is also part of the strategy we choose and not part of our option of underlying. That leaves us with two inputs that will mainly drive the success or failure of any offered trade. These two inputs are stock rate and implied volatility.

Let's first take a look at the stock rate and its effect on our choice of underlying. If you have an understanding of the option Greeks that are originated from the option rates model, you will understand that the option's delta forecasts the change in an alternative price for each $1 move in its underlying. Eventually, it is, in fact, the motion of the underlying that has the best influence on whether a trade is successful. Why do we invest so much energy and time talking about an option's implied volatility? To answer this, let's spend a few minutes to think of the ramifications of making trades entirely around our forecasts for the underlying's future movement.

The concern that must be responded to is whether you can regularly predict the instructions and magnitude of a stock's motion within a particular timespan. An option has a restricted life expectancy. We will discuss this in more information; later on, we must consider this reality now. If you think XYZ stock will rise in the future, that belief alone is not adequate to require purchasing a call choice with 30 days left till expiration. You need to, in truth, think XYZ will increase higher than a certain amount within the next 30 days for that details to be beneficial in your options trading. Does that mean we should disregard our beliefs about what a stock will perform in the future? It is tough to consistently predict a stock's instructions and magnitude of move within a given amount of time.

There is a term you might often hear used in financing, which name is "mean reversion." Some analysts will state a stock's price is mean going back. Simply put, what goes up need to boil down. When we speak of a stock's rate, there is little evidence to support this claim. For instance, even if we talk about a stock's rate movement being random, we quickly also to assert the stock's cost distribution has a favorable drift. That means that a reasonable stock price will drift up with time. In truth, if we think about stocks like Lucent or WorldCom, we acknowledge that some stocks may not just fail to drift upward but also, in truth, go to zero. That is, these businesses may declare bankruptcy, clearly breaking our upward drift theory. The point I am making is that stock prices usually are not as mean going back as many individuals believe. I find that thinking about stock prices as being mean reverting in the short term often gets in the way of developing a regularly rewarding options trading approach.

Why speak about mean reversion at all if I do not believe stock rates are mean-reverting? Well, in truth, I believe implied volatility is among the most mean reverse functions we see in finance. Let's take a better take a look at this statement.

Bring up a stock chart that spans one, two, three, or five years, for any ten underlying that pop into your head. As you move from one chart to the other, you will probably discover numerous charts that do not have a specified top end and bottom end within which the stock's price oscillates. On the other hand, if you bring up a suggested volatility chart for the same underlying with the same amount of time, you will most likely see that the implied volatility tends to oscillate within a variety. Looking more closely at these charts, you should be able to recognize a much tighter range within which the stock's suggested volatility generally lives. When selecting an underlying to trade, it is an expectation that a stock's implied volatility will return to this tight range over time that we can rely on. When we talk about indicated volatility being a mean going back function, this is exactly what we mean.

How can we use this in our trading? If we recall in time and prevent- my own a "regular," a high, and a low expectation for a stock's implied volatility, we can determine where in this range the current meant volatility lives. There are two ways that traders do this. The very first is to identify where the present implied volatility is as compared to its range for the time frame in which we are looking. So the computation would appear like this:

IV Range (or IV Rank) = (IV Current – IV Low)/(IV High – IV Low)

So, for example, if we are using a one-year time frame and the highest the implied volatility has been is 40, the lowest it has been is 20, and the current implied volatility is 25, the stocks IV percentile would be as follows:

(25 – 20) / (40 – 20) = 5/20 = .25, or 25th percentile

Some traders will mistakenly call this metric "IV Percentile." Mathematically, that is incorrect, and I will call this "IV Range." Although this calculation makes intuitive sense, it does not always reflect wherein its normal range the current implied volatility currently resides (and is, in fact, a ratio and not a percentile). To illustrate this, let's assume that the underlying represented earlier trades typically in the 20 to 25 IV range. Let's assume that in the past one year, or 252 trading days, the implied volatility for the underlying exceeded 25 in only one day. On this day, the implied volatility stood at 40 due to some unusual event. If today the implied volatility of this underlying stands at 25, the other calculation shows it to be in its 25th percentile. Yet it surely is trading at a reasonably costly implied volatility for the underlying as on all, but one day the implied volatility was less than or equal to its current reading. And this defines the second means of calculating the implied volatility percentile. Again assuming we are using one year, we can take the current implied volatility and determine how many days the implied volatility has exceeded or been beneath the current reading. Using this calculation, our implied volatility percentile for the other stock would be 99 percent or 100 percent, as the 25 percent IV was exceeded only once in the past year out of 252 reading days. While these two calculations do not always show such a dramatic difference, it is essential to take note of the strengths and weaknesses of each, as some software packages you will encounter may use one or the other of the calculations.

So how do we use this number in our trading? It would seem logical that if the underlying was trading at more magnificent than its 50th percentile, we might be interested in selling premium. And if the underlying was trading at less than its50th percentile, we might be interested in buying premium. After all, if we believe that implied volatility is mean reverting, doesn't that mean we believe the implied volatility will trend back toward its 50th percentile? In practicality, it is not that simple for three reasons.

First, as we have discussed, our option trades have a limited life span. So though I believe in mean reversion for implied volatility, It shouldn't be assumed that an option will complete its mean reversion before the option's expiration.

Secondly, when the market gets quiet and realized volatility slows, most underlying will fall to below their 50th percentile. It is often the case that during those times, the selling option premium gives us the best edge (the most extensive margin) between implied volatility and realized volatility. And unlike periods of high implied volatility in the general market, these quiet periods tend to last for long periods. They often last for over one year and have been known to last for as long as two years. If we traded underlying only when their implied volatility percentile was higher than the 50th percentile, we would have very little to do during these quiet periods. We would be missing out on money-making opportunities.

Lastly, underlying that are trading high in their IV percentile are often trading that way for a reason. Perhaps the stock has earnings coming up or some other type of announcement. Or maybe the stock's volatility has increased for another reason, such as the stock breaking out to new all-time highs or falling below its 52-week low, or simply because the industry the stock's business falls within has come upon hard times. Whatever the reason, recognition of the "event" and its timing will help you to make more informed trading decisions.

Rather than keying all your trades off that 50th implied volatility percentile, it is advisable to often compare an underlying's implied volatility percentile to that of the overall market. You will generally use either the SPX or the SPY as the representation of the global market. In general, you want an individual equity's IV percentile to be at least 15 percent higher than that of the overall market. That is required because a personal investment is subject to what I call "binary moves," whereas the SPX, as a diversified portfolio of stocks, is not nearly as affected by such events. It is also required that the IV percentile of the individual stock by over 35 percent. In this way, if the stock does mean revert in a short time frame, you do not get hurt too much by the volatility move. And this allows you to still build a short premium portfolio during the extended, low volatility environments we experience.

This implied volatility percentile, or implied volatility rank if that is all you have to work with, is the first thing you look at when trying to find an underlying you wish to trade. It allows you to compare underlying' implied volatilities on a relative basis, one against the other, and choose the underlying whose implied volatility is particularly high or unusually low for itself.

Having an underlying trading high in its range does not guarantee you will find a trade that you like, but from experience, this is the best place to start looking. So, begin your search with the underlying having the highest IV rank and continue through your watch list until you get to the name whose IV rank is 15 percent higher than that of the SPX. All of those underlying are potential premium-selling candidates.

Continuing our discussion of how to choose an underlying, let's assume we found XYZ stock to be high enough in its IV percentile to warrant further research. What do we do next? The first question that comes to mind is, "Why is XYZ stock trading with such a (relatively) high implied volatility?" So we do a little research. The first thing to check is when earnings are due out. We will spend time later discussing earnings in detail. As profits approach a stock's implied volatility, the percentile will appear high as it builds in other IV for the potential binary move to come. If you find XYZ will be reporting earnings within the next two weeks, you will move on to the following underlying in your list. During earnings season, this can get a bit tedious and frustrating, as most stocks that are high in their implied volatility percentile are top due to upcoming earnings. It is beneficial if your broker's trading platform in some way flags those stocks whose earnings dates are approaching, as mine does. But if revenues are not approaching and XYZ's implied volatility is high for other reasons, we need to continue our search.

Though we already know that one-year implied volatility percentile is high in its range, as that is the reason we got this far in our research, to begin with, the additional time frames add color to the picture. For example, if 11 months ago, some news came out on this particular stock that caused a great deal of price fluctuation, and the implied volatility rose for 45 days, a 9-month picture would exclude that event. I may consider the past nine months as a more typical picture for the stock, or I may not, but at least I have that choice when I look at multiple time frames.

We now turn our attention to the term historical volatility, or realized volatility as it is sometimes called. Unlike implied volatility, which is a measure of future stock movement as predicted by (or built into) an option's price, historical volatility has nothing to do with options. It is not a predictor of future stock movement at all, but rather it is a reporter of past stock movement. The industry norm, if you will, is the 20-day (or 21-day) historical volatility of a stock's movement. Though I find historical volatility to be a useful indicator, at times, its value can be deceptive. To understand this, we need to review how historical volatility is calculated once again. Historical volatility is the standard deviation of an asset's returns over a past period of time. If the stock closes at the same price every day for 20 days, its historical volatility is zero. If the stock rises (or falls) 10 percent every day for 20 days, its historical volatility is also zero. So a stock that is trending steeply will have an historical volatility that is lower than one might expect. Thus, you should always be careful to review the stock chart to ensure you understand the stock's past behavior. If the stock is trending steeply, you discount the value of the historical volatility calculation.

Now let's assume that the historical volatility calculation seems to show the past behavior of the stock fairly. What good is it to our trading process? Many traders will say it has no value. They will say, "You have seen the disclaimer that past performance may not be indicative of future performance, have you not? In the same manner, looking at past stock performance has little bearing on future stock performance, and therefore, the historical volatility tells us nothing." Though I understand their point, I disagree. Indeed, past performance has some predictive value, or why would we prefer to sell KO implied volatility at 25 before we would sell FSLR implied volatility at 32?

For this reason, many traders simply look for a significant difference between an option's implied volatility and its underlying's historical volatility when lining up trades. Though I find this information to be useful, you need to remember that historical volatility is calculated using only 20 days of data and can, therefore, change quickly. What is found to be even more meaningful is the trend in the historical volatility.

Many traders will debate whether historical volatility leads to implied volatility or whether implied volatility leads to historical volatility. I often see historical volatility lead on the way up, and implied volatility lead on the way down. But before I change the nature of my portfolio, I like to see historical volatility trends going in one direction or the other. After all, the historical volatility calculation requires 5, 10, or 20 days of data, whereas the implied volatility is a snapshot in time and can whip back and forth much quicker.

Making an Assumption

An assumption of some kind drives every trade. It might be a directional assumption or implied volatility-related. Though most of my trades are driven by volatility assumptions (after all, that is the "edge" option most readily provide), most traders will be driven by directional hypotheses when making trades. This is true of technical analysts, fundamental analysts, contrarian traders, and your average investor. And this kind of directional trading can be done with virtually any instrument, options included. The advantage of directional options trading is the leverage you receive. The disadvantage, unless you are trading deep in the money options, is that to obtain an unlimited upside for your trade, you must purchase options (as opposed to selling them). As earlier discussed, when you are buying an option, you are paying more than the option is currently intrinsically worth. So your underlying must move a certain amount in your favor just for you to break even on the trade. If you are trading stocks or futures, this is not true. So purchasing options for a purely directional trade is akin to running the first 20 meters of a 100-meter dash in sand.

When you execute a directional trade by selling options, you have a limited profit potential with the possibility of unlimited losses. Of course, you gain the advantage of selling extrinsic value, and thus the underlying can actually move against you a bit, and you still make money. As such, you put the odds in your favor as a premium seller. But as you can see, this discussion has quickly moved away from using options as a directional vehicle to using options as a strategic vehicle. And that is as it should be. I will leave others to spend hundreds of millions of dollars trying to find a way to continually predict market direction more accurately than "Brownian motion with an upward drift" would predict. However, the bulk of your decision-making process, your trade assumption if you will, is not based on a directional assumption but a volatility assumption. This is the beauty of options trading. You can be as bad at choosing a stock's direction and still be highly profitable. Volatility assumptions are much easier to make, leave more room for error, and have a tendency for mean reversion that can guide you on your way. None of these things can be said of directional assumptions.

Each trader is different. There is a well-known trading psychologist by the name of Dr. Van Tharp, who begins each one of his newsletters with the statement, "I always say that people do not trade the markets; they trade their beliefs about the markets." I agree with Dr. Tharp, 100 percent. You may be thinking, "If every person reading this book is trading his or her own beliefs, and they differ considerably, how can we all be profitable? Isn't it the market that pays us?" This is to my point. It is your strategy and not the assumptions that can make you a consistently profitable trader. If you believe that statement, doesn't it make more sense to spend your time and money choosing and refining a strategy that can continuously grow your account, instead of wasting your time and money trying to predict the direction of a stock or the market in general? For me, the answer is a resounding yes.

Though the trade might begin with an assumption that may or may not be correct, it will always be supported by a volatility assumption, a proper choice of strategy, and a mathematically supported, positive expectancy exit strategy. And this is the crux of trading success, in my opinion.

Fundamental analysis holds excellent merit, in my opinion. If a company is growing at a long-term growth rate of 17 percent and its stock is trading at a 12 P/E, I find that pretty attractive. Based on those numbers, you might scoop up some stock, or you might sell some puts below the market in hopes of either capturing that premium or buying stock lower than it is trading. Those are rational actions to take based on the information given. But to assume the stock price will move up in the next 30 to 50 days is overreaching the limits of what fundamental analysis can do for you. The current price of the stock, in an efficient market, theoretically takes into account all known information. To assume that the marketplace is mispricing a company so dramatically that you think the stock will move considerably in the next 30 to 50 days is a fool's errand, in my opinion. So, though I believe in the validity of fundamental analysis, I think it has little application in the short time frame world in which my options trading resides. In other words, it is a timing issue and not a problem with the analysis itself.

The third means of arriving at a directional assumption is what we term contrarian trading. Contrarian traders generally take the other side of extended moves in a stock or in the overall market itself. They try to take advantage of markets that are overdone on either side. When a stock catches fire, so to speak, and runs up very far, very fast, a contrarian trader will often step in and get short that stock, hoping for a turnaround in its price. As I said, the same is right on the downside. When they feel the "baby has been thrown out with the bathwater," and the stock has taken more abuse than is warranted, they will be there to get long the stock. It has been observed that many contrarians have a decent track record when measured by the percentage of time they are correct. Unfortunately, when measured by their profitability, they seem to have less success. Intuitively those statements don't seem to go together. But thinking about the nature of those stocks, we can make some sense of it. A stock that has run up very far, very fast, is what we term "in play." It has acquired significant velocity, and the farther up it runs, the more speed it seems to pick up. We used to term getting in front of these moves, "picking up nickels in front of a steamroller." In other words, when you are wrong, you are dead wrong. Due to the velocity of the stock at the time the contrarian steps in, when one is wrong, the losses can be brutal.

The primary point to note here is that unless you can predict stock movement in a time frame that matches your trades' timing, spending a lot of time and money trying is wasted effort. And even if you believe you can learn to predict the direction and magnitude of short-term moves, I still think option strategy is easier to learn and provides a better outcome.

.

CHAPTER NINE

ExitingTrades

Majority of traders exit by "fear" rather than by mechanics. They stubbornly refuse to take a loss and think that makes them much better traders in the end. As a person who believes strongly in the power of mathematics, I would like to change that. We will discuss what an appropriate mechanical strategy looks like and how to create one. We will likewise take a look at when it is allowed to deviate from the plan and when it is crucial not to depart. This will happen in the context of a method with a favorable span. We will examine the three situations that lead us to exit the trade and dissect what each suggests to our probability presumptions.

•The Variables

What variables must we resolve for (or a minimum of comprehend) to produce a positive expectancy trading method? It sounds like a challenging question; it has an easy answer. Even the traders who work by gut feel have an understanding that the "edge vs. odds" relationship is essential to success. In other words, the higher the chances of success or the more significant the edge in the trade, the bigger the threat you should take on with the business. What is essential to take away from this explanation is that there are three carefully linked inputs to the decision. They are the possibility of winning, the average benefit when you gain, and the average expense when you lose. These are "3 legs of the stool" that make up your strategy, and all three are inexplicably linked. When someone asks me, "When should I take my losses?" it is difficult to respond to that without the context of when they are taking their earnings and how regularly they are benefiting and losing.

You may be questioning if you will ever have the ability to understand how to develop a winning technique with all these interconnected pieces complicating the issue. How are they interconnected? How will I know if my method has a definite span? Thankfully, there was a researcher by the name of John Kelly operating at Bell Labs who, back in 1956, obtained a formula to help in a sound reduction for long-distance calls.

People rapidly realized Kelly's method (or Kelly's Criterion, as it is typically called) had applications for gambling and position sizing in trading. Let's analyze this little gem and see what we can discover.

The Kelly Criterion

As we discussed, the Kelly Criterion can help us stabilize the three legs of the stool connected with our trading technique. The simplified formula, used for position sizing, looks like this:

Kelly percent = W – [(1 – W)/ R]

Where;

W = portion of winners (or if forecasting, probability of revenue).

R = average gain of our winning trades/average loss of our losing trades.

How do we use this formula for position sizing to assist in building our technique? Let's begin by taking a look at where Kelly percent is equivalent to zero. This would indicate the method is neither for a loser nor a winner; however, instead is a breakeven. We can "back off" one of the three variables to produce a winning formula.

Replacing 0 for Kelly percent, we can streamline our formula as follows:

$0 = W – [1 – W/ R] R = (1/W) – 1.$

$W = 1/(R + 1).$

These identify the break-even relationships between our three variables. Given any two of the variables, you can figure out the break-even value from the 3rd. Let's look at a few examples. In these examples, we will presume we have made short premium trades and that the overall credit gotten on each trade will be represented by 100 percent. If we offer a strangle for $4 and we let it end useless, we make 100 percent. We have a 75 percent earnings ($ 4-- $1)/$ 4 =.75 (or 75%) if we purchase it back for $1.

To Log Your Trades or Not to Log Your Trades

Typically a topic of intense debate is whether it is worth the time and effort to log your trades. You will remember your genuinely painful businesses without the requirement to compose them down. And if you make a note of the right trades, this may keep you from successfully embellishing the stories over cocktails at a later date and time. So, why trouble with all the small trades or trades that had little impact on your account? As I hope you keep in mind by now, alternatives trading is a probability-based activity. Here are a couple of reasons you need to keep a detailed trading log and a couple of methods you need to use your diary to guide you as you progress.

1. Though the option chain anticipates your possibility of earnings for you, there is no guarantee that your outcomes will match them precisely. If you collect your trading data for an

extended amount of time and discover that your real percentage of trades that pay does not match what the option chain anticipated, you have a flaw in the method you are picking either your underlying or your trades. However, it is generally the option of underlying that triggers the possibilities to veer off the predicted path, from my experience. Going back through those areas of this book that cover "picking your underlying" or "picking a strategy" needs to help you in determining where you are going incorrect. If not, you may need a session with an excellent choices coach to point you in the right direction. The excellent news is that for any decent alternatives coach, this is usually a quick fix.

2. A "three-legged stool" that helps us produce a trading strategy that has a favorable span (i.e., it specifies a rewarding trading methodology). And among the three legs is our likelihood of revenue. Without this piece, we can not determine the appropriate levels to close our trades, both on the earnings side and the losing side. Using the probabilities from the option chain is an excellent place to begin. Over time, if we study our logs and the data that come out of it, we can get better possibilities to guide us in our exit levels. Traders who are against keeping a diary are usually not using any kind of exit strategy based upon probabilities. If they are and are not logging their trades, they are trading so infrequently that they can track them in their heads. And that is an entirely various problem, as

you require a sensible variety of occurrences for the possibilities to work. Back to my point: If you do not log your trades, it is challenging to abide and remember by your Kelly Criterion exit methods.

3. Though this may appear silly, I discover that without logging trades, it is a lot more difficult for a new trader to think the discipline of trading is as simple and as necessary as I discover it to be. And when that holds, it is a lot easier for a trader to drift off strategy. So, a trade log can hammer house the point that trading is indeed a "discipline." Checking out six or nine months of trades and seeing that your trade likelihoods are within a couple of percent of what was forecasted by the choice chain can be an eye-opening workout for newer traders, and even for knowledgeable traders. They try logging their trades for the very first time.

4. This is a close analogy to number one; a log is the simplest way of discovering errors in your method. Patterns you might not anticipate to see will frequently pop out of a cautious evaluation of your record.

So, what type of info is beneficial in a trading log? The more information you select to log, the more of your time the registration uses up. And since time is money, it makes good sense to attempt to keep this data collection to a minimum. But no one ever stated trading did not require some effort. The beautiful part of creating a trading log is that it can be occupied after trading hours or after work hours. Though a few numbers may alter throughout the day, you can easily either re-create or insert those numbers in the evening or on the weekend. Of course, the closer to the trade time you log the trade, the more comfortable and more accurate it will be. And the more details you gather, the better the log will be to your trading. So, this is a place I would not skimp. I would collect all the details you feel you may require. It is far simpler to gather it in advance than to attempt to go back in time and re-create the numbers.

When keeping your log, bear in mind that the primary purpose is to be able to compare expected probabilities to actual likelihoods over a prolonged duration of time. As such, you will be logging information from when you made the trade and expectations from the profession, as well as recording your exits and the actual probabilities you incur.

Here are a couple of fields I discover work for a trade log and how they can be made use of.

1. Trade entry date: I always log the year I made the trade. This will work in a couple of ways, which we will detail later.

2. The sign of the underlying traded: As we discussed previously, when we do our "trade forensics" after a minimum of several months of data are gathered, among the things we look for are symbols that regularly do not carry out as their alternative chain

predicts. Hence, we need to be able to sort by the logo in our spreadsheet to accumulate this information quickly.

3. The trading strategy employed: Not only do I like to see how my strangles, my iron condors, and my long straddles are doing. However, I also want to code whether my trades are undefined or specified threat techniques. I can then see how my probabilities are tracking expected results on a number of various levels.

4. The rate of the underlying at the time of the trade: This enables one to see the magnitude of the relocation in the underlying from trade entry to trade exit. You might begin logging your trades (or begin trading, for that matter) right at the start of some high historical volatility. If that is so, these numbers will assist you to figure out.

5. The strikes traded: This is handy when managing your trades, but can end up being a tough thing to track if you roll your sell any manner. There are a plethora of methods to follow this if you do run a trade. Analyze the best way to set up your own log.

6. The variety of agreements traded: This is crucial in tracking your success and to recall to ensure you are sizing your trades correctly. If your probabilities are following well, however, you are not making cash sizing is the most common cause—more on this during our section on portfolio management.

7. The possibility of earnings as defined by your option chain: This is an essential piece of information for the way we use our logs. Remember that this is not the likelihood of ending up out of the cash, but rather the possibility of breakeven. With brief premium techniques, the probability of breakeven will be higher than the likelihood of expiring out of the money.

8. The implied volatility at the time of the trade: This can be tracked in a number of ways. You can either keep the implied volatility of the at the cash option for the expiration cycle you are trading or keep the implied volatility of each strike you trade. The latter offers far more details; for the starting trader, I discover the information to be extreme. The extra data can be used in discerning alter and other changes in the distribution curve. But determining that information is hard. I discover keeping the at the cash implied volatility is enough.

9. The premium invested or got throughout the trade: Having the net rate of the business is very vital if you are going to use the spreadsheet to track your trade exits as specified by your Kelly Criterion. It is likewise required if you are following your earnings and loss details.

10. I like to set up my log so that I either input the portion of max profit at which I wish to take my earnings and the edge I want from the anticipated likelihood (typically in between 10 and 15 percent) or input both the portion of max profit at which I want to take my earnings and my piece at which I want to take

my loss. In either case, I compute the costs, both profits and loss, at which I desire to leave my trade. Whichever price the trade strikes first is my exit point. By having this calculated at the time I enter the trade into my log, I know instantly where my exit points are. And by having them in my log, I can describe them at any time.

11. Specific pieces of info on the exit: The very first piece of information is the date we make the exit trade. From that date, we can determine and log the number of days we were in our trade.

12. The rate at which you close your trade: From this information, you can determine your actual possibility of earnings for comparison with what the choice chain anticipated. You can also identify your profits or loss for the trade.

13. Some other fields: We can determine profits and losses, number and portions of winners and losers, and percentage differences from anticipated. We can break these fields down by classifications, like defined risk trades versus undefined risk trades, or by particular trading methods, like strangles or iron condors. We can find out how we are doing with our long premium trades versus our short premium trades. We can see if we work with our profits trades. We can find underlying that are carrying out well or performing inadequately. The kind of information you can pull from your log is limited just by your creativity.

As you can observe, a trade log is a beneficial tool for helping fine-tune and track our trading techniques. I use Excel for producing my log, however a few of the traders I coach use Google Docs spreadsheets, FileMaker Pro, or other shows languages to track their trades. So, it can be an elementary program or a more complicated means of accumulating the information. Start basic and grow your log as you please. The goal is to get the very best return for your time. Once you begin logging your trades and pulling info out of it, it becomes quite addicting. It is a vital tool to assist you in your trading.

CHAPTER TEN

Portfolio Management

We have discussed how to choose individual trades, how to best exit your trades, and when to exit trades both as winners and losers. Once you have many trades on your sheets, what should you do to manage your overall portfolio's danger? How do you know what the total threat is?

We will start our conversation by exploring a more academic viewpoint on the concern and continue to a more practical method. I need to warn you that for each educator you check out or listen to, you will more than likely get different answers regarding the very best method to control your risk.

What I will provide to you is a solid structure for how to see your threat, some possible trade concepts to help reduce the portfolio's risk, and some general rules as to how to size your trades. You may be questioning why sizing your trades appears in a portfolio management conversation.

Two Types of Risk

Many people hear the term threat and believe it refers to how much they can lose. That is not wrong; there is much more to the story. And knowing a few more of the information will help you much better comprehend the nature of your portfolio.

People, by nature, are risk-averse. The majority of us would choose not to take any danger, all else being equal. There are those couple of risk-takers out there who take on risk solely for the sake to rush opportunities. I would extremely recommend those individuals to stay away from trading. They will get their rush and then the call from their broker, letting them know their account is closed due to a lack of funds. Every trade is a moving danger. By lining up trades where the implied volatility exceeds its norm and its historical volatility, we feel appropriately compensated in the majority of circumstances. But we need to comprehend a bit more about the risk to handle it properly. There are two types of risks of which every trader should understand.

• Unique Risk

The very first type of danger is a unique risk. This refers to risk specific to a company or a stock. They consist of management changes, quality of management, company profits surprises, lawsuits, bad press, and getting outcompeted, among others. When thinking about distinct risks, imagine an event that will affect just one company or a small circle of associated companies. This risk can likewise be broadened to a market, though the market threat is a little a hybrid. The point you need to be familiar with is that distinct risk can be diversified to restrict the quantity of danger new trades may contribute to the portfolio.

• Systematic Risk

The second type of risk is systematic; this refers to macro-level threats, such as that provided by political events or large financial policy occasions. Examples may be war breaking out, oil prices increasing, a surprise rate trek, or health issues of a high-ranking authorities in the federal government or Federal Reserve. These occasions impact essentially on trades. This is the kind of danger that can not be diversified away, frequently comes unexpectedly, and need to be mitigated, in the majority of circumstances. Your portfolio ought to preserve some type of balance concerning direction, property, industry, and volatility class. That is not to say you must be perfectly balanced. It simply means you need to be familiar with the level of systematic risk your portfolio carries and guarantee you feel you are getting adequate threat premiums for the level of danger you bring.

The Goal: Diversification of Minimizing Unique Risk

At this point, we will look in more depth at the theory behind the diversification of special threats. First, as options traders, we are noticeably knowledgeable about suggested volatility as a threat in every trade we make. And, as we have discussed, implied volatility is nothing more than the basic discrepancy of the distribution curve of our underlying's movement. Each specific underlying has its own, distinct standard difference. In modern monetary management courses, we use that basic discrepancy as a measure of threat in a business. We can recall over a minimum of a 60-month (5-year) duration and identify what that basic deviation is? Any statistics book can assist you with this if you are not knowledgeable about how to compute it. You can use a spreadsheet, like Excel, and use its built-in standard deviation function to show up at a solution. We can also calculate the fundamental discrepancy for a varied portfolio, such as the S&P 500 (as represented by the SPX). I have selected to compute the standard discrepancy for twelve securities for a 20-year duration to help in our conversation. These 12 securities consist of 11 members of the SPX, and the SPX itself. See the next table for the information.

Looking at this data, we see a wide variety of necessary deviations, and therefore risk, amongst our underlying. The one thing that must stand out is that the diversified portfolio of stocks, the SPX, has the lowest step of risk. If we were to take all 500 securities, determine their essential variance, and average (weighted or not), the typical basic variation would be far more significant than the basic discrepancy of the SPX. In reality, that is not diversification works. Diversity is the phenomenon where the typical basic disparity of the parts of a portfolio is much greater than the standard discrepancy of the combined portfolio. Why is this? It is because the distinct threats are canceling each other out! One caution to be familiar with is the underlying in your portfolio needs to be diverse. That means they should be reasonably uncorrelated or inversely correlated. If you are trading two related securities, the distinct risks will not cancel.

Option Trading Software - Why You Should Never Analyze Option Stocks Manually

Whether you are an experienced trader or anew comer in the field of stock trading, using Option Trading Software to trade will significantly boost your capability to trade correctly in the stock market.

If you are searching for an automated software application to trade with, then you ought to have been familiar with the term options trading.

This section of the book will teach you the essentials of options and what to look for when searching for automated software, especially the ones that are used for trading options. Why trouble trading manually, trying to find out complicated stock analysis, when there are software application packages readily available to fix this.

Options are contracts or financial contracts that are comparable to stocks. In truth, they can be traded similar to stocks. Options offer various trading solutions for traders that are more open to new ways to trade efficiently in public markets.

Options can, at times, be perilous, and even the smart investor can lose cash on a wrong trade choice, without evaluating the opportunity rapidly. Stock options are time delicate and will end quickly. Quick analyses of options are required to be effective.

Options end extremely rapidly at times, dramatically affecting the cost of the choice. That is why using option trading software to examine robust and complex factors of the marketplace quickly, is vital to a trader's success. Stock values can alter quickly at times, and using manual methods to trade will trigger you to be at a downside.

Options trading software application will correctly select the ideal stocks for you. You can materialize money fast if you use options trading software application, but you should remember that the software is not totally automated. Human intervention is required at times. The important point that you ought to remember is not to completely depend on automated software applications to do the work for you, but using trading software will give you the very best chances for success.

Although automated trading software application is used for trading stocks, you need to learn and understand how it is done, in the event you need to do it by hand. There are free and paid software applications offered for use, but paid ones will have more alternatives available.

Options trading software application is available as online services, or software that is installed straight on your computer. Both have advantages and disadvantages. Software application set up on your computer will probably not require a month-to-month subscription charge for use because you would be using your own computer system resources. All you have to be sure of is that the software application vendor uses totally free updates and upgrades to your set up the software application.

Using online alternative trading software application affords you the chance of not having to fret about updates to the software application. The creator of the software application will look after all updates and upgrades, given that you will be using the software application from their computers. The only disadvantage may be the continuous regular monthly membership fee.

Another advantage of using alternative trading software as an online service is that your trade history will be conserved and instantly backed up by the owner of the software application. If you use the software set up on your computer system and your computer system crashes, you may lose information if not doing a day-to-day backup.

Manual trading is excellent, however, using options trading Software is better. Why waste valuable time by manually trying to find out the complexities of discovering exceptional Option Stocks.

CHAPTER ELEVEN

Why do You TradeWeekly Options?

Weekly options have remained in existence for long, but in numerous stocks, a week represents over 30 percent of the total option volume. The development is still exponential, and that has brought liquidity and a fantastic chance. I have been an options trader for years, and more than 95 percent of my income has come as a direct outcome of trading stock choices and futures choices. In those years, I have never seen an item with the potential to offer the typical investor a possibility to compete on relatively equivalent footing with the expert traders.

Trading choices, stock, and futures are all zero-sum video games. Simply stated, when I offer or purchase something in an auction market, I must find a buyer or seller who is ready to do the opposite side of the trade. In the end, among us will win what the other loses. If I make this trade to infinity, both of us will have the very same P & L, minus commissions. Because our capital is not infinite and commissions are, both people will ultimately wind up broke.

When you are thinking about making trading your profession, that is a critical note! Let's go back to a game of possibility once again-poker. You enter a game with nine other players. Each of you needs to invest $100, and you must play the video game to the end of each hand. The home" rakes" (commission) $1 per hand. How long does the game last? In this circumstance, the game would last around 1,000 hands. At that point, the home would have taken all the players' money in the form of commission. This is a zero-sum video game plus commissions, extremely much the like trading alternatives.

I discussed what makes a possession tradable. The first thing that I require is that it is liquid. I define liquidity as the ability to get in and exit a property effortlessly to the possible gain. If our possible benefit, usually, is $100, but the quote offer spread is $10, that asset is not liquid. It will cost us $10 to enter and $10 to exit, and if our commission is $10, we are giving up a 30 percent edge to our possible gain. On any private trade, you might generate income, but in the long run, no matter how excellent you are, you will lose. On the other hand, if our quote--use spread is just $1 and our commission is $1.00, is it possible to conquer the edge and turn a profit gradually?

I have now developed what it takes to conquer the zero-sum choice market. You need to have a combination of fast quote--provide spreads, low commission, and more ability than your opponent.

Weekly alternatives are a little variation of the longer-term serials, but that is where the resemblance ends.

CHAPTER TWELVE

Traits of a Successful Options Trader

Regardless of its numerous benefits, options trading brings considerable risk of loss, and it is extremely speculative. Like any other business, being a successful options trader requires a certain capability, character type, and attitude.

1. Be Able to Manage Risk

Options are high-risk instruments, and it is necessary for traders to acknowledge how much danger they have at any point in time. What is the optimum downside of the trade? What is the specific or implicit position with regard to volatility? Just how much of my capital is designated to the trade? These are some of the concerns traders always have to keep in their minds.

Traders likewise require to take proper procedures to manage risk. If you are a committed short-term options trader, you will frequently stumble upon loss-making trades. You need to be able to reduce the risk of your positions at any time. Some traders do so by restricting their trade size and diversifying into several trades, so all their eggs aren't in the exact same basket.

An options trader also needs to be an excellent money supervisor. They require to utilize their capital wisely. It would not be wise to obstruct 90% of your capital in a single trade. Whatever technique you adopt, risk management and cash management can not be disregarded.

2. Be Excellent With Numbers

In the course of trading in options, you are always dealing with numbers. What is volatility? What's the break-even of the trade? Options traders are always answering these questions. They likewise refer to option Greeks, such as the delta, gamma, vega, and theta of their options trades.

3. Have Discipline.

To become successful, options traders need to practice discipline. Doing a comprehensive research study, recognizing changes, setting up the best trade, sticking and forming to a technique, setting up goals, and developing an exit method are all part of the discipline. An easy example of deviating from the training is following the herd. Never rely on an opinion without doing your research study. Instead, you need to devise an independent trading method that operates for it to be an effective options strategy.

While formal education in the kind of higher degrees can be related to elite traders, it is not always the case for all. You must be informed about the market. Active traders take some time to find out the basics and study the marketplace-- numerous scenarios, different trends-- anything and everything about how the market works. They are not normally newbies who have taken a three-hour trading seminar on "How to get rich quick trading," however rather make an effort to discover from the marketplace.

4. Be Patient.

Client investors are willing to await the marketplace to offer the best chance instead of attempting to make a big win on every market movement. The very same is not the case with amateur traders. They are restless, unable to control their feelings, and they will be quick to go into and exit trades.

5. Establish a Trading Style.

Each trader has various personalities and needs to embrace a trading style that fits his or her characteristics. Some traders might be good at day trading, where they purchase and sell options several times during the day to make small earnings. Some may be comfier with position trading, where they form trading methods to benefit from distinct opportunities, such as volatility and time decay. And others can be more comfortable with swing trading, where traders make bets on rate movement over durations lasting five to 30 days.

6. Analyze the News.

It is vital for traders to be able to analyze the news, different hype from truth, and make suitable decisions based upon this understanding. You will discover numerous traders excited to put their capital in an option with promising news, and the next day they will proceed to the next huge story. This distracts them from recognizing larger patterns in the market. A lot of effective traders will be truthful with themselves and make sound personal options, instead of just passing the significant stories in the news.

7. Be an Active Learner.

The Chicago Board of Trade (CBOT) reported 90% of options traders would understand losses. What separates successful traders from typical ones succeeds traders are able to gain from their losses and execute what they find out in their trading methods. Elite traders practice until they discover the lessons behind the trade, and see the market behavior as it is taking place.

The monetary markets are constantly changing and developing; you need to have a clear understanding of what's taking place and how all of it works. By ending up being an active learner, you will not only become great at your current trading techniques, but however, you will also be able to recognize new opportunities others may not see or might pass over.

8. Be Flexible.

You can not stake a claim on the marketplace but should opt for the market or get out of it when it is not the type that fits you. You need to accept losses take place which it is inevitable that you will lose. Acceptance rather than battling the market is vital to understanding, clarity, and finally winning.

9. Strategy Your Trades.

An options trader who prepares is most likely to be successful than the trader who operates on instinct and feel. If you don't have a plan, you will place random trades, and consequently, you'll be directionless. On the other hand, if you have a plan, you are more likely to stay with it. You should be very clear about what your goals are and how you plan to attain them. When to book profits, you will also understand how to cover your losses or. You can see how the plan has actually worked (or not worked) for you. All these steps are important to establishing a strong trading strategy.

10. Keep Records.

A lot of effective options traders keep persistent records of their trades. Maintaining proper trade records is an important habit to assist you to avoid making costly decisions. The history of your trade records likewise supplies a wealth of info to assist you enhance your odds of success.

The Bottom Line.

Top options traders get joy from scouting and enjoying their trades. Sure, it's excellent to see an option come out on top, however, just like sports fans, options traders delight in viewing the entire game unfold, not just discovering out the last score. These attributes will not guarantee your success in the options trading world, but they will definitely increase your chances at it.

The Psychological Component to Options Trading

Being successful with options is not always the simplest thing to attain. Sure, there are some that have made a great success in their endeavors into the world of options trading. These individuals are among those that lots of will look towards as motivation for their options trading adventures. There will be those that will look towards these success stories for more than motivation. They will look towards effective options traders as those to replicate. Or, more properly, they will attempt to replicate the trading techniques and techniques of the trader.

While it is definitely a wise thing to look towards the trading methods of an effective trader, replicating the actions of the trader alone might not prove to be the best technique. The reason for this is that there are other factors that go into the process of establishing a trading method than simply the execution of the trades. Individual aspects will enter into the development of an approach. In some circumstances, there will be mental factors that will be turned into the trading strategies. Understanding such parts is essential to exploring a trading approach to make sure it is critical to your goals.

It would not harm you to explore your psychological aspects and elements before seriously at trading. Now, some might presume such assessments are little more than 'psycho-babble' that look at options trading from an over-analytical perspective. This might be the case in some instances, but as a general description of what inspires people towards options trading, it is not something you want to overlook. By having a clear understanding of your mental makeup, you can develop the appropriate insight into how to be efficient in the art of trading.

Some people are more cut out for options trading than others. Those that are conservative in their investment techniques may want to restrict options trading to a smaller sized part of their general portfolio. Those that can be thought about rather aggressive in their method might look towards possibly using options as a hedge to their portfolio. Again, your own personal psychological makeup regarding comfort levels of trading in important in options. This will definitely help promote your capability to find the correct response to whether you are cut out for options trading.

How can you discover whether you have the frame of mind of an options trader? The initial step includes truthfully answering whether you are somebody that possesses the discipline to be an options trader. Some might believe they have the discipline to succeed. Thinking you possess specific attributes to a specific degree and, in fact, having those attributes to the proper degree are two completely various things. Understanding exactly where you stand in regards to your mindset and your levels of discipline will help in improving your chances of success.

Somebody who requires to keep fiddling with their account by purchasing and offering every few days isn't somebody who should be investing in options! The commissions alone will eat you up. Someone who likes a lot of excitement in their trading must probably remain away from options.

Having a quality options trading technique is handy. Putting the options trading strategy through to fruition is a lot more valuable. Then again, there is a big difference in having the desire to follow such a procedure and actually following through with it. Those that have the ability to follow through with such steps may be limited in number. No, that is not stated as a method of weakening anyone's morale, motivation, or desire. Rather, it is a method of effectively forecasting the management of your endeavor and examining the danger of getting included with options trading. You also need a strategy for when the market goes against your method so that you do not make options due to the fact that you're panicking.

Yes, trading in options needs to be looked at from the point of view of managing a small company. When running a small company, you require to assess the risk connected with a venture. You also require to assess the capacities and dangers related to the success or failure of the business. This same ideology needs to be put towards options trading. If you can honestly assess yourself as someone with the self-discipline to follow through with a reliable options trading method, then you may extremely well be very successful with options trading.

How well can you handle losing trades? Are you able to manage losses and pick things up and begin the procedure over again? If you are, then you might effectively embody the proper psychological makeup for being successful with options trading. Those that can not handle the pressure of the periodic loss would be much better served looking towards another investing strategy.

It has actually been stated success begins with the ideal mental makeup. You might discover success is not as elusive as you believe if you can adjust your frame of mind to your psychological approach to trading.

CHAPTER THIRTEEN

Selecting a Portfolio trade

Finally, you have actually learned how to do lots of things trading weekly options. We have examined how markets are organized and how they buy, identified the numerous market participants, and how they shape the market results. The book has explained why it is necessary to continually sell liquid markets and how to recognize the qualities that constitute liquidity. The phases of the marketplace were identified, and a mathematical explanation was provided to describe how and why they rotate around the mean. The option model was dissected, and you were taught how to price it like an expert market maker. Easy trades were recommended that would permit you to effectively trade in any market conditions. Finally, the trades were wed to the marketplace conditions and the ones that work best when it is in any of the market stages.

All of the preliminary information is now in place, and it is time to discover how to arrange and trade a portfolio.

All of the technical work that has actually been done so far will not help you if you do not know how to arrange a portfolio of stocks. This is among the essential aspects of trading, due to the fact that your portfolio represents all of your liquid properties, cash! If you are not aware of where to invest your money, the possibilities of beating the market will go to absolutely no. The portfolio that you pick need to be in proportion to the amount of danger capital that you have to deal with; in addition, the diversification of the collection is essential.

The option procedure will be performed in 4 actions, and it is a screening procedure that is universal. By that, it indicates that the only thing that alters is the quantity of risk capital that you need to trade. The principles remain the exact same.

■ Liquidity

By now, you are most likely tired of finding out about liquidity; however, acknowledging liquidity in a portfolio is a little different than cash in a single trade.

When establishing a portfolio, the three aspects concerning liquidity are: the quote-- use spread, the expected series of the stock, and the size of the hidden security.

You will be trying to find stocks that are somewhere in between Priceline and Bank of America. There are hundreds of stocks that fit that mold, and they are constantly changing. Years ago, Facebook didn't exist as a public company, and now it is! Tight spreads, cost of over $50 a share, and excellent varieties. Look for stocks that are priced at $50 or higher or have a unique history of volatility.

■ Volatility

Liquidity was the first quality that we looked at; the 2nd characteristic is volatility. Volatility is the amount of air in the balloon in relation to the underlying stock cost. As an example, two stocks can be priced at $50. One is a utility that has been trading in a $5 variety for the past year. It is a dividend stock and is extremely stable. It is possible something could take place that would alter the price of the stock unexpectedly, but the opportunities are slim. The average anticipated variety for a weekly alternative would most likely remain in the $1 range.

This segment of the market has an excellent degree of unpredictability. The stock has actually more than quadrupled in price in the past year, and you would believe that it would have a much wider anticipated range; based upon history, you can be sure that the anticipated variety will be at least $4 and most likely more.

When we price a portfolio, in addition to liquidity, you need to consider volatility. If you are picking between 2 stocks with similar dollar rates, the more unpredictable stock is the one you desire in your portfolio.

If you are a financier, you like to have an extremely smooth trip in which you rarely trade in the marketplace; you don't care if you get a great deal of rate motion, you just desire long-lasting return. A trader needs a great deal of rate movement to offset the slippage that is lost in quote-- offer commissions and spreads.

■ Diversification by Product

Diversification by list is the next action in the procedure of establishing your portfolio. You want to ensure that the stocks that you are selecting are all not from the same group (duplication). This needs to be logical; you want to make sure that if one sector of the market is bullish, and another is bearish, you stabilize your portfolio in between the two segments.

As an example, if you choose that you desire to trade a financial stock, you can take a look at a variety of them and put the first two steps, liquidity and volatility, to the test. You then can decide from your technical indications which one appears to offer you the best possibility presently to cash a ticket. Place that stock in your portfolio and then go on to the next group. You are prepared to start trading when you have at least five stocks from various groups in place.

In addition to trading your portfolio, you need to watch extra stocks in the groupings to make sure that you are keeping your portfolio approximately date. If you are trading at the maximum portfolio size of $100,000+, you ought to be observed at least 50 stocks that fit the requirements of liquidity and volatility at all times. Even if you are trading at the minimum size of $1,000, you need at least ten stocks in your observation list.

■ Diversification by Dollar Risk

This is a fundamental principle and one that is frequently misused not just by first time traders, however by lots of veterans. Dollar diversification is used to offset the likelihood of risk.

Here is how it works.

We are back in the casino once again, playing blackjack. This time we are in your house, and there are two players against us. One is wagering $500 a hand, and one is betting $5 at hand. We understand the chances are somewhat in our favor, as we have the mathematical edge, so in the long run, we must anticipate the very same outcomes no matter which player wins. As a matter of truth, we enjoy seeing the enormous shooter, because, in theory, he must lose more to us in the long run. But here is where the problem comes in. Expect the vast shooter is an expert card counter, and the $5 gamer is having fun. The $5 player is there to take pleasure in the adventure. He is out the door; it does not have any impact on him if he loses his $50 bankroll. The $500 gamer is attempting to beat your home, and in the long run, possibly he suffices to do it. Given that the players are so out of balance, the casino could win its theoretical drop; however, lose money-- not an excellent scenario to be in.

If you do not account for the dollar distinction in your portfolio, this is the same problem that you will experience. The reason I used the $50 stocks earlier was to show you that diversification by rate and group is not enough. Suppose that your portfolio holds 100 shares of the $50 energy stock that has a typical weekly move of $1 and 100 shares of the $50 green energy stock that has an average variety of about $4. You must have the ability to see that you are not balanced; you would require to win four times as much in the energy stock on average to balance out one theoretical loss in the green stock, assuming the loss was understood at the expected relocation.

One might win 75 percent of your trades and still lose cash! An unbalanced dollar portfolio is more dangerous than one containing a lot of stocks of the same grouping. One hundred shares of Caterpillar are not like trading 100 shares of Netflix, and you need to accommodate this in order to balance your portfolio.

Balancing your portfolio is performed in steps:

Step one.

Take the stock with the highest Weekly EV and designate it a value of 1.

Step two.

Divide the EV of all other stocks buy the EV in the most significant stock.

Step three.

Trade the rest of step two and appoint it the correct number of contracts.

Consistently round to the nearest number of agreements; do not be concerned if your ratios are slightly off; unless you are trading hundreds of contracts, the rounding will have no result. The concept is to stabilize the dollars in the portfolio as close as you can to the current EV levels.

Handling money is the most crucial part of trading. If you wish to contend with expert traders, you need to know how they take a look at the marketplace. They are always trying to figure out a method to reduce their exposure. Unless it is a market-making function where they are your home, they are not going to get included in illiquid markets. They will trade a well-balanced portfolio, and you must likewise purchase one.

CHAPTER FOURTEEN

Stock Options Trading Newbie Mistakes

Error 1: Choosing the wrong options

Lots of options trading newbies choose to buy "cheap" options. Well, that person decision alone had resulted in much of the preliminary losses when a stock moved up insignificantly, and the position stays in a loss. Suppose you anticipate the stock to move powerfully in that instructions. Buying options of low amount of money also the reason that many options trading beginners lose all their money in one go. This takes place when the options they bought never turn into profit.

Error 2: Making complex positions as your first couple of tries at options trading

Many options trading newbies begin making sophisticated positioning strategies such as iron condor spread or butterfly spreads as their very first few options trades and then totally mess up as they did not understand how to keep the position and some don't even understand how to set up the positions correctly. When your trading experience is as detailed as they are, sophisticated techniques are just excellent.

Error 3: Buying options that do not conform to your expected trading horizon

The majority of options trading novices have no idea what an expected trading horizon is in the top place and typically find the options they purchase expiring before the underlying stock made the move they expected it to.

Error 4: Placing the wrong orders

Yes, when under pressure, specifically when real money is included, newbies tend to make silly human mistakes such as clicking an incorrect button, purchasing an incorrect option, purchasing an incorrect expiration month, or positioning a wrong stop-loss order that got the position sold right away. Such beginner human mistakes can only be lowered through an extended period of virtual trading practice on your selected options platform and, after that, gradually practice using only really little cash in order to get used to the sensation of trading genuine money. Unfortunately, we are all human, while skilled options traders tend to make lower of such mistakes, they still do often. It is more widespread in rookie trades and definitely injures trading self-confidence. Regularly give yourself a couple of months of virtual trading practice on your chosen platform before going on genuine cash.

Error 5: Trading with obtained money (or money you can not manage to lose).

There is a saying, "you can't pay to win if you can't manage to lose." This is incredibly true in trading, not just options trading, but any type of trading. If you trade using money that you can not pay for to lose, the mental pressure will minimize your odds of winning when your chances of winning are currently meager as a beginner. This is why we continuously encourage people to trade just with cash they can pay for to lose.

Error 6: Trading without assistance.

Would you discover to drive a car and truck without anyone guiding you? Why then would you try to trade without anybody guiding you? Yes, a teacher or a mentor is very crucial to a newbie in options trading not since they can provide you "tips" but because they can shed light on your scenario and reveal weak points that you might not have discovered. Newbies trading without assistance frequently repeat mistakes over and over again, and if you have traded option before, you know it don't take a lot of those mistakes to wipe your account out.

There you have, the leading six mistakes that newbies make in stock options trading. Take note of these frequently made mistakes, and you will prevent the disappointment of losing money unnecessarily.

Is There Liquidity Risk?

During durations of high volatility of option and stock bid/ask spreads expand. Regularly play out a worst-case scenario in your head and attempt to determine what the damage might be.

The key is attempting to get a much deeper understanding of the danger related to the position, what option elements affect (time, volatility, stock price motion) it, and how.

Nevertheless, I understand that a few of you have a little bit more danger tolerance than me, so I wished to reveal to you what else to consider when taking on more risk by sizing up.

Don't forget experience is the very best teacher, but I'm likewise here to assist.

Discovering Or Creating Your Own Options Trading System That Works

Stock Options are lovely! This smart derivative of the equities market has to be among the most artistic developments of modern-day times. For the trader who can discover how to win at trading choices, there are many high-ends in life that can be experienced.

Success in options trading needs a consistent approach for long-term success. This declaration is not meant to be grand, idealistic remark made by some 'trading theorist'; instead, it is a declaration born out of the problematic knocks and success experiences of the author and numerous other long-lasting, active trader contemporaries.

This "constant technique" to options trading can also be called a "trading system" or an "option trading system" in this case. The term "trading system" is not always restricted to a series of computerized "black box" trading signals. A trading system might be something as simple as "buy an option on a stock in an uptrend that breaks the high of the previous bar after a minimum of two days of drawback down movement that makes lower lows." A trading system is merely an organized method that benefits from a duplicated pattern or event that brings net revenues.

Considering that an Option is a "Derivative" of the stock, you need to derive your choices trading system from a stock trading system. This indicates your trading system should be based around real stock price movement. That stated, your trading system does not need to work for all stocks. It merely has to work for particular types of stocks, inevitable volatility of stocks and specific cost levels of stocks, etc. Focus your trading system on particular stocks that have cost habits that is predictable to the net results you want to abstract from a stock.

You can design a trading system, a trading method, and a trading approach by determining a price movement pattern (or lack of cost motion pattern) or some occasion that occurs on some sort of routine basis. This means you can trade rate behavior patterns on cost charts such as traditional chart patterns, trends, swings, pivot points, boxes, etc. or you can trade occasions that encourage stock rate such as earnings runs, post revenues runs, stock splits, seasonal aspects, etc.. Bottom line to make the maximum earnings in options trading you desire your stock to relocate your favor quickly, and you want it to move far. A relatively little motion in the rate of a stock can double your money in options!

There are so many various methods and strategies that you can trade with options. You can also enter into ratio back spreads, condors, and butterflies. And if you're feeling insane, you can sell 'naked' options (just better use a stop loss or you'll wind up like among my old trading buddies who ran an account to $20 million then offered everything back offering naked alternatives.)

Directional options trading systems are the very best. Keep it simple, purchase calls for and upside trade or buy puts for a downside trade. But this suggests you need a directional stock trading system to trade directional options.

Here are a couple of various techniques for directional systems:

Establish a choice trading system that trades the swings in stock rate motion. There are lots of excellent swing trading systems available today. We suggest you get one. The bottom line with swing trading is that you wish to swing trade with the trend. Options brokers nowadays have advanced order technology that will allow you to go into swing trades based on the rate movement of the stock, so you do not have to see this stock throughout the day. That significant improvement to swing trading options.

Swing trade the day bars: The majority of swing trading systems are based on daily bars on the stock cost chart.

Swing trade the Intra Day Bars! Their other high systems based on intraday charts that pinpoint swing trading entries.

Establish an options trading system that trades 3 to 6-month trends. This is where the vast money is. Trading the significant patterns is where numerous can place larger amounts of money to develop their net worth.

Develop an options trading system that trades pivot points. Pivot point trading is perhaps the best way to trade choices, since cost action is typically explosive, and occurs rapidly in our instructions when a trade works. Because you can use shorter-term options and take advantage of yourself a little much better, this is good. And it's also excellent you can make fantastic gains in 5 days to 4 weeks typically, so time decay problems end up being less of a worry.

There are various directional trading approaches you could use to trade alternatives. You need to select one, work it, and never use more than 10% options position size per trade on little accounts 1% to 5 % max position size on larger accounts. This exact method of cash management trading options is the fastest method to possibly quick account development, helping you avoid needless setbacks.

STOCK MARKET INVESTING FOR BEGINNERS 2020

A Simplified Beginner's Guide To Starting Investing In The Stock Market And Achieve Your Financial Freedom

Nathan Bel

INTRODUCTION

Before you study how you can turn the stock market into a goldmine, you should first have an excellent foundation of the fundamentals of investing in stocks. Stock Investing has been an honor for me to write. I'm grateful that I can share my knowledge, information, and experience with such a devoted and large group of readers.

Although the stock market has served countless financiers for nearly a century, recent years have shown me that an excellent investing lorry such as stocks can be quickly misunderstood, misused, and even mistreated.

Recently, millions of investors lost an overall of over 5 trillion dollars. Financiers at the tail end of a bull market frequently think that stock investing is a secure, carefree, specific method to make a fast riches. The many stories of investors who lost improbable quantities of cash hypothesizing in tech stocks, dot-.coms, and other fancy stocks are lessons for everyone. Successful stock investing takes thorough work and knowledge like any other significant prematch. This book can help you prevent the mistakes others have made and can point you in the right direction.

CHAPTER ONE

Stock Market

A stock market, to say the least, is a place for trading stocks. It also functions as a sign of the financial cycle. When the economy is performing well, the prices of commodities tend to increase in the market, typically. When the economy is down, the costs of stocks also decrease; this can be true even for a very high share. It is also worth noting that the costs of stocks mainly depend on the efficiency of a business. When a company is succeeding, the price of its stocks will also tend to increase; the opposite would take place if the business is not earning well. There are odd cases where speculators are buying stock that is not performing well at all, which will result in a high stock cost even for a lousy business, but that is another story for another time. Now, the question is: Why using stocks? The reason is that it assists businesses to raise funds to finance their tasks, whether for the expansion of the company, or for their day-to-day activities, or just to please their stakeholders. Money, after all, is the brain behind every investment.

Stock

A stock, also known to as a share, represents ownership of a business. When you purchase stocks from a company, you get to work out ownership rights of the company, for instance, a claim on the company's properties and revenues, and ballot rights.

Remember that there are different kinds of stocks. When you see investors talking about the stock market, they usually refer to a typical stock.

Stock Market Index

You might hear them talk about how the market increases or falls one day when individuals talk about stocks. The way to view this is to know the stock market index or indices.

There are many stocks present in the stock exchange. Similar stocks are grouped to form an index.

Having an index is an excellent way to sort the various kinds of stocks in the market. After all, the stock exchange is composed of several stocks. It will be confused if you fail to sort similar stocks in the same place. It is also a thing of reference for contrast. You can compare the tendency of the index worth with the pattern of the cost of specific stocks that fit into that same index. You can as well compare one index with another and see which industry might be a rewarding investment.

Considering that there are many stocks in the market, and the index can sort all of them out in an orderly manner, an index acts as a good representation of the whole market. If you look at the index of the IT industry, then you will know the average performance of the stocks in the IT market. This applies to other markets. There are different ways to make contrasts, depending on how the shares are arranged in an index.

How the stocks are organized together identifies the type of category of the index. For instance, in a world stock market index, such as in the S&P Global 100, you will discover stocks that are found worldwide. These are stocks from different countries in the world, such as Asia and Europe. There is also what is known as the national index.

As the name suggests, this type of index considers the performance of the stock market in a particular country. You can likewise discover a more specific index that reveals the habits of the stock market on a local level. When analyzing the stock market, it is advisable to study various indexes so that you can have a much better understanding of what is truly going on in the stock market.

Long-Term versus Short-Term Stock

You can choose how long you want to purchase the stock market. Many traders invest just in one day. Therefore they are known as day traders, but it is also typical to discover people who purchase stocks for more than five years. This depends on your preference, along with how you want to approach the stock market. When to categorize an investment as a short- term or long term, there is no quick and challenging guideline for that.

Some financial investments start as a short term but then grow into a long time while doing so. For beginners, the majority of people specify a short-term investment as any investment that lasts for a year. For this reason, all other investments that lasted for more than one year are considered as a long-lasting investment. Again, such meaning is approximately you.

It is worth noting that the stock exchange, in general, does not fluctuate too quickly. You can not anticipate a significant return on a short-term investment as much as you can get from a lucrative long-term investment. Numerous short-term investments only last for a month or some months.

The problem with long-lasting investing is that it is more difficult to predict how the market will respond during your investment. Even though the market is doing terrible now, it can do well after a year. Of course, the difference can take place.

The purpose of the investment also matters. If you desire to save for retirement, then a long-term investment is the best.

It is to be noted that the market takes some time to respond. This is among the issues why day trading might not be the right choice considering that the market might take more than 24 hours before it reacts to your prediction. Another separating factor is the technique that you change. For short-term savings, technical analysis would be valuable to you; however, for a long-term investment, the fundamental analysis would be the much better option.

Stock Investing versus Trading

It is rather safe to state that there is no difference between investing in and trading stocks. A view drawn from a fundamental perspective, they are interchangeable. Nevertheless, for the word Nazis out there, investing and trading stocks might have some distinctions.

You can trade many stocks on a single day. On the other hand, investing means a less active approach where you purchase particular shares and hold on to them for a more extended period so that you can sell them later for a profit.

Remember that this book uses both words synonymously with no reference to any practical implication. After all, before you can buy anything, you first need to have money to purchase your goods. And, when you buy stocks, you also need to sell and trade them afterward for you to earn an income. Short-term investing likewise consists of the habits of day traders who trade stocks within a single day.

Is it for you?

Anybody can invest in stocks; this type of investment is not for everybody. You have to earn it if making revenue is your intention (which should always be). Real expert financiers spend hours of research and study regularly. Yes, you can earn money in the stock market by just relying on mere luck without any investigation. But, you cannot expect to make a continuous profit by merely relying on mere luck or guesswork.

To make the stock market a rewarding place for you and your company, you require to devote severe time and effort into discovering the craft of investing in stocks. This indicates that you need to be ready to spend hours of research study and be sure you are following the stock market on a routine basis.

Fundamentals Of The Stock Market

Owners of business have been raising capital through the sale of equity interests for many years. But the auction of equity interests via a public market dates back more detailed to four-hundred years.

In the early 1600s, a Dutch shipping business sold shares of itself to increase the capital it required to broaden business operations. Other companies began offering shares of themselves for sale, and innovative business owners started trading commodities, stocks, and other monetary instruments in personal markets. A stock market opened in Amsterdam in 1611 in response to the increase in the trading of products and financial securities. Over the next couple of centuries, other markets opened in Europe only.

In the year 1792, brokers assemble under a buttonwood tree in Wall Street to formulate rules for buying and selling stocks and bonds-- the precursor to the New York Stock Exchange. The following bullet points will tell you enough about the most crucial exchanges, so everyone will not assume you're checking out Wall Street for the first time.

- -American Stock Exchange (AMEX)-- For some years, the smallest of the three primary U.S. stock markets. The American Stock Exchange, frequently called Amex, offered itself to NYSE Euronext in 2008. While the mom's and dad's business changed Amex's name to NYSE MKT, the old name has remained. This exchange centers on small-cap stocks, exchange-traded funds, and derivatives.
- -Chicago Board Options Exchange (CBOE)-- The world's largest market for choices on stocks, indexes, and interest rates.
- -Chicago Mercantile Exchange (CME)-- The country's largest futures exchange, and the second most prominent worldwide.
- -Nasdaq Stock Market (NASDAQ)-- Commonly called just the Nasdaq; this market is a subsidiary of Nasdaq OMX Group, which operates 24 markets on six continents.
- -New York Stock Exchange (NYSE)-- The earliest, and some state still the most prominent, stock exchange in the United States. The NYSE is a subsidiary of NYSE

Euronext, an international conglomerate that controls those markets that sell more than 8,000 equities and account for nearly 40% of the world's stock trading.

Most big companies and many little ones trade on exchanges to make it easier for investors to buy their shares. Exchangers need the business to satisfy specific criteria, such as the variety of shares readily available, market cap, share price, and financial rules, before they will note the stock for trading. However, thousands of companies do not list their stocks on exchanges either because they can't satisfy the listing requirements or merely choose not to pay the exchanges' charges. Those stocks trade via networks of securities dealerships who work out deals among themselves. Such stocks are said to be OTC or buy on-the-counter.

As OTC stocks tend to be small and less accessible than those that trade on exchanges, they have obtained a reputation for threat. Naturally, lots of OTC stocks make suitable investments and lots of big foreign business trade non-prescription. Novices, nevertheless, might want to steer clear of OTC stocks, particularly cent stocks-- stocks that trade at meager rates.

Both exchanges and OTC markets welcome foreign companies. Companies situated outside the United States can sign up American depositary receipts (ADRs) or other customized securities that sell their stocks on U.S. exchanges. Various U.S. companies take advantage of comparable systems to trade on markets in Canada, Europe, or Asia. Not before having financiers delighted in such flexibility to buy and sell securities.

What You Should Know

Once you start investing or even looking into investments, you'll likely encounter different terms specialists in the field anticipate you to know. If you read about the Wall Street Journal or enjoy CNBC, reporters will frequently toss around expressions like "bull market" and "penny stocks" without specifying them. If you don't know what you encounter in the financial media or something your broker tells you, ask for an explanation or check the term above. Don't be ashamed of your lack of knowledge. Ignorance can be dangerous to your success, and smart investors won't buy anything or fill out a form, answer a personal question, or make a monetary pledge until they know the consequences of their actions.

The exchange names provided above are a good start when it comes to learning the vocabulary of investment.

Q&A-- Important Questions

There is more to investing than memorizing many terms. For answers to 10 questions that beginner stock investors typically ask, keep reading.

Question # 1: How do I start capitalizing in stocks exchange?

Answer: Open an investment account with a stockbroker. While some companies allow you to purchase your first share of stock directly from them, most businesses trade their shares just on dealer networks or through stock exchanges. A brokerage account will give you a chance to access many stocks and shared funds and other financial investments.

Question # 2: How much do I need to start buying stocks?

Answer: In an ideal world, you'll jump into the market with $100,000-- enough to purchase a diversified portfolio of stocks at once. Even if you can spare just $5,000 or $1,000, you can still invest in stocks.

Naturally, limiting yourself to just one business's stock, or small stocks call for danger. However, while you handle some risk when you purchase only one or two shares, choosing not to invest exposes you to another kind of threat-- poverty.

If you have an account at a discount broker charging $10 per trade, acquiring $1,000 in stock will cost you 1 percent of your income in commissions. That means your inventory must return about 1% before you recover the expense of the investment. As a guideline, investors should try to minimize their charge costs below 0.5% of the portfolio worth for the year. As the collection grows, your investment commissions should reduce as a percentage of the resources (See Table below).

Portfolio size	Cost to build 20-stock portfolio @ $10 per trade	% of portfolio	Cost to build 20-stock portfolio @ $50 per trade	% of portfolio
$50,000	$200	0.40%	$1,000	2.00%
$100,000	$200	0.20%	$1,000	1.00%
$500,000	$200	0.04%	$1,000	0.20%

Table 1.0-- Errors of Commission

If you have $1,000 to invest, leap, and pay the commission. You've got to begin somewhere. You'll be including new cash to the account over time if you dedicate to investing. Invest some years enjoying your stocks increase in worth, and after a while, the commissions will not take such a huge bite out of the whole.

Question # 3: I want to purchase Apple, but the stock expenses any dollars per share, and I don't have enough cash to buy 100 shares. Should I stick to cheaper stocks?

Answer 1: This concern needs two responses. Relating to the question of buying 100 shares. Some decades back, purchase shares in great round deals of 100 count. Brokers do not like dealing with smaller trades, and often they charged lower commissions for round lots. Some full-service brokers still choose to handle round lots, however with securities trading digitally and discount brokers charging a fixed rate for many trades, today, you can purchase eighty-seven shares of Stock A and forty-two shares of Stock B, without encountering a tough time.

Dollar-based investing centers on the size of the stock point in dollars, not shares. Think about putting $2,500 in each stock, which relates to fifty shares of $50 stock, eighty-three shares of $30 stock, or twenty-nine shares of an $80 stock. Holding equivalent dollar of all your stocks not just minimizes the threat in lopsided portfolios (if your highest holding falls, it triggers an out of proportion decrease in the worth of your whole collection), but also makes it easier to examine how your stocks are performing.

Answer 2: The second answer addresses the problem of cheap stocks. Many financiers, particularly those who began buying stocks during the days when everybody bought shares in round lots, still see a $100 inventory as more expensive than a $50 stock. Experts value stocks relative to revenues, money flows, or sales, and so should you do.

Question # 4: Which one should I purchase, bonds, or stocks?

Answer: For many investors, the intelligent answer is both. Both bonds and stocks play an essential role in a portfolio. While stocks offer superior development capacity throughout good years (in addition to many drawback potentials during bad years), bonds provide higher income and steadier general returns (though they can't match stocks for possible advantage).

While not all stocks follow the same path, they do tend to relocate comparable instructions. If the S&P 500 Index has returned 15% in a particular year, for example, many stocks-- even those outside the index-- have most likely published positive returns. Some tread more quickly than others, naturally.

Bonds also tend to relocate the same instructions as other bonds. However, different classes within the bond group (such as long-term business bonds, Treasury expenses, high-yield bonds, and so on) will see their incomesdeviate.

While bonds and stocks tend to run in loose packs, a reality investors ought to use to lower volatility is that those packs do not frequently run together. How much should you put in stocks against bonds? The equation means a 30-year-old must hold 80% stocks and 20% bonds, while an 80-year-old needs to hold 30% stocks and 70% bonds.

Question # 5: How do I know the stocks to buy?

Answer: Whole books have been written on this subject, however most stock analysis comes down to a few key styles:

Worth.

Even the fastest-growing stock is not worth buying if you have to pay too much. Beginners, in particular, should not mess around with expensive hyper growth stocks. Before you buy, think about the stock's key valuation ratios (price/earnings and operating money circulation).

Growth.

If the business can't increase its earnings, even the least expensive stock isn't worth purchasing. Rising sales, revenues, and cash flow recommend the company's products sell well enough to increase its penetration of the market.

Success.

Any business can grow if it spends enough cash. A well-run business can keep their profit margins while still growing.

Investors should target stocks with steady or increasing success.

News.

What type of headings does the stock create? Both great news and problem can impact a stock's price before any changes drip down to the income statement or balance sheet.

Convenience level.

Do not buy it if a stock will keep you up at night for any reason. This guideline uses even if the capital escalates or if all your friends fill up on the hot name. No investment, even a profitable one, makes good sense for an investor who can't buy into the idea with the shares.

Question # 6: How do I identify when to trade a stock?

Answer: Whole books have also been composed on this topic. Because they only buy stocks they like, most investors find the sell choice harder than the buy decision. As soon as you purchase a stock, you take pleasure in owning; you may find it difficult to do away with the investment.

That said, there is nothing like a permanent buy. Eventually, every stock outlasts its energy in your portfolio. All stocks move up and down with time, but the unsightly plunge of bank stocks in late 2008 and 2009-- far worse than the drop in the broad market-- highlights the risks of sticking with stocks when their environment changes substantially.

Rudiments of the Stock Market

Figure above - Don't Buy It

1) If you bought the capital because of its appraisal, does the valuation still look appealing? If growth drew you in, has that development continued? Consider selling if the response is no.

The business has radically changed. Often that drug company you acquired because of its pipeline of asthma drugs changes its instructions and starts to concentrate on mental-health treatments. Do not be scared to sell if you like the first method, but not the second.

In late 2007 and early 2008, when some enemies started grousing about banks overstretching themselves, lots of financiers bailed out on their stocks. Financiers who heard the train coming and sold their paper stocks in 2004 and their bank stocks in 2007 benefited from their ability to see and from their willingness to accept the new reality.

Question # 7: My stock has dropped, but I can't find any news on it. What triggered the dip? Answer: You might not know. First, you should recognize that the stock market reflects the collective will and viewpoints of millions of financiers. If enough of them choose to sell Acme Widget-- no matter their factors-- the shares will decrease in value.

In some cases, people sell a stock because it has yielded well, and they want to schedule some profits. Since shares have begun to fall and they fear further declines, stockholders might also sell. In some cases, problems from another business in the market will trigger stock to decline because the reasons behind the weakness in the other stock might affect the first stock.

And sometimes stocks sell in compassion-- perhaps when a close competitor has taken a substantial loss-- even when the news does not impact them directly; in such cases, they often rebound quickly.

Often stock will increase or decrease not because of any company-specific news but because the market itself has taken a turn. Keep in mind that stocks tend to move in a pack. As with any bag, you'll see bold names that bolt to the front while plenty of laggers hang back. If you have stocks, you should expect them to decline when the broader market declines.

Expect the broad stock market dips 10% for some months. History recommends that it could still decline even more, but ultimately most stocks will recover. They constantly do. If your capital falls 10% in a prevalent market decline of 10% without giving any unfavorable news, you can blame the broad market for the decrease.

Question # 8: How do I trail my portfolio?

Answer: Twenty years ago, most big papers printed everyday stock prices, and investors followed their financial investments in the article. With the proliferation of sites using the same information in a more modern style, often at no charge, many papers have avoided the stock pages. These days, the Internet merely uses more info, and many commercial websites do an excellent task of stocking pricing and trading data.

You can have a look at the efficiency of your stocks on your discount broker's site. While each broker does little task differently, they ought to show you the value of your stock positions and allow you to see the stocks' history-- how they have moved considering that you bought them.

Use a third-party site to track all your investments at the same time if you do not buy all your investments through the same broker. Simply input your stocks' ticker symbols, and you can have a portfolio of the stocks you own in addition to stocks you want to view.

Interested in more detail than today's share cost? You can likewise get on the date you purchased the stock along with the purchase cost and the variety of stocks. If you input your transaction details, the website you selected will show you the profits of each stock considering that you bought it-- essential information for assessing your portfolio.

Question # 9: Should I register for a newsletter or go to a broker for help about picking stocks? Or am I much better off making my own investment decisions and not paying for guidance?

Answer: The response to this question depends upon the answer to two other concerns. How much time will you commit to dealing with your financial investments? And how comfortable do you feel evaluating numbers?

People who claim to have discovered the single technique of making money in the stock market shoot emails all over. Even if a financier makes a 932% return on a stock once, you can't assume he'll do it once again.

Real stock analysis-- the kind of research carried out by experts who handle other people's money and can get fired if they mess up-- takes some time. You don't need to spend 40 hours a week, but unless you know you'll invest at least three hours a week learning about your investment, following market news, and comparing one stock with another, do not try to do it alone. Find somebody you trust-- a newsletter editor, a monetary organizer, or an online master who gives suggestions without spitting through the computer screen-- and pay attention. You do not need to follow anybody's tips precisely. Still, you'll make much better choices when you can begin your analysis by examining the stocks other people like, or when you can use somebody else's strategy to check your own decisions.

Now, about the numbers. More mathematics geeks regulate the universe. Stock analysis is not rocket science, and you don't need a Ph.D. in data or mathematics to analyze stocks. The job simply requires a versatile mind, a desire to learn a few originalities, and a calculator.

Question # 10: The stock market is dropping, but I like the Acme Widget. Should I get the shares now or wait till the price dips further?

Answer: Plenty of investors buy and sell choices based on a stock's price action-- a process known as a practical analysis.

Practical analysis looks at a stock's price chart and conclude where it will go based on where it has been. Some people make cash by doing this, and some lose it. Even professionals will concur that forecasting and timing short-term stock or market motions are very tough.

This book gives you the tools to examine stocks from an essential perspective: by looking at their operating data or appraisal ratios. You take a threat by not acquiring it instantly as soon as you get a stock with strong investment potential at its current rate. Sure, the stock might dip, providing you an opportunity to snap it up at a bargain. However, the price might also increase, eating away some of your possible earnings. As a practical matter, financiers who enjoyed a stock at $50 per share tend to discover it more difficult to shoot on the purchase after it jumps to $60, even if it increases on relevant news, and the future still looks intense.

Markets often shift direction unpredictably, and just because stocks have declined over the last week does not mean they'll keep decreasing anymore than it implies they'll reverse course.

You simply can not predict. Unless you have some personal perception about the direction of the stock or the market in the coming days, don't hold back on your purchase in the hopes of purchasing a better cost.

After buying, the market could always go up or go down. Do not kick yourself for acting too quickly if the demand decreases and do not pat yourself on the back since you purchased before an upturn. If you bought the best stock, you'd enjoy your reward in time, regardless of what the market does after you make your transaction

Why Invest?

Everyone invests. From the smart stockbroker on Wall Street to the assembly line employee who avoids breakfast every Friday because he runs out of cash before his next income, everyone invests their time, effort, and attention in what they find valuable.

You're investing in your health if you spend your Saturdays' training for a marathon or tackling 50-mile bike trips. If you spend your weekends with family activities, taking the kids to swimming practice or attending Little League video games or checking out museums, you're buying your kids. And if you go to classes in hopes that a college degree will assist you in getting a better job, you're purchasing your career.

While each of these types of investing appears to support different objectives, all of them-- and dozens more-- share a common purpose: to provide for the future. Investing in your family now can develop relationships that will sustain in times when you might need more from others yet have less to give in return.

Many people enjoy the wealthiest rewards from their investments after retirement, but the earlier you start preparing, the better you will be in the future. Making a little dedication to different kinds of investing-- the monetary strategies presented in this book-- can put you on your journey to a longer and more influential retirement.

Common Motivations.

Motivations behind financial investing are almost as many as investors themselves. Naturally, your concerns may vary from your neighbor's, however for the many parts, motivations for investing tend to fall into three classifications:

-Investing in build wealth.

-Investing to support a family.

-Investing in preparation for retirement.

Financiers concentrated on building wealth, i.e. tend to focus more on the future than other financiers. Wealth makes you to establish and maintain a comfortable lifestyle. For some, that comfort might imply a nice-sized house, a couple of reliable vehicles, and a journey to somewhere warm for a week every January. Numerous investors are more than happy with such a lifestyle, while others set loftier objectives. By building wealth gradually-- the safest and best way to do it-- you can enhance your way of life along with your net worth.

Financiers who focus on supporting a family frequently seek to build sufficient wealth now to pay for a property in a community with good schools, the periodic trip, and things like ballet slippers, algebra tutoring, and summer season. You know the type-- the type that works hard for 40 years, climbing up the business ladder. The supreme goal for these investors is a smooth transition to retirement, where even without an income, they can maintain the standard of living they invested all those years making.

Whether you seek to support a healthy lifestyle, buy a happy home for your children, or just buy enough and keep so you will not have to work till you turn 80, you can enhance the chances of reaching your objectives by putting your money to work. Whether you're 20, 40, or 60, you'll like more options decades from now if you invest wisely-- starting today.

People who keep investing until it's hassle-free spend their golden years consuming ramen noodles. You've got to start today.

Uncertain how to continue?

Do not panic. After reading this book, you'll know all your monetary goals and some tools needed to reach them. The primary step is to avoid making a foolish-- but frighteningly common mistake.

Don't Kid Yourself.

Lots of expert financiers-- even some who have accumulated millions of dollars in assets-- don't comprehend what is affordable to expect from their investments. All too often, they state things like, "I want yearly returns of about 20%. Greed, wrong choices, and stubbornness have torpedoed many financiers, but the most considerable difficulty inactive investing may be unreasonable expectations.

Over the last eighty-seven years, big-company stocks have balanced annual returns of 11.8%. Long-lasting government bonds returned an average of 6.1% a year given that 1926, while

Treasury expenses-- about the lowest-risk investment readily available-- handled just 3.6% returns. Small business stocks published higher highs and lower lows than large companies and bonds, and they were also more likely than big stocks to see returns vary considerably from year to year.

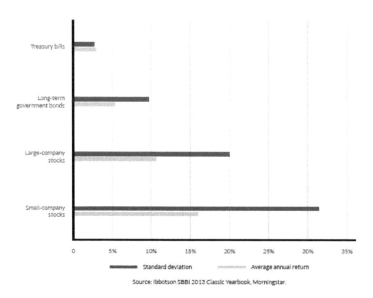

Figure above - Stocks Outperform Bonds.

If you wish to become an active investor, commit this idea to memory:

" High threat, high return. Low threat, low return.".

Like many essential realities, the investment mantra above is easy to comprehend; but, not always easy to actualize—still, the relationship between return and risk is the foundation of capitalizing.

Every investment has its ups and downs; nothing plans a straight course. However, some paths are rockier than others. The more danger you take, the higher your opportunity for a high return-- or a significant loss.

You've probably found the wrong man to help you with your investments if a stockbroker or financial consultant informs you he can make high returns with little threat.

Set Attainable Goals.

Now that you know the importance of investing and the different kinds of returns a few of the most common financial investments grow; it's time to proceed to your circumstance. Every person has various investment needs and strictures. No investment strategy, no matter how wise or well-considered, applies to everybody. To tailor your financial plan, ask yourself the following questions:

What are my goals? Be specific. "Get rich" will not cut it. Your objectives must set specific targets, such as, "Retire with $1 million in assets.".

What time do I need to reach those objectives? A forty-year-old mother with a daughter who will begin school in ten years must go for an investment that diff from a forty-year-old with no children who won't touch her finances till she retires at 65.

Some financiers can tolerate more risk than others. None of the approaches is right or wrong, but you'll sleep much better if you customize your investment technique to your personal feelings about risk.

What must I do to fulfill those objectives? Now you've attained the million-dollar question. Even if you set uncertain goals, you won't reach them overnight. As Table 1.3 shows, the time it needs to feather your nest depends on how quickly your financial investments grow. Split 72 by an investment's rate of return, and you know approximately for how long it will need to double your money. Earn 4% a year, and your salary increases in 18 years. An 8% return doubles the cash in 9 years while making 12% reduces the doubling time to 6 years.

Investment development ratio	No of years to increase in price

4%	18
6%	12
8%	9
10%	7
12%	6

The above table;

Assuming you have $100,000 in your 401(k) plan and hope to retire in 40 years with $1 million in properties. According to the Law of seventy-two, if you grow a portfolio that yields six percent in a year, your account would double to $200,000 by year 12, increase to $400,000 by year 24, redouble once again to $800,000 by year 36, and leading $1 million at the end of year 40. In the nick of time to satisfy your objective.

You can't ensure yourself a 6% return. And in some cases, even if you do manage a 6% annual return, you'll sustain a lot of twists and turns along the method-- a 30% profit this year, a 15% loss next year, then a flat year followed by an 8% gain.

Taking the natural unpredictability of investing into account, you must overengineer your investment portfolio. In other words, if you want to build up a particular quantity by a specific time, plan as if you need, state, 20% more than your target. Many of all, keep those targets affordable.

For example, a 30-year-old with no cost savings and a job paying $40,000 each year who desires to retire a millionaire at age 65 should not need much risk to reach that objective. A 40-year-old with no cost savings and a task paying $40,000 annually who wishes to retire a millionaire at age 65 will just have the ability to obtain that goal if she wants to handle some threat. A 50-

Year-old with two children, no savings, and a task paying $40,000 annually who likewise wishes to spend for his child's' college educations without loaning and then retire a millionaire at 65, merely do not have an affordable objective.

At this moment, you may be asking, "How can I know whether my goal is affordable?" The figure below ought to help.

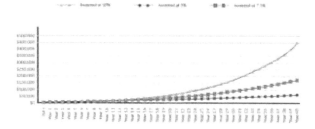

The Power of Time.

Too frequently, investors concentrate on the gulf between what they have and what they end up being and want to be discouraged. Do not fall under that trap, since you have not embarked on this investment journey alone. You have a capable ally: time.

The image shows the power of time on investment. If you invest at the rate of 7.5% annually, $10,000 will increase to more than $20,000 in 10 years, and then to $42,000 in 20 years. After 40 years, that $10,000 will have turned into a $180,000 nest egg.

Investments seem to grow quicker in later years because of the results of intensifying. The investment showed in the image never really accelerates its growth on a portion basis, but as the numbers get bigger, the nest egg appears to grow faster. Suppose you invest $10,000 and make a 10% profit. In the last month of the year, you have a rate of $11,000. If you repeat the 10% return in the second year, you'll acquire not only another $1,000 but an extra $100-- the 10% return on the $1,000 you gained in 2015. With time, the excess return made on previous gains will enhance your portfolio's value significantly.

Don't panic. People with 40 years to invest enjoy many options. And while financiers with much shorter time horizons may have fewer choices, this book can help you make the best decisions possible.

CHAPTER TWO

Myths and Misconception about Stock Investment

There are some myths and misinterpretations about investing in stocks. To have a more understanding of what it truly means to be a stock financier, be sure that you understand the truth behind the misconceptions: Investing in Stocks is Having a bet

This is why people run away from the stock market. Take note that the costs of stocks in the market depend on particular variables, such as the economic climate, organization performance, customer habits, and technical advancements, among others. The costs of stocks do not rise and fall arbitrarily.

Whether the securities market is betting or otherwise depends on how you approach it; if you merely pick the stocks randomly and simply depend on pure luck to be successful, after that, you are gambling. You can expect the same effects as you would definitely when you wager in the online casino. Nevertheless, if you come close to the stock market expertly where you place a short time, effort, and research, in all your transaction, if you take into consideration every act as an investment choice, then you are not wagering yet investing. Gamblers depend on luck, while real investors understand what they are doing and have a side over the stock exchange.

Buying Stocks will undoubtedly make you a Multi-Millionaire Investing in stocks is similar to any type of different other business: You can make money; nevertheless, you can also shed money. Like any investment, there are risks involved. Indeed, some of those can grow their cash, but many financiers lose their money. To be successful, you need to know the stock exchange and apply particular methods. Indeed, a significant component of success is to carry out a considerable research study.

It is worth noting that you will just gain a specific portion of your financial investment. Naturally, you may earn more than 100% or perhaps 200% of your investment. Do not expect it to happen overnight. For that reason, the more cash you spend, the more income you can make.

If you are in a particular exclusive group, the Stock Market is Only for the Rich People Some assume that you can only invest in stocks. This is not true. The securities market is open to every person given you are of age, and there are no other legal prohibitions relevant to you in your state. Especially today where you can buy stocks by just opening an account with an internet broker, you can invest despite only $300, or perhaps much less.

You Need Connections to Succeed

With all the links that Warren Buffet has, there is no surprise he can determine the appropriate stocks to spend in. Well, if this is what you believe, then you are wrong, absolutely incorrect. Yes, having great connections can help you leverage and also increase your possibilities of choosing the right stocks and also earn a profit, but handling the stock exchange is more than building links. In truth, several investors make appropriate amounts of income even without connection with anyone whatsoever. Many thanks to the Internet, which essentially makes our world smaller, you can quickly access different sites and also gather details from the convenience of your house. There are also many evaluations and evaluations shared by other financiers that you can use as an additional recommendation. Here is the reality: You do not require links.

Duration.

What you need is to find the securities market and deal with your winning approaches.

You need Extensive Financial Knowledge

This is one more myth that needs to be broken. Indeed, having financial knowledge is something that you require to help you to pick the most active stocks to purchase. This is real, mainly if you use financial analysis-- which is one of the most typical investing strategies. There are various other approaches that you can use without you having to look at any number. This, naturally, does not mean that you need not to bother establishing your financial understanding. However, it just shows that you can still make and spend cash by buying stocks, even if you have minimal expertise in business finance. It needs to remember that you do

You can establish your financial expertise just by researching stuff online. The crucial part below is to analyze what you currently know.

Quick way to earn money

If you have significant funding and also can deal with many shares, then you can earn money by buying stocks rapidly. However, just some people have the true blessing of having millions or billions of funds in their checking account. Likewise, if you are a beginner, the best way is to begin small no matter how much capital you have.

An Easy Way to earn money

Considering that you just have to pick stocks and also invest in some cash, wait for some time, and after that market to enjoy your earnings, after that generating income with the securities market must be very easy, best? I am afraid that is a No. You can do all these with merely a few clicks of a mouse, investing in stocks is not as straightforward as it looks. The main problem hinges on selecting the best stocks to purchase, in addition to the appropriate timing. Now, for you to recognize these two significant points, you need to apply severe initiative and also the time in research and analysis.

Your Partners in Crime; For best stock trading experience
Before you can spend in the stock market, you need to open an account with a broker. The issue is, with all the brokers out there convincing you to sanction and make a financial investment, how do you identify the broker that can suit your requirements? Make sure that your broker passes this type so that you will certainly have the ideal investing or stock trading experience.

Banking

This is a fundamental part to consider before you even transfer any money right into your account. Make sure to inspect the down payment methods, in addition to the approaches for making a withdrawal. It is not unusual to locate brokers that use even more alternatives when making a deposit but just have limited choices for making a withdrawal. You would certainly not wish to have your cash locked up in your account with no way to withdraw it right into real money.

A broker will typically ask you to submit a copy of your identification papers before it also processes your withdrawal. Before you make a down payment, see to it that you recognize what these papers are, which you have them in your belongings. Otherwise, you may not be able to withdraw your cash.

Minimum Deposit and Withdrawal Limit

Take note of the minimum down payment calls for. Some brokers need a minimum down payment of a minimum of $250, while others may approve a small amount of just $25. You should be aware of the minimum and maximum withdrawal limits. A broker may also bill a low withdrawal cost, which is normal. If you mean to make several withdrawals in a week, after that, the withdrawal charge is something that you must pay attention to.

Demonstration Account

Your broker ought to give you a free demonstration account. This is an excellent means to get a feel of real trading in a real-time stock market setting without running at lost.

Costs

These fees usually are just a tiny amount, they can quickly load up swiftly, mainly if you make huge sales in a short period. Be sure to contrast the different brokers that you locate online and look for the one that stocks the least expensive fees.

Trading Platform

Every online broker will certainly give you an investment platform where you can buy and sell stocks with just a click of a mouse. Your broker must give you an expertly created platform with useful attributes. The best brokers will offer you cost-free information or details concerning the securities market to help you make the best financial investment decision. Your broker also needs to provide you with charts and even graphs in case you intend to make use of technical analysis.

Trading Restrictions

Some brokers will also put a constraint as to the number of stocks that you can sell or buy.

You need to only work with a broker that will allow you to invest on your own.

It also needs to permit you to trade as many stocks as you want.

Before you also sign up for an account with any kind of broker, be sure to examine the testimonials given by various other financiers. A secure way to do this is to use your favorite internet browser to search for the name of the broker and add the word testimonials. It is not scarce for brokers to employ freelance writers to come up with a positive review of the broker's organization.

Pay attention to the time when the latest testimonials were done. If the most current favorable evaluations were made about a year ago after that beware. After all, the management group and also the policy of a broker might change periodically.

Mobile Feature

These days, people access the Internet using their cellphones. It is less complicated and more convenient. Your broker should also give you a platform that has a mobile feature. This implies that you need to have the ability to manage your account and make investments by only using your mobile phone, and also, the procedure must be as convenient as you are when you use a desktop. Do not fret; brokers with a high score always have a mobile feature. Having a mobile feature is among the reasons people like specific brokers.

Customer Support

Remember how you can call the customer assistance group. Exists a number that you can call any time? Also, inspect if the broker provides a live conversation feature on the website. If the broker can only be contacted through email after that, evaluate how fast it can respond, and focus on exactly how specialist it handles your inquiry. When you make your first withdrawal, an excellent way to do this is by sending a message to client assistance asking for any kind of alternative documents that you might send requests. Ideally, the consumer support should be able to respond with an answer to your query within 24 hours.

CHAPTER THREE

What to Do to Be a Successful Stock Investor

Using strategies alone is insufficient. To also boost your opportunities of earning a profit, you need to observe the best techniques complied with by capable stock capitalists.

Sufficient Research

It is not shocking why so many people lose their cash when they purchase stocks. Although books on the subject always stress the relevance of doing findings, just a few can research appropriately. Regrettably, many financiers assume that only because they have investigated the market for two hours, then it would be enough to come up with a sound financial investment choice. This is wrong. Make sure that you do adequate research. A research study should be an all-natural component of your day-to-day life if you are serious about a successful financier.

Start Small

It doesn't mean the amount you have in your account that you want to invest in. It means that you first use a demonstration account so that you can examine the water without running the risk of any cash.

Always start small. Your objective is to acquaint on your own with the real technique of trading stocks, also, to create a winning strategy. Do not worry; when you have a reliable approach in place, you can always enhance the quantity of your financial investment, which will also improve your possible profit.

Diversification

Expanding your investment is just one of the best means to minimize your losses. As they say, you must not place all your eggs in one basket. The factor is that no matter how a lot you examine the securities market, it can just boost our possibilities of success. It can never ensure the return of positive earnings. The fact is, there is a possibility that you might also lose your financial investment. Investing in stocks has its threats, just like any various other rewarding financial investment possibilities. By expanding your financial investment, you can reduce your danger and minimize your losses.

The most common means is to purchase stocks from different companies and not put all your money into a single business. An industry that is blossoming today might no longer be considered a rewarding financial investment tomorrow. Spread your financial investment over different markets.

Possession class diversity is an additional means to branch out. You do this by buying the various property class, such as in bonds, products, others, and stocks. You must discover how to time it well when you apply this approach. For instance, in the situation of economic healing, shares may be your best asset to buy. In an example of recession, investing in bonds might be a much better option than investing in stocks. Technique diversification is an additional efficient way to lower your risk. Depending on where you wish to spend or how you want to invest (short-term or long-term), particular approaches may be more relevant than others. In an instance of a lasting financial investment, you can not disregard the use of business evaluation.

When it comes to a temporary financial investment, technical analysis might be one of the very best approaches that you can use. You may also make use of geographical diversity. Some capitalists are quite partial and purchase a business that lies in a specific territory. Remember that no industry in a particular geographic location can outmatch others continuously—Ups and downs are standard in the securities market. You can also expand regarding time. Remember that you do not need to invest all the cash in your account in one trade. You can scatter your investments over time. For example, you can spend 20% of your money today and then follow it up with 30% in the following month. Much like anything in the company, proper timing is vital to success.

Diversifying simply means spreading your financial investment and not placing it in a single basket. Bear in mind that branching out alone is not a trick to revenue. One vital part of expanding is choosing where to diversify and place your money. Consequently, you can not sacrifice the value of studying and analysis.

Avoid complying with Expert Advice at all times

When you are a novice, you may find it handy to search the web for pieces of advice coming from the supposed "specialists." This is a standard error because not all of these "professionals" are actual professionals. These days, it is reasonably straightforward to spread a word and advertise one's self online. If you are good at advertising, you can quickly project an image that you are a professional stock financier of which you have not invested in any stock before. It is also worth noting that even the real experts commit blunders from time to time.

The best way to avoid depending on experts is to create your understanding of the stock market. What separates an expert from a complete novice is that an expert has his very own view of the stock market and can sustain his sight with sensible defenses. At the same time, a beginner generally counts on what other people say.

Beware of the Pump and Dump Scheme

A business or somebody that possesses stocks advertises his stocks and spread favorable reports about them. When this takes place, other investors will use to acquire the shares, assuming that they are a significant financial investment. The result is that the seller of the stocks makes a revenue, while the purchaser has a stock whose price is frantically dropping down.

Remember that the pump and dump scheme is not a bad thing. You can gain from it and earn an income.

The secret is to purchase the stocks before or quickly after the preliminary part of the pump and dispose of the scheme. The right way to do this is to sell the shares after you small amount of revenue. Don't wait for the increase to stop.

Do Not Hold the Stocks for Too Long

It deserves keeping in mind that not all financiers lose their money for choosing the wrong stocks. Some lose their money because they want the right stocks yet hang on to them for too long. Do not ignore the volatility of the stock exchange. See to it to market your stocks before their price drops. Take your revenue while you still can.

Understand Volatility

You should have a proper knowledge of what volatility is. Many people think about volatility as something where the costs of stocks merely rise and fall nearly arbitrarily. They frequently believe that after a massive surge, then a considerable fall can be expected, and the other way around. This is not always the case. If it were so, then instability would be very easy to foresee. Numerous pressures influence the volatility of the stock market. This means that even after a substantial decrease in the costs of stocks, it is still possible that a further decline will occur. This likewise implies that the outcome of a specific trade depends on previous sales or purchases. Regrettably, some people believe that given that their last three financial investments did not work out, after that, it is most likely that the next trade will bring profit with a positive result as long as they use the same approach. This is wrong.

There is an excellent chance that the succeeding trade or investment will also be a loss. The reason depends on the strategy that you are using. It is a sign that you must change or at least modify your technique if the method maintains on shedding. Real expert capitalists do not count on pure good luck. They recognize that if they come up with the right winning method, then the possibilities of raking in some earnings would be high. Keep in mind that if you have the right approach, there is still a possibility that you might shed an investment. No strategy can guarantee 100% the return of favorable revenues. However, with consistent research, hard work, and technique, you can turn a favorable outcome to your side and develop a winning edge over the stock exchange.

Maintain a Trading Journal

Even though it's not called for, keeping a trading journal can be useful. Don't worry; you do not have to be a professional writer to maintain a trading journal. Nevertheless, you need two things:

One, you need to be completely sincere.

This means that you must admit and accept your difficulties and weaknesses, in addition to the result of every financial investment that you make with no bias.

And two, you need to upgrade your journal regularly.

Preferably, you should write in your journal the reasons why you want to invest in stocks, and your short-term and also long-term goals. Your journal should likewise include your techniques, the financial investments that you make, and even your objectives.

It will make it much easier for you to detect any weak point or component of your method that still requires to be changed. Again, the essential thing is for you to be straightforward with every detail that you compose in your journal, and also update it regularly.

Do Not Approach Investing as a Hobby

The depressing fact is that many people who purchase stocks approach the securities market as a hobby. Although you are always totally free to consider it a simple pastime, you can also anticipate getting a fair result equally as when you come close to any different other services as a mere leisure activity, with no dedication. You need to take it as a business or an occupation if you want to get the right quantity of regular earnings from your investment. The issue with those that consider this type of investment as a mere pastime is that they fail putting in the right initiative and findings that will enable them to increase their possibilities of making a profit.

Wait it Out

Occasionally the best method to deal with the stock exchange is simply to wait it out. When the market is merely going down, it is unavoidable that you will soon come across a time. As opposed to being too worried and putting speculative financial investments, simply wait it out. Waiting investment out does not mean that you would neglect the market. It means that you ought to follow what is happening in the market, yet do not make any kind of move or financial investment. Wait for the best time to act. When the market recovers, then make sure that you want to make the most of it.

Do Not be an Emotional Trader

When you invest, it isn't enough that you feel good and also make regarding it. Instead, you need to be confident of your investment since you have done the right study and research, and that are good reasons to believe that it is the best financial investment. Anytime you feel like your feeling is getting in the way of your decision making, quit, and don't spend in any kind of investment whatsoever.

Capitalize on a Bull Market

An advancing market describes the securities market. It indicates that the prices of the stock on the market are rising-- which is good. On the other hand, when the prices are falling, it is called a bear or bearish market.

You should know how to make use of a bull market. Of program, the key right here is to be able to acknowledge that a bull market in the present situation of the market or when a proceeding market is just about to take place. You need to place your settings (financial investments) as early as possible to make sure that you can capitalize on the increase in the prices of stocks. A bull market usually occurs after a bearish market. You must know as soon as possible when a bear market would end, and a booming market would start. To do this, you have to meet up with your day-to-day study and valuation. A decree market may be promoted on the news; the best way to take advantage of it is by placing your financial investments at its creation. The factor is that an advancing market is usually complied with by a bearish market. It may currently be too late for you if you wait for a bull market to be introduced before you act up. Take note that the means to be in advance of the securities market is to be ahead of the competitors. Be the first to get hold of every possibility.

Examination and Develop your Strategy

Always evaluate your approach and also examine it several times before you use it with actual cash entailed. If you just change a minor part of your technique, take note that you have to repeat this process. The best way to do this is by using a demonstration account or by investing the minimum amount.

Remember that as a beginner, your primary objective is not to gain money right away. When it comes to success in the stock market, the more knowledge you have, the more your possibilities of hitting the appropriate financial investment. It takes time to know the best investment choice.

Never chase after your Losses

This is a general advice offered to speculators: Do not chase your losses. A fantastic reality about this is that lots of people who run after their losses are well aware of this advice. Despite the understanding that it is not a good idea to run after one's injuries, they still fall into this mistake.

So that you will not lose control of yourself, make sure you have the strength to stop making any kind of financial investment when you come across a considerable loss. Give yourself time to forget everything concerning the stock market. People generally chase after their losses by placing a more substantial investment with the hope that they will recover what they have lost and have more profit. After all, they have currently spent some time and initiative. The secret below is that rather of chasing what you have already lost, you should be composed and focus on your winnings or income. Bear in mind that every investment that you make is one-of-a-kind from all the remainder. When you run into a loss, simply admit and approve the damage, and move on. After all, the best strategy in the world will lose from time to time. Once you add up every little thing, the vital thing is for you to end up with a positive profit.

Only Invest the Money that you can Lose

Another standard rule given to casino players is to only play with the cash that you can lose. Well, although you will certainly not be gambling, you have to understand that this is still an investment. And, like any other type of investment, there is an opportunity that you may not make any profit or even lose all your cash.

Do Not Be Tired

The great stock investors have their own unpleasant stories to tell. They have experience of being overwhelmed in the stock market. As you go and spend more time investing in stocks, you will also encounter countless challenges.

Relax

Give yourself a break. It is so straightforward to obtain addicted to the stock exchange, especially when you realize some profit. But you have to give yourself time to relax. If you bear in mind that you can come up with much better financial investment decisions, allow your soul to rest. Likewise, it requires time to make a substantial profit in the stock market. As a result, give yourself time to loosen up every time, and afterward come back to work more durable.

An Overview of Different Strategies

You can not have a constant stream of income by investing in stocks unless you have a reliable approach. You are not limited to using one strategy. You can combine the policies, modify them, and come up with your plan. The important thing is that you make use of an approach to transform the odd in your favor.

Fundamental Analysis

Anybody who has invested in stocks or any business has probably experienced this method. This is one of the most common and practical strategies that you can use. Fundamental analysis emphasizes on the basics of the company concerned. After all, the performance of stocks in the market only depends on the performance of the business. Hence, this strategy involves examining the cash flow and financial statements of companies. To a certain degree, this strategy also considers the quality of the company. But, the main focus of this strategy lies in the performance of stocks in the market, which depends on the efficiency of the company. When you use this strategy, your goal must not be simply to gain from the capital gains but to receive all the advantages of possessing a prosperous company.

Practical Analysis

This strategy deals with analyzing graphs and charts, which show just how the rates of stocks change within a specific time. It is believed that many variables that affect the performance of stocks have their accumulated effect on the scale.

When you use this strategy, the secret is to seek a pattern or trend. You must then benefit from this pattern. Take note, nevertheless, that models come and go

Sometimes you may not see some pattern at all. A common blunder committed by many investors is that they force a design. Don't look for a pattern if it is not visible.

Value Investing

This method has to do with buying a company that is presently trading below its real worth. As an example, if the actual cost of the stocks of Company A is $25 per stock, but the stock exchange only reveals that its stocks are just worth $15, after that, it has to be a profitable investment. The trick here is to be able to take the evaluation and benefit from it.

When using this strategy, you need to look for stocks that have solid basics. If the true worth of a stock is $25, but it is rated at $15; after that, its actual rate will soon increase.

Remember that when you use this approach, you do not only look for a stock that is selling at a low rate. If the stock of Company A uses to sell at $23 per stock, however then they now go down to $14 per stock, it does not mean that they are good stocks to invest in.

Development Investing

This technique was accepted in the 1990s, when industrial firms were on the increase. At that time, several financiers who used this technique were able to obtain a considerable profits. It is to be noted that this approach is riskier than other methods.

The best means to know this strategy is to compare it with worth investing. This is the reason why a growth capitalist might buy a stock that is presently trading higher than its actual worth.

Again, a great investor looks into the future to see if a particular stock will be selling at a higher rate in the future, after that, the investment that you make today can be taken into consideration a successful one.

When you make use of development investing, the best stocks to buy are those that have a high capacity to grow. Growth financiers pay close attention to new and little business. This is because small and largescale enterprises have immense potential and space for development.

Qualitative Analysis

This approach provides a vital focus on the high quality of a company. It also takes into consideration the management approach of the company or the style by which the people of the firm mean to achieve its objectives. Appropriately, there is an excellent opportunity that the rate of its stocks will increase, which makes it a good investment.

Stock Split Advantage

A company usually proclaims a stock split when the price of its stock gets too high that is no longer eye-catching to investors. When the rate of capital is too expensive, it tends to project a picture that it has currently reached its top and makes people think that the stocks are no longer an excellent financial investment.

So, how does a stock split work? If you have thirty stocks at $20 each and a stock split is announced, then you will be with sixty stocks at $10 each. It is a fair division. The stocks will increase after the split, yet their rate will also decrease. It worth noting that a stock split is not limited to dividing a stock into two. A stock split might divide a stock into three or more divides

How to use this strategy is to check out a business that has simply declared a stock split. The stocks of that company might be an excellent investment if the stock split was legally done due to a growing investment. Naturally, you ought to also discover as high as you can about a company and also make your analysis. Counting on a stock split alone is not a good idea.

You need to understand the inverse split. The reverse split is also known as stock split but in the opposite. Compare to a stock split, and a reverse split is not a good sign. Keep in mind to run away from a company that uses a reverse split.

Right here is exactly how the reverse split works: if you have ten shares of stock at $10 each in Company X and a reverse split is performed, after that, you will have five shares at $20 each. As you can see, the cost of the stocks has increased significantly. A firm might make use of a reverse split to tempt investors to make a financial investment. As you can see, it is a deceitful relocation. The boost in the cost of stocks is not caused by any kind of progress or growth in the company but only by simple control. Indeed, a company that exercises a reverse split may be successful in the future. Such an act is a sign that the company is already having a hard time at present.

Revenue Investing

Take note that when you spend in stocks, you come to be a part-owner of company service. When you use this method, look for a huge and well-established company that no longer look for expansion. Instead of using the investor's profits for the growth of the company, these companies pass dividends to investors.

An important thing to note is that when you gain income from dividends is that in most states, such earnings that you receive from revenues are taxed at the same rate as wages. You can anticipate a higher tax than the ones enforced on capital gains. Check the regulations of your state to have more knowledge about the tax regulations that might be suitable for you.

Stock Mastery

You can adapt this strategy for a long time. How this works is that you need to pick a specific stock or company, and you need to learn about it every day until you have a perfect knowledge of how that stockwork. Remember that the more you know something about a stock, the far better you will be able to predict its actions-- and this is the key to incomes.

Can Slim

Can slim is an acronym that means Current quarterly incomes, Annual revenues growth, new products, services, management, or high rate, demand and stock, Leader or Laggard, Institutional sponsorship, and Market direction? According to this technique, by just looking at these factors, you can determine the best stocks to purchase.

How do you use this method?

The first step is to identify the stocks that have a quarterly revenues increase price of at] at least 25%. Because you also need to be particular with the growth of the company for the long term, you need to even think about the development of the annual income of the company. This technique means that you ought to search for a business that has 25% yearly revenue growth (minimum) for the past five years. You need to also watch out for companies that stock something new to the market. Researches show that out of the typical characteristics of the best stock performers is that their firms have something new to stock to the market. You must also bear in mind the rule of stock and demand. If a minimal item has a high requirement, then the effect is that its price will rise. In a company, this rule of stock and demand is always present.

The next thing that you need to determine is the origin of the stocks. Does the company known as a leader in the industry or a laggard?

Of course, your purpose is to obtain your stocks from a leader. When you use this strategy, only receive your stocks from reputable companies. Many activities in the stock market also come from mutual funds and pensions, so also watch institutional sponsorship.

Buy and Hold

This is the usual means of buying stocks. It is thought that although it is challenging to say the instructions of the stocks market for a short-term period, you can expect the costs of the stocks to increase in the long run. Since everybody in the stock market intends for those instructions, this is. Therefore, it is said that so you can hang on high stock for a more extended period, then you can enjoy profit in years to come.

This is the expected outcome bearing in mind that an investment society is included. Remember that you will be holding the stocks for a more extended period; after that, it means that you will not always be investing.

Therefore, you will have lower costs and taxes to worry about.

CHAPTER FOUR

How to Buy Your First Stock?

Buying stock is not such as getting much else. When you go to the book shop and purchase a book, there are some threats. When you are buying stocks, you usually pay a great deal even more than what it would set you back to purchase a book, and also the danger of losing it is also more higher.

Before you start buying stocks, you need to know 100% of what you are doing. I would recommend you set up a brokerage firm account now so that it's ready when you're ready, but make sure you do your finding and also shops around there.

First, learn about stocks. Learn what they are, how they work, how they give you money, and how to know them.

Stocks aren't complicated, yet they aren't easy. They will take a little time to figure out, and you will need to understand how they work.

How can you earn money from something if you do not know how it works.

You can start choosing and researching companies as soon as you know the system. Look at different markets. For adequate diversification, you have to ensure you possess stocks in various industries. When you knowhow the sectors you choose affect each other and also work with each other, and as soon as you have them chosen, explore different company, you have an interest in. Look for companies you know and understand. You do not have to buy from them for them to be good stocks. Take a look at companies that you have seen development in and see a great future with.

When you've selected some stocks, research them. If they do not look good, do not buy the stock.

You need to be all ready before you buy your first stock. You can start investing in stocks.

Purchasing Your First Stocks Can Be Confusing

People who don't understand much about the stock exchange commonly search for information online. They browse for things like "stocks for novices" because they feel overwhelmed and confused before they start. If you do not know the stock market, the excellent point is that you don't have any money in it and also have not lost anything this last year. Now, anybody that has money in stocks possibly feels sick right now because of how much they have lost.

You need to gain from this horrible market change that absolutely nothing is risk-free in the stock market. Some people have shed a lot more than they should have because they were overconfident and had most of their income in stocks. Also, some lost because they had too much in one specific stock or one particular sector.

When you spend in the stock market, you should always acquire a range of stocks. When you buy stocks that are in different sectors, you make sure that you will not shed every little thing if one of those markets happens under challenging times.

Today the securities market means down from its highs some years earlier. A ton of money has been lost, along with lots of people's retirement cost savings. If you are in the stock market, it must feel like your pocket has been selected. The issue all of us face is that at some factor, the market will reverse the program, and many people will not have anything to return in to make some of the lost. Currently, it looks like the market will not go up, yet it will, and you have to be ready. If you have nothing left from now fiasco, nonetheless, there will be nothing you can do to reclaim some of your losses.

Buying Your First Stock - Hints, And Tips For Those New To The Market

The stock market is an exciting place. If you're thinking about entering it, you're probably excited about the possibility of making some money.

Before you purchase, do your study. I can not worry about this enough. There are lots of professionals available who can give you handy advice. Still, there are also many people out there that believe they are professionals, and their information may not be as reliable as you think. If a friend gives you advice and also urges you to buy because such a company is warm, make sure you didn't follow their guidance.

I would recommend any beginner to start with stable stock. Select a company that has been around for a long time and research them. Financial publications are practical, as are sites such as Reuters. Look at how the business of your choice is doing, and what the state of the market look like in general. This will assist you in making your choice.

The reason for choosing a company and stock that has been around for a while is because you'll be much more likely to forecast what will certainly occur in the future. New companies might be superb to buy, and we are all aware of how people can make a grand revenue out of them, but the threat of losing your cash is substantial.

For that reason, the more strong stock could not offer a great deal of excitement, buy it can give a bit of satisfaction while you discover what's acquaint on your own with the world of finance and stock profession. There is a lot to learn, and this takes some time.

The stock market is affected by so many outside influences, including lawful events. The tort system has had a significant impact on the market in the past, and huge decisions are collective.

Another piece of recommendation is to start small while you are finding out. It real that the securities market can be seen as a little bit of a wager, and there is always a certain quantity of threat included. Absolutely nothing is inevitable, but you can reduce the risk of monetary loss by doing your study and by maintaining a close eye on the influences that could influence your stock.

How to Prepare for Your First Stock Market Trade

Action 1: Set Up an Account with a Broker

If you're planning to make your professions, your best option is to opt for a discount broker online. They are much more affordable than complete brokers because they don't offer you all the new services like financial investment advice and various other services you probably don't need. If you're making your stock decisions, you should simply pay for the profession.

If you want to be a short-term trader, also known as a day investor, look for a website that gives affordable professions if you trade frequently. Look for a broker that specializes in providing cost-effective long-term professional charges if you want to invest for the long-term.

Action 2: Learn the Ropes

You can miss this step if you're ready to trade. If you just decided you want to invest, but you don't know how to take your time on this. It is incredibly crucial to understand what you're doing, or else you'll simply be gambling.

Step 3: Set Up a Strategy and Choose your Investments

Stock investing is everything about approach, despite how simple or complicated you make your way. Use the details you discovered from step 2 to set up your strategy—use the guidance from successful financiers like Warren Buffett to construct a method that will work.

Bear in mind that regardless of how excellent your technique is, there will always be a risk. Because one stock choice was terrible doesn't mean you're a terrible investor and must give up. Just put yourself together, change your method as possible, and move on.

Step 4: Money

Place money aside to invest. It's vital to invest in the stock market because, without it, you won't have the ability to purchase any type of financial investment. Start saving your income as soon as possible and be adding money to your portfolio on a routine basis.

Step 5: Buy

The last action is to acquire stocks and also get going. You made your options, currently go to your broker agent account, and make your professions.

A First Lesson in Learning How to Trade Stocks

For anyone learning how to trade stocks, it is essential to know the difference between investing and trading in the securities market.

The discussion here is directed not to the investor but to the neophyte investor, a person who has yet to discover how to trade stocks, one who is thinking about putting their cash at risk. A risk that can be lessened by complying with some useful standards rules pointed out but disregarded in the excitement, success, failure, or greed, that the present sector of stocks market exhibit.

The trader is typically more active than a financier in acquiring and marketing stocks, holding the stock settings for a shorter period in the attempt to make gains when they occur or to lessen the inevitable loss that belongs to speculative trading.

Yes, substantial profits can be made when investing in the stock exchange, to the extent that somebody can be financially independent.

It takes time and initiative to discover the principles of stock trading and determination to follow reasonable standards to handle risks and make the needed action in those standards. When encountered with the demand to act, to offer a losing placement, the lure is to simply wait for a little while, "perhaps it will recover" is the thought that supersedes the rule that brings about"sell!".

When they are wrong and allowing revenues to run when they are right, great investors take high-risk examining by limiting losses.

There are many reasons stocks change in price at the time, and it is the goal of the investor to buy or sell stocks and benefit from those changes to purchase stocks at a lower cost from which they will rise or sell stocks at a rate where they will fall. This way, when transactions have been completed, if an expected total revenue has been achieved, a receipt a minimum of close or equivalent to the expected target profit, it can be taken into consideration that the purpose has been met.

No formula can guarantee revenue, and successful investors approve the reality that they will indeed make unprofitable and profitable investments. The requirement, regarding possible, is to reduce the losses and to optimize the gains to make sure that the overall outcome will be rewarding to the level that the return on the capitals at risk will be more than if they were used to purchase another investment.

Buying Stocks - Making It a Smart Financial Move

Joining the stock market can be a smooth economic action. The different factors you ought to discover about previously making this financial step is how the stock market works, the ups and downs of the stock market, knowing what to buy and how much to buy, understanding when to buy and when to sell, and many more.

Investing in stocks can be a very profitable business if you learn all of this before you sign up with the stock market or the stock exchange. This is the reason why investing your cash generally is a good idea. There is the potential for high returns to any kind of investment. Stocks are not the only things that people can purchase. People can buy companies, personal home mortgages, property, and many more. Nevertheless, among the most popular investing strategies includes stocks.

Purchasing stocks can be so profitable that many people make earning from it. They make their cash by buying and selling stocks. One way to maximize your gain in a stock profession is buying many shares of a stock when it has reduced and afterward selling all the stocks as quickly as it increases in worth. When you buy the stock when the price is low, then you reduce your risk as well because the loss will not be significant in that situation.

You should also have the ability to forecast how well the stock will perform. Your opportunities for losing money will increase if you buy a stock that is predicted to execute poorly. On the other hand, you may obtain a stock that increases in worth; in that case, you stand to gain a significant amount of money. An investing consulting company focusing on the stock exchange can guide you on which stocks to buy. It is also a good idea when purchasing stocks to spend in a sector that you have experience with. By doing this, your wishes about buying a stock or selling your stocks are more probable to be correct.

Stock investment Tip

Do this: put your money in a stock, then for the rest of the year, don't look at your account or learn what's happening in the stock market. What do you think your report will look like after the years?

Do you think you'll be a millionaire?

Below's what's going to happen.

If you are lucky, you'll have some gains. You'll lose most of your cash if you run into bad luck.

"Take or leave it" method is no different than betting. Throughout a year, a whole lot of things can happen that will affect the stock you own. You have to take note of these things, or you might regret it.

Despite winning stocks, they claim their breakthroughs are short term. The significant gains in these uncommon stocks will last from one to three years. Like all other stocks, they decline and also are no longer attractive to buyers that wanted it.

On the other hand, a champion stock will give you many chances to contribute to your position and produce better gains. If you practice the "set it and neglect it" approach and did not pay attention, you would have missed an opportunity to pyramid your setting.

Simply look at how many people lost in the recent stock market crash. You would have found out near the leading and gotten back in near the base that generated lately if you pay attention to the markets.

Buying stocks isn't an easy search. If we want to minimize our losses and optimize our gains, it calls for energetic engagement and taking decisive action.

CHAPTER FIVE

Mechanics of OwingStock; How to Choose a Stock Broker

You've done the tricky part. Picking stocks-- without a doubt, is one of the essential products of the equity-investing process-- requires more time, initiative, and belief than any other parts of the task. But your responsibilities don't end there. They didn't even start with stock selection.

It is assuming stock picking as choosing a path to the journey of financial liberty, understanding, of training course, that the course will frequently change to accommodate the detours and weather condition risks that are market instabilities.

In this session, you'll learn how to choose a broker, how to buy and sell stocks with that broker, and how to limit your tax obligation. Consider it a quick glimpse of this book. Pay attention to the journey. With some patience and persistence, you'll get where you want to go.

Who Does Your Trading?

Have you ever asked the question, "So how can I find an excellent broker and not someone who will jet off to the Cayman

Islands on my penny?" Words "broker" doesn't load people with confidence, and many people have captivated that, though, mainly because a few brokers have absconded with investors' funds. Realistically, if you make use of a traditional brokerage home, you need not bother with funding for a thief's permanent vacation.

Securities Investor Protection Corporation (SIPC) works to help investors hurt by crooked brokers, saying to have returned assets to 99% of investors qualified for defense. The SIPC doesn't help you recover your losses if you buy the wrong stocks and lose your tee shirt. Simply put, if you get scammed or suckered in a worthless investment, that's your problem. But if a broker steals your money or losses it in the process of doing something unethical or illegal, that's the SIPC's issue.

So do not lose sleep over a broker stealing your money. Instead, focus on picking the best stocks, and concentrate on what kind of broker to use.

Discount brokers, such as TD Ameritrade, E * Trade, Charles Schwab, or Scottrade, buy and sell stocks on behalf of investors at lower rates. While the four noted above represent some of the best-known price cut brokers, dozens of others give online trading services for less than $10 per deal. For the majority of investors that want to focus and pick their stocks or act on advice from a third-party specialist, such as a newsletter, a discount broker will do the trick.

Full-service brokers.

On top of making professions for you, full-service brokers might also give guidance or do various other solutions. If you look for stock advice or your economic circumstance requires customized help, a full-service broker might make good sense. Be ready to pay more for your professions-- in some instances $50 per deal or more.

To compare brokers, just visit their internet sites and sneak around. Processing stock purchases have come to be an asset company, meaning that all the companies do it well. When you study brokers, try to find features relevant to you, such as:

-Minimum account dimension.

Many brokers sales price cuts for accounts over $25,000 or $100,000, but low rollers don't get specialized treatment, and all brokers need minimum balances of accounts. If you are ready to start small, make sure your broker can accommodate you. Minimum account sizes usually differ.

-Web site style.

Each broker website features its interface. You'll find some even more intuitive than others, and the ones you choose might not attract another person. When it comes to navigating a broker's site, rest lesson suggestions from others and more on your own

-choice.

Quantity discount rates. If you wish to make a lot of investment (as a beginner, you should not), some brokers lower their fees for regular traders.

-Range of safeties.

All brokers sell stocks and ETFs. If you intend to purchase standard mutual funds, look around. Some brokers stock a multitude of shared funds available for a no-deal cost, but the choice and rates differ significantly from company to company.

-Research study solutions.

Some price cut brokers provide access to online devices, stock screeners, and research records. Some allow clients to interact in online neighborhoods where investors share ideas.

If you 'd rather stay away from brokers entirely, you can buy stocks directly from the company that provided them (or directly from the transfer agent the company hires).

Dividend reinvestment plans (DRIPs) permit capitalists to buy stocks without a broker. Many of the strategies state that you must already possess at least one share of stock in your name before you can participate. DRIPs do not bill brokerage commissions, but the majority of them examine small charges for buying and selling shares.

Alternately, when you purchase stock with a broker, it certainly belongs to you. Because the broker has custodianship of the shares, they are held in the broker agent firm's name-- usually referred to as the road name-- for easy buying, selling, and transferring. Instead of allowing the broker to use its road name, you can pay to sign up the shares in your name and have the physical certificate sent to you.

Investors like DRIPs because they allow the reinvestment of money dividends in company shares, also if the payments are smaller than the share rate. For instance, if your holdings in a stock trading at $50 per share pay a $5 dividend, you can buy and reinvest the reward 0.1 shares of the stock. Many DRIPs also allow you to add money to the account in percentages-- sometimes as low as $10 a month.

The ability to slowly add money to multiple stocks with time interest investors who do not have much money but who plan to allot cash for investment regularly

DRIPs bring in investors that want to develop a wide range gradually and that don't plan to trade often. Because many small stocks and big ones don't provide the plans, DRIP financiers appreciate fewer choices for numerous investors; 1,000 shares still look like many choices.

Essentially, beginners ought to deal with their stocks at the original price.

Before you make a transaction online, see your broker's web site and click the trading link. The site will ask you the number of shares you want to buy, and whether you wish to make a market order or a limit order.

The broker will make the deal at the best available cost when you place in a market order to buy fifty shares of Acme Widget. If you've examined Acme Widget and like the stock at $40 per share, it shouldn't matter the price whether you buy at $39 or $41.

Limit orders, on the other hand, are for investors who want to buy or sell only if the share price reaches a certain degree. For instance, if you take into consideration Acme as being expensive at $40 yet would acquire it at $35, you can submit a limit order with a $35 rate, and the broker will buy the shares if they dip to $35 or below. Restriction orders give higher control over the price paid for a stock, yet they can keep investors out of stock. If Acme goes down to $35.01, then climbs to $50, the financier with the $35 limit order will not purchase the stock and share in the gains.

Investors also use restriction orders on the sell-side to secure gains. Intend Acme trades for $40 per share, yet you would certainly such as to sell and book your revenues if the rate rises to $45. A limitation order to offer at $45 will get you out of stock at a price not less than $45, as long as the stock climbs to the target degree before the order runs out. Brokers usually charge higher compensations on limit orders than on market orders.

Reading a Stock Quote

When you open a financial web site and enter your ticker, you'll see a web page with some numbers. While each website makes its pages in different ways, you can trust seeing the majority of this info:

-Inquire rate: The lowest price a seller is ready to accept for a stock. For most huge, heavily traded stocks, the bid and ask price will be close with each other. For sparsely traded stocks, the bid-ask spread can be vast.

-Quote cost: The highest possible cost a customer agrees to pay for a stock. At any given time, brokers handle countless deal orders, a few of which means a particular charge to sell or buy a stock.

-Present rate: This number reflects one of the most recent deal prices, though free websites normally run on a delay, so their names are a bit obsoleted.

Day's range: The low and high rates in the current day's trading.

Fifty-two-week range: The high and low prices over the last year.

Volume: The number of shares traded.

Last, note that if you access a quote web page after the market closes, you'll see end-of-day numbers. You'll see intraday numbers if you go during trading hours.

Some investors like to make use of stop orders-order that turn into market orders after the stock hits a limit. If the shares rise and fall below $35, the stop order starts, and your broker sells the stock at the prevailing cost.

Regrettably, stop orders have limitations. You'll sell at around that price if negative news breaks, and the stock instantly dips to $30 per share. A sell limitation order will not assure you a sale at $35, just that you'll market the shares at the going rate once the cost dips below $35.

Investors who make use of stop orders likewise run the risk of buying or selling stocks simply because of the market relocations. Suppose you set a stop order at 10% below the stock's present rate to safeguard against hideous losses because you are afraid the company will lose a patent lawsuit that might cost millions of dollars in sales. What happens if the market falls 15% and your stock slides with the rest of them? No trial has surfaced, and the reasons you bought the stock is still intact. Yet the stop order would have sold you out of stock, which probably stands a high chance of recovering when the marked retrieves its momentum.

In short, limits orders allow you to get into stocks if they fall or get out of stocks if they rise. Stop orders will enable you to get out of stocks if they fall or get into stocks if they increase.

Your broker will give you many trading options beyond the market, limit, and stop orders. As you gain experience, feel free to expand your horizons and try new ways to trade. But anything you do, no matter your investment goals, don't forget the most critical trading rule: If you don't know how the trade works and why it makes sense, don't make the trade.

Come to think of it, that rule applies to many aspects of investments.

Limit Your Taxes

Only a fool makes financial investment decisions without considering the tax implications. On the flip side of that coin, only a fool allows tax obligation problems to be the principal driver of those same decisions. Because they don't want to pay tax obligations on the profits, many investors decline to market stocks at a revenue. But when the situation changes, and it no makes sense to hold the stock, failure to sell might cost them.

The good news is, managing tax obligations on your financial investments is more annoying than it is hard. With that in mind, below are three questions about taxes that every investor needs to be able to address.

- First Question: How much will I pay in taxes when I collect rewards or sell my stock?

Answer: Because Congress can change tax rates, this question has no permanent solution. According to tax obligation prices that took effect at the beginning of 2013:

Many stock returns and bond rates of interest settlements will be exhausted at the taxpayer's average earnings price.

Temporary capital gains (profits on the sale of stock or other securities) will be strained at the average income price. You owe tax obligations at the short-term rate if you sell a possession after holding it for one year or less.

Long-term resources gains will be taxed at 0%, 15%, or 20%, depending on the investor's income.

As always, you only accumulate tax responsibility when you sell your shares. If you buy stock for $1,000 and it skyrockets to $10,000 in a year, as long as you hold it as stock, you don't owe a dollar of tax obligations on it.

- Second Question: How can I protect my investments from tax obligation liability?

Answer: personal retired life accounts (IRAs) allow financiers to postpone taxes on investment proceeds. Some salesmen sell IRAs as if a unique company can set them up, and after that, direct financiers to companies that charge huge fees to handle the accounts. That's not how IRAs work. IRA can be set at any type of brokerage, and you can buy stocks, bonds, mutual funds, and other monetary properties within an IRA.

Recently, financiers under age 50 can add a maximum of $5,500 to their IRA; payment restrictions have increased over time, and this trend is likely to continue. You can deduct contributions to an IRA from this year's taxes.

However, if you or a partner contributes to another retirement plan through a job, you probably can't. And you can only add to an IRA if you or your partner earns taxable income.

Investors can start taking cash out of their IRAs at age 59 1/2, and they need to start after they turn 70 1/2. IRA circulations undergo government earnings tax, and also, if you get rid of cash from an IRA before the age of 59 1/2, you'll owe federal income tax obligation plus an extra 10% charge.

A special kind of IRA-- the Roth IRA-- enables investors to grow their money tax-free. Roth IRAs need some hurdles. You can't deduct the contributions, your income and tax-filing status might limit how much you can contribute.

- Third Question: My job offers a 401(k) retirement plan. Should I sign up for it?

Answer: Almost definitely yes. As long as the strategy gives you the investment alternatives that do not stink, the advantages of a 401(k) are too appealing to neglect.

The 401(k) strategy allows your employer to deduct a portion of your salary before taxes and spend it-- usually in mutual funds-- and some employers will match your payment to a particular degree. The business could match 50% of your contribution to 6% of your income.

While your contributions, your company's contributions, and any type of dividends and also gains in the portfolio are not subject to income tax obligation promptly, similar to IRAs, you'll pay tax obligations when you withdraw the funds-- after retirement.

CHAPTER SIX

Building your Perfect Portfolio

Since you have a sense of the power and significance of diversity, it's time to create your target profile. While this book can provide you with a structure, no formula or cookie-cutter technique will churn out the best possession allotment for each financier. To do this right, you'll need to make a couple of judgment calls. Start by asking yourself the following four questions.

- ## How much Do You Need?

Investors can make several sorts of errors as they prepare for the future. But perhaps the most usual-- and the most harmful-- is not understanding how much you need.

IS $1million enough? That depends on when you retire, how long you live, and how much you want to invest. Check the following table, assuming you manage to sock away $1 million by the time you retire, and after that, spend enough to gain 5% per year after inflation.

Portfolio at retirement	$1,000,000	$1,000,000	$1,000,000
Annual living expenses, rising 3% per year with inflation	$120,000	$100,000	$60,000
Year 1	$930,000	$950,000	$990,000
Year 2	$856,500	$897,500	$979,500
Year 3	$779,325	$842,375	$968,475
Year 4	$698,291	$784,494	$956,899
Year 5	$613,206	$723,718	$944,744
Year 6	$523,866	$659,904	$931,981
Year 7	$430,059	$592,900	$918,580
Year 8	$331,562	$522,545	$904,509
Year 9	$228,140	$448,672	$889,734
Year 10	$119,548	$371,105	$874,221
Year 11	$5,525	$289,661	$857,932
Year 12	$0	$204,144	$840,829
Year 13		$114,351	$822,870
Year 14		$20,068	$804,014
Year 15		$0	$784,214
Year 16			$763,425
Year 17			$741,596
Year 18			$718,676
Year 19			$694,610
Year 20			$669,340

The table - Living off $1 Million

Somehow $1 million doesn't look like a tremendous amount after you crunch the numbers.

If you plan to amass a $1 million after retirement, and after that live on $120,000 a year each year after you retire, you would be ready to work until you're 75-- or die reasonably young. (For the document, the retired person who can live on $60,000 a year and sustain a 5% financial investment return after inflation might extend his $1 million for 36 years.).

- **When Will You Need the cash?**

This question has a straightforward answer if you do not plan to touch your financial investments until retired life. On the other hand, if you need $100,000 for college expenses in 10 years, or if you want to buy a holiday habitation years before you retire, now is the time to make it up. As a general policy, the shorter the financial investment time, the lesser you can depend on stocks, which tend to be unpredictable.

Between 1926 and 2012, there have been 66 periods of 20 years-- 1926 through 1946, 1927 through 1947, and so on. Neither stocks nor bonds have ever posted a decline for20 years. Large-company stocks lose worth in just 4 of the 78 periods of 10 years, while neither corporate neither government bonds ever had a negative return. When it comes to five-year periods, the image changes substantially. Large-company stocks decreased in 12 of the 83 five-year periods, or roughly 14% of the time. Long-term corporate bonds declined in just 3 of the five-year periods, and it hasn't taken place in more than 40 years.

Keeping primarily stocks in the profile makes sense if you're looking 20 years out. You possibly need some extra bond exposure if you're going to need the cash in five years or less.

- **How Much Can You Invest?**

The answer to this question depends on two things: how much you realize, and how much you spend to live. You have more control over the second than the first.

When it comes to this question, you have to be sincere. Who doesn't think he's worth $100,000 per year? But, most Americans won't smell that annual salary.

You can build up a nest egg even if you don't make $100,000 per year. Don't believe it? The table below demonstrates how swiftly you can develop a financial investment portfolio.

	$100 per month	$200 per month	$500 per month	$1,000 per month
Year 1	$1,200	$2,400	$6,000	$12,000
Year 2	$2,496	$4,992	$12,480	$24,960
Year 3	$3,896	$7,791	$19,478	$38,957
Year 4	$5,407	$10,815	$27,037	$54,073
Year 5	$7,040	$14,080	$35,200	$70,399
Year 6	$8,803	$17,606	$44,016	$88,031
Year 7	$10,707	$21,415	$58,537	$107,074
Year 8	$12,764	$25,528	$63,820	$127,640
Year 9	$14,985	$29,970	$74,925	$149,851
Year 10	$17,384	$34,768	$86,919	$173,839
Year 11	$19,975	$39,949	$99,873	$199,746
Year 12	$22,773	$45,545	$113,863	$227,726
Year 13	$25,794	$51,589	$128,972	$257,944
Year 14	$29,058	$58,116	$145,290	$290,579
Year 15	$32,583	$65,165	$162,913	$325,825
Year 16	$36,389	$72,778	$181,946	$363,891
Year 17	$40,500	$81,001	$202,501	$405,003
Year 18	$44,940	$89,881	$224,701	$449,403
Year 19	$49,786	$99,471	$248,678	$497,355
Year 20	$54,914	$109,829	$274,572	$549,144
Year 21	$60,508	$121,015	$302,538	$605,075
Year 22	$66,548	$133,096	$332,741	$665,481
Year 23	$73,072	$146,144	$365,360	$730,720
Year 24	$80,118	$160,235	$400,589	$801,177
Year 25	$87,727	$175,454	$438,636	$877,271
Year 26	$95,945	$191,891	$479,726	$959,453
Year 27	$104,821	$209,642	$524,105	$1,048,209
Year 28	$114,407	$228,813	$572,033	$1,144,066
Year 29	$124,759	$249,518	$623,796	$1,247,591
Year 30	$135,940	$271,880	$679,699	$1,359,399

The Above Table - Building Wealth a Month at a Time.

These are not wrong numbers, and they assume you never get a raise-- and hence never enhance your month-to-month financial investment. The more you can save, the extra you'll have when you need it. And also herein lies one of the most vital keys to developing wealth: Spend less than you make.

Despite what your investments do from year to year-- and you definitely can't trust them delivering such stable development-- if you invest less than you make every year, you'll have enough to support on your own and set some aside.

- **How many risks Can You Handle?**

Some investors need a 10% yearly return to meet their monetary goals. That's a high obstacle. People have handled it, however accomplishing 10yearly returns over a long time would exhaust both the ability and the good luck of many expert financiers, not to mention that of beginners. What happens if the kind of securities required to make a run at 10% annual returns will keep you up in the night? You have two options:

- Live in anxiety. (This is not ideal.).
- Alter your purposes so you can meet your goals with a less risky profile.

Many people select option one, but option two makes the most sense, both for your portfolio and your nerves.

In the most investment business, fear of unpredictability is called risk hostility. The term applies to fear of investment decreases or volatility. Everybody worries about losing all their money, but that isn't the issue below. Stocks are likely to give exceptional returns over a 20-year duration, but you can't sit in your rocking chair and wait 20 years. Purchasing the stock market entails dealing with the movements of your stocks day-to-day and year-to-year. This's where risk hostility can be found. Everybody has some level of risk aversion. The higher your degree of risk hostility (the better your fear of loss), the less risk you can tolerate.

Your degree of riches also influences your risk tolerance. If you have $1 million in the bank, make a great living, and also won't require your financial investments for 20 years, you can pay to take even more risks than somebody with $10,000 in the financial institution.

Running the Numbers

You'll better comprehend what you need from your profile when you address the four essential concerns. And with that knowledge comes power.

Questions one and two-- how much money do you need, and when do you need it-- will help you identify your needed price of return. The list below formula will give you a rate of return for any starting and ending factor, assuming you want to grow a basket of cash and don't want to add any kind of new funds:

(What you require What you have) ^ (1 Year till you need it)-- 1

If you need $1 million, and you have $100,000, and you plan to retire in 25 years, it looks like this:

($ 1,000,000 $100,000) ^ (1 25)-- 1 = 0.096 = 9.6%.

What if you have nothing, yet you can devote funds to invest over time? You can quickly produce a table like the wealth-building one earlier to plot different situations. Here's the formula:

[Portfolio value X (1 + Rate of return)] + Annual financial investment = Portfolio value a year later.

The following is an example of the beginning of a wealth-building table, starting with the following assumptions:

Begin at the end of the first year, putting a year of investment contributions in your brokerage firm account.

You contribute $500 monthly.

Your investments grow at 8% a year.

Year 1: $6,000.

Year 2: $6,000 X (1.08) + $6,000 = $12,480.

Year 3: $12,480 X (1.08) + $6,000 = $19,478.

Construct that formula in a spreadsheet, and you can see the length of time it will take to reach your objective. Alternatively, if you recognize when you need to achieve that objective, try different prices to determine the kind of the returns required to get you there at the right time.

Before you move on to the last action, ensure you've avoided these four pitfalls:

- Unreasonable expectations.

If your required rate of return is more than 10%, change your presumptions. Even 10% of profits will be adamant, and any type of plan based on the possibility that you can gain more than 10% will fail extra frequently than it does well. Don't kid yourself. Ensure that your investing estimates reflect inflation.

- Neglecting expenses

Try to add extra amounts to your budget. You may be ill. Your house could refute. Your brother-in-law may guilt-trip you to backing his restaurant, even though you understand most restaurants fail. Life happens, and things that cost money are part of life.

- Underestimating your needs and lifetime

Plan for $70,000 if you think you'll require $60,000 a year. Plan for 25 if you think you'll live 20 years before retirement. The more traditional your estimates, the most likely your investment plan will accomplish its objectives.

- Deciding

OK, now, you have an idea of what you desire and the type of returns that are wanted to get you there.

That leaves just one question: What goes into the profile?

At this moment, go back to the rule of thumb that you need to deduct your age from 110 and put that portion in stocks, and after that build from there:

Are you ready? If so, add 5% to 10% to the stock allowance, depending on how comfortable you are with your level of riches.

How's your risk resistance? Add or subtract as much as 10% from the stock allowance, depending on your strength for danger. Risk-takers add to the allocation, risk-avoiders deduct.

When do you need the cash? If your time perspective is greater than 15 years, amount to 10% to the stock allotment. If you want to use the money in less than ten years, subtract 10%.

While previous instances have used average returns for quality, below, you have to depend on annualized returns. And over the long haul, large-company stocks have taken care of annualized returns of about 10%, long-term government bonds of over 6%, and Treasury expenses about 3.5%.

Why Use Annualized Returns?

Annualized returns assume stable development without any variants, and also they will certainly always lag the average annual performance. In actual life, investment returns differ from year to year, and the better the variance, the higher the difference between annualized and ordinary returns. For example:

The perfect world. Invest $100 at 10% this year and next year, and you'll have $121 at the end of two years. That's a two-year annualized return of 10% and an average return of 10%.

Messy fact. Spend $100 at an unfavorable 20% this year and a favorable 51% following year, and you'll have $121. That's a two-year annualized return of 10%, but an average return of more than 15%. A return of negative 35% for the first year and a positive 86% for the second year gets you to $121, but with an ordinary yearly return of more than 25%.

Annualized returns to say a more accurate story. Because approximating the variance in yearly returns over long periods is impossible, the majority of long-term projections assume annualized returns.

While it takes a lot of effort to compute annualized profile returns, those three historic returns allow you to approximate the yearly returns using large-company stocks, long-term government bonds, and short-term government bonds. The target annualized return of your profile is 8.8%.

Here's how to get there:

Equation.

(Stock allowance X Stock returns) + (Bond allocation X Bond return) (70% X 10%) + (30% X 6%) = 7.0% + 1.8% = 8.8%.

Remember, this is just an approximate portfolio return based on approximated stock and bond returns. It's a work in progress-- and at best a rough estimate-- today you have enough to contrast your expected return (the performance you require to obtain where you wish to go) and your target return (the yield implied by your target allocation). If your needs exceed your target, you'll either have to tackle more risk-- as in selecting a higher stock appropriation-- or scale back on your financial investment targets.

No one likes to reduce their objectives or realize they can't indulge throughout retirement. It's better to make an effort to discover how far your resources can take you. After that, you can change your objectives to match your fact.

Life is great if your target exceeds your requirements. You can reduce your danger to boost your possibility of accomplishing your goals, or you can try to construct a new wide range-- potentially providing increased flexibility in the future.

Closing It Out.

Whew. It took some work, but by now you should have a good idea about how to reach your financial location without running out of cash. After you understand the principles in this book, take the campaign to increase your understanding of investing. It's not far too late to begin working toward your objectives for the future, and despite how you learn, you'll not figure everything out.

The trip never finishes. Thankfully, the techniques in this book must get you off to a great beginning.

CHAPTER SEVEN

How to Minimize Losses and Maximize Gains with Stocks?

When it comes to money, what matters most is not how much you earn, but how well you handle what you have. Being able to enhance the cash you have considered is the hallmark of real money management, and also one of the most efficient ways to accomplish this is to invest in stocks. Market researchers assert that for five years, buying stocks can produce, at a minimum, a 20% return.

To earn money by investing in stocks, an individual should first know the rules of trading. These rules are mandatory and are regulated to secure both financiers and the trading industry itself. Considering that somebody can face prosecution for bending or damaging these policies, investors might find it helpful to find out more about the regulations on the specified website to have more understanding.

There are two primary means you can buy stocks.

The first is investing, which is where a specific search for long-term gains in the stocks market, and purchases companies that offer potentially higher growth. This strategy calls for in-depth research of firms to determine the best ones to invest in, yet brings relatively little risk. The downside is that not everybody has the time or the ability to recognize all the financial details of a company.

One style is called trading, which is where the investor tries to benefit from the ups and downs of the stock market. The success of this approach will depend partly on the personality of the investor, as the short-term volatility of the stock market can be stressful. While this design of trading can stock considerable returns in a short space of time, it's not for the fainthearted.

Before investing, think of a strategy that includes plainly defined objectives, creates a personal risk profile, and establishes a long-time for investing. Knowing when to sell is as vital as understanding when to buy. Don't to time the market, but enter it in stages, benefiting from the market volatility.

Stock market investment has some kind of fundamental threats in it; this kind of investment is one of how you can make some money. You might start to spend in stocks when you are young to be safe for risks entailed in the stock market.

Securities Market Manipulation - How To Protect Yourself

Stock exchange control is among the most significant problem in today's financial world. Despite having Obama's determined relocate to stop such acts, we need to deal with the truth. No matter how risk-free and safe we think the market is, there are always those higher up that will abuse their power and use it to their benefit.

For the amateur traders, this is somewhat frustrating. Once it starts looking stronger, hands begin reeling costs in, and by the end of the days close, the market back to where it began.

These include:

1) Spend a week examining price patterns and see when bigger great deals of volume been available during the day. This is probably the more significant players attempting their hand to trick you.

2) During the day, be careful of Amateur hr. This is the first hr of the day when the brand-new novice investors come in and coldly start buying every little thing.

3) Always scale into settings and out of positions. These will reduce loss and optimize your gains.

4) Avoid chop time. This is a quiet time in the market do not trade it. Cut time got its name in the old days by amateur investors that got their accounts cut to items when they tried to buy during lunchtime in the market.

5) Always set your stop losses in the market in case something goes wrong. Take it on the chin, get up, and you will live to fight one more day.

6) Make sure you never trade alone. Always work with investors that are better than you. This will help you become much better. With the control that takes place, you will need all eyes on you.

7) Get a mentor. Get somebody who knows the ropes to educate you about how the manipulators work their magic during the day on the stock exchange. This can save you a lot of distress, but most notably, it can conserve you from losing your account.

When developing a departure technique, there are three things that we should take into consideration.

1. How long are we intending on being in this trade?

2. How much risk are we willing to take?

3. At what cost point do we want to exit?"

The answer to the first question is:

A) Set revenue targets to be hit in some months, which will certainly lessen the number of trades you make.

B) Develop tracking stop-loss factors that enable earnings to be secured periodically to limit the disadvantage capacity. Bear in mind, the primary objective of any type of trade should be to protect resources.

C) Take revenues in increments over time to minimize volatility while liquidating.

D) Allow for volatility to make sure that you maintain your trades to a minimum.

E) Create leave approaches based on essential aspects geared in the direction of the longer term. Let's claim you love the company model of ISRG, and you think the company's growth possibility to be enormous. In this situation, you may wish to hold the stock long term and create a price target based on future income development. Nevertheless, if you are in a trade temporarily, you should not bother yourself with these things because they do not matter on a short-term basis. Too many short term investors try to trade on fundamentals, and it does not make good sense to do that. Fundamentals only work in the event you wish to invest in a company as opposed to trading their stock.

F) Set near-term revenue targets that perform at favorable times to make the best use of earnings. Right here are some common implementation points:

- Pivot Points (A technical sign acquired by determining the numerical average of specific stocks high, low, and closing rates.

- Fibonacci/Gann degrees

- Trend line breaks.

The secret is to learn a system that helps you and one that creates solid stop-loss points that get rid of stocks that do not work in the right manner

2. How much threat are we willing to take?

This will certainly establish the size of our trade and the type of stop-loss we need to use. Those who desire less risk tend to develop tighter stops, and those who presume more risk offer the position more area to maneuver or work as they state.

It is also essential to set your stop-loss points so that they are protected from being set off by average market volatility. This can be done in several ways.

The beta indication can give you an excellent concept of how volatile the stock is relative to the market in general, but these are great for longer-term traders that can endure 10% losses. An example would certainly be if the beta is within 0 and 2; after that, you will be risk-free with a stop-loss point at 10-20% lower than where you got the stock.

3) Where do we desire to obtain out?

You may ask, why would you want to establish a take-profit factor or limitation order where we sell when our stock is doing well? The answer is. Ideally, we do not intend to do something like this, but there are times when it for your benefit. Lots of people are crazily connected to their placements and hold the stocks when the underlying basics or technicals of the profession have changed. The only thing excellent about a limit sell order is the reality that it takes the feeling out of the trade. It either strikes your sell restriction order, or it hits your stop-loss point, and you can deal with your service after you enter your decrees and not have to stress over how your position is doing while you are away. If you are to sell this way, your exit point must be evaluated at a critical price level such as rate resistance, trend line resistance, or other technological aspects on the chart such as particular Fibonacci levels.

Leave strategies and various other money monitoring techniques can significantly improve your trading by getting rid of emotion and reducing risk. Before you enter a trade, take into consideration the three inquiries noted above.

CHAPTER EIGHT

How to Start Investing in Stock at $100? Or Less

The majority of people assume that you require thousands of dollars to start investing, but that's not true. I started investing with just $100 when I began working my first job in high school (of course, top institution).

It's possible to start buying at high school, in college, or even in your 20s.

Much more something to chew on - if you spent $100 in Apple stock in 2000, it would be worth $2,300 today. Or if you invested in Amazon stock at that same time, it would be work over $1,000 today, which's if you spent $100 as soon as— assuming if you paid $100 month-to-month given that 2000? You would have over $20,000 today.

Hopefully, that's pretty motivating for you and confirms that you do not need a great deal of money to start investing. Just look into this graph:

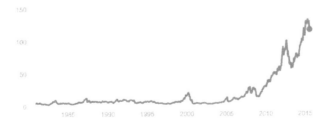

Remember, the hardest part of beginning to spend is only getting going. Since you're starting with $100 doesn't mean you need to wait, just. Begin investing now!

Allow's break down just how you can begin investing with only $100.

Where To Start Investing With Just $100.

If you want to get going investing, the first thing you have to do is open an investing account and a broker agent company. Do not allow that fear in you - brokers are just like financial institutions, except they focus on holding financial investments. We even maintain a list of the best broker agent accounts, including where to find the most affordable fees and best motivations:

Best Online Stock Brokers.

Given that you're just beginning with $50 or $100, you will desire to open an account with zero or reduced account minimums, and lowered costs. $0 payments, and you can invest in every little thing you wish - for free!

Remember, lots of brokers bill $5-20 to place a financial investment (called a compensation), so if you do not want an account with reduced expenses, you might see 5-20% of your first financial investment disappear to costs.

There are also other areas that you can spend on complimentary. Here's a listing of the best areas to allocate free of charge. Just keep in mind, many of these locations have "strings connected" where you have to purchase their funds or buy.

What Type Of Account Should You Open.

There are many different account types, so it truly depends on why you're investing. If you're putting your money for the long term, you need to concentrate on the pension. You need to keep your money in taxable accounts if you're investing for a shorter time.

Here's a graph to help you understand this:

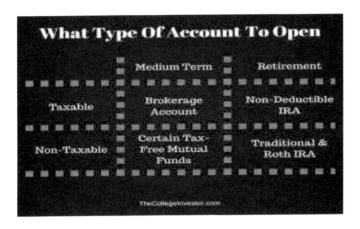

What To Invest In

$100 can expand a great deal over time, but only if you invest wisely. It's unusual to lose all your money in an investment.

To get started, you must focus on investing in a reduced expense index-focused ETF. Over time, ETFs are the least high priced means to spend in the broad stock market, and given that a lot of financiers can not beat the market, it makes sense to simulate it.

Think About Using A Robo-Advisor

Consider using a robot-advisor like Betterment if you're still not sure about what to invest in. Improvement is an online solution that will handle all the "investing possessions" for you. All you need to do is deposit your money (and there is $0 minimum to open an account), and Betterment takes care of the rest.

When you first open an account, you respond to a collection of questions to ensure that Betterment knows more about you. It will indeed, after that, develop and keep a portfolio based on what your needs are from that questionnaire. Therefore, robots-advisor. It's like a financial advisor managing your cash, but the computer system deals with it.

There is a cost to use Betterment (and similar services). Improvement costs 0.25% of the account balance. This is less expensive than what you would pay a traditional monetary consultant, specifically if you're only getting going at $100. Practically all financial consultants would most likely pull out from assisting you with just $100.

Alternatives to Investing In Stocks

There are options if you're not sure about getting started investing with just $100. Remember, investing just means placing your cash to help you.

Below are some of our preferred options for investing in stocks for $100.

- Cost Savings Account Or Money Market

-Cost savings accounts and cash market accounts are risk-free investments - they are typically guaranteed by the FDIC and are held at a financial institution.

-These accounts earn interest - so they are a financial investment. Nevertheless, that interest is less than you 'd make investing over time.

-You can't lose cash in a savings account or money market - so you have that going for you.

The most effective interest-bearing accounts gain up to 1.50% rate of interest now - which is the highest possible it has been in years!

Take a look at these cost savings accounts listed below:

Open A New Savings Account

Another choice to investing in stocks is investing in the certification of down payment (CD). This is where you loan cash to a financial institution, and they will pay you interest for your finance. CDs differ in size from three months to ten years - and the longer you spend your cash, the higher interest you'll get.

That's a little more than their high yield financial savings account - but you have to "link" up your money for 11 months. The cool thing is that the CD is penalty-free so that you can withdraw your money any time without penalty.

Look into the list of the most effective CD prices, or compare on the table below:

-Peer To Peer LendingYou could look at being a peer-to-peer lending institution on a website like success or LendingClub if you're worried to start investing in the stock market with your $100. Peer-to-peer loaning is much like it sounds: you provide your money to others, and they pay you back with interest.

The reason why peer-to-peer borrowing is excellent for borrowers with a tiny quantity of cash is that you can separate your investment into little loans. You can lend as low as $25 per credit if you're going to start investing with $100. That means your initial $100 can be invested into four various loans. Each month these loans pay back principal and interest to you, which you can then invest right into other lendings.

With time, your first $100 might be borrowed out to multiple lendings past the first 4, and you will continue to see your growth compounded over time.

Financial Investment Options To Avoid

There are many investments available that promote beginning investing for $5. We desire to ensure that you have a "customer beware" mindset when it comes to using these firms, and you fully know what you're entering into.

Stock Investing allows you to invest for as little as $5. However, they charge $1 per month cost on accounts of less than $5,000. If you're only spending $5 monthly - and paying $1 in fees each month, your portfolio return is likely to suffer (or loss) money.

You'll have dedicated $60 if you just spend $5 per month for a year. However, you'll have paid $12 in fees - leaving you with $48. That's 20% of your money given up to prices.

Only in 32 of the last 100 years has the stock market returned over 20% in a given year (and that year generally complied with a bad year). The average return has been around 11%.

That's why you need to avoid services that charge you substantial costs to invest. $1 monthly could not look huge, but it is as a percentage of your $100 financial investment. That's why we like services like M1 Finance, which use commission cost-free trading without annual fees.

Simply Get Start Investing

Bear in mind, the reason that you're investing is to expand your cash over time. That means you're leveraging the power of time and compound rate of interest.

Time services your side. The earlier you begin investing, the better. Even if you only have $100 to spend, just get started.

How to Invest $100 in the Stock Market

Investing can change your life for the better, and the earlier you start, the more you'll have in your investing account over time. Several people wrongly think that unless they have thousands of dollars in your account, there's no better area to put your cash.

The reality is that even if you only have a small amount of money, you can start investing. Consider these five perfect ways to spend a few hundred dollars. By selecting the one that attracts you based on your risk tolerance-- or by blending and matching several concepts-- you can jump on the path towards long-term economic protection and develop a nest egg that you'll have the ability to tap whenever you need it.

Five Best Ways to Invest $100.

If you've managed to save up to $100, here are our five best things to do wit:

- Start an emergency fund.

- Consider using a robot-advisor to help choose financial investments for you.

- Invest in a stock index mutual fund or exchange-traded fund.

- Find high individual stocks for your brokerage account.

- Open an IRA.

1. Start an emergency fund

It's easy to understand if your first idea was to start by taking your $100 and purchasing percentages of stock. There is much engaging evidence that investing in stocks is the best means for ordinary people to have economic self-reliance. A lot of people do not know how vital it is to have a substantial margin of safety and security with their finances. For most of us, the ideal way to have that margin of safety and security is by having cold, hard money.

If you do not have 3 to six months' worth of living expenses set apart-- possibly more if you have a mortgage and a family-- after that, the best way to start with that $100 monthly is putting it in an interest-saving account as an emergency fund.

With an emergency fund, you can not expect much of a return on your cost savings. Having that safeguard isn't about getting returns; instead, it's about keeping you from entering into financial debt or having to touch your long-term investment accounts if you have a fund emergency.

This is true if you were to lose your job or suffer an unexpected sickness or mishap that affects your income for weeks or months. Having some months of income readily available in cash will imply that life's unforeseen occasions won't affect your monetary plans. Rate of interest on savings accounts isn't high, but this is concerning securing your drawback-- not recording high returns.

2. Think about using Robo-advisor to choose financial investments for you

You're in a much better position to start investing once you have financial emergencies covered. If you like an automated method that needs as little initiative as possible, then making use of a Robo-advisor can be just what you're searching for.

Robo-advisors use apps or websites to learn more about your financial needs and, after that, come up with an investing method to fulfill them. They'll commonly use standard details like age, family risk, size, and income tolerance to design a portfolio to your demands. Robo-advisors, after that, deal with all the features of selecting investments, making sales and purchases, and keeping you informed.

The Motley Fool believes you can gain far better returns by managing your financial investments. However, numerous Robo-advisor algorithms do an excellent job, and you're likely to improve long-term results from Robo-advisors than if you never spend anything.

3. Purchase a stock index common fund or exchange-traded fund

Putting your money into a stock index common fund or an inexpensive exchange-traded fund is a great way to start investing with just a little money. Both of these investment drivers offer you diversity by allowing you to buy percentages of many different stocks with a modest investment. The general concept behind both ETFs and stock investments is to enable you to invest in the whole market or picked parts of it through a single financial investment.

You can, after that, branch out and find other investment alternatives when you've built up a strong structure in these index-tracking funds. An index-tracking fund could be all you'll need to do well with your investing.

4. Buy private stocks through a brokerage firm account

Thanks to the current approach, commission-free stock trading, buying private stocks with just $100 a month to invest is now a cost-effective choice to start investing. To begin purchasing individual stocks, you'll just need to open an investment account with a broker agent company and start making regular deposits of your $100.

Finding stocks for your portfolio can be challenging, but you can comply with some basic principles to help you get going. Primarily, don't buy any investment if you don't know its company. By sticking with acquainted firms, you'll be able to inform when they're doing well and when they're doing inadequately. Choosing a portfolio of at least 10-12 stocks will reduce the risk of significant losses if you make a poor choice with 1 or 2 of your stock choices, and avoiding stocks that make big moves in both directions is also smart when you're first getting going. Over time, you'll discover what to look for in business economic statements, and as you find out, you'll be even able to separate solid stocks from weaker ones.

Private stocks offer you an opportunity to outperform the broader market standards in the future. When you're talking about years or decades of holding high-quality stocks, the advantages of buying the best companies in the stock market can pay life-changing benefits to long-term stock investors. Also, a single share can expand all over the years to worth a considerable quantity and assist you in reaching your financial objectives.

5. Open up an IRA

Finally, the kind of account you choose to spend in can be more crucial than what you decide to buy. You should consider doing it in a tax-advantaged account like an IRA if you intend to spend

$100 per month. Either a traditional or Roth IRA can offer you valuable tax obligation advantages.

Let's say that you stash $100 a month in a Roth IRA for 30 years. If you are in the 24% tax obligation bracket at retirement, having this cash in a Roth IRA can mean $43,200 in financial tax savings-- and that doesn't mean the returns and capital gains taxes you did not have to pay along the way. If you want to save more, you can put up to $6,000 into an IRA every year for 2020 and 2021 -- or up to $7,000 if you're aged 50 or more.

Don't wait!

So if you've been holding back with your investing, don't wait any longer. Take your hundred dollars and select one or more of these five means to get started.

CHAPTER NINE

Turn your Stock Portfolio to a "Cash Flow Machine"

Personal finance masters are always speaking about how to come to be economically free genuinely, and you must have enough passive income to exceed your costs. That's great, yet what is passive income, and how do you get it?

In its most straightforward way, income can be broken into four groups: earned income, portfolio income, leveraged income, and passive income.

--Earned income, as you possibly figured, is income that requires you to show up to get money. Cash is earned from your time and energy. This is how lots of people make their living - as an employee.

--Portfolio income is the interest, rewards, and capital gains that originates from the possession of stocks, bonds, and shared funds.

--Leveraged income is produced when one activity earns more cash with bigger caught target markets. A speaker at a conference, for instance, may put in as much initiative to give a speech to 20 people as 1,000 people but can gain more money with the bigger team.

--Passive income is income that calls for an advance financial investment and keeps paying over and over while the needed participation wastes. The first effort creates a money machine that brings money many times over, though the participation becomes marginal.

As you can tell above, gained income only pays you what you put in. In other words, it requires your time, and you can earn raises and promotions, yet your income is restricted because there is just one of you.

With passive income, on the other hand, you can create multiple streams of income that continue to generate cash long after you did the job once. As you continue to include a growing number of cash-flowing machine, your passive income streams increase along with your wealth.

Let's consider a couple of instances so we can begin making passive income streams.

-Money Flow Positive Real Estate: Passive income can be generated from commercial or residential properties. When it comes to passive income, real estate is what many people think of. It's just passive income when the rent you receive is more than your home mortgage, taxes, upkeep, and expenditures. Or else, your rental property is simply a responsibility that costs you money - not makes you cash. You are probably speculating to make money off the appreciation.

-Certificate a Patent: Got a terrific concept or a creation? License it and make money anytime any person uses your accredited license.

-Come to be an Author: Copyrighting products that make nobilities, such as e-books or books, music or lyrics, Images, or pictures, is one more way business owners produce passive income.

-Automated Fulfillment Websites: Build an e-commerce site that can effectively process and fill up orders with little involvement to generate some passive income.

-Spend For Use Items: Vending equipment, quarter car, coin laundries, washes, video clip arcades, and storage space systems can all gain passive income.

-Build a Successful Business: A successful service in these terms means an organization that can run with or without your heavy involvement. However, for example, do you see the owner of a McDonald's franchise business on location? A franchise that is cash circulation favorable and has a team to run the market is gaining passive income;e for the proprietor.

Realize that passive income does not necessarily mean that there is no participation on your end. Producing passive income streams typically involves a substantial financial investment upfront, but in the long run, it needs little or no interaction.

Also, just because you make an earned income now (as opposed to a passive income) does not mean you should quit your day task and open a quarter car wash. To begin building passive income streams, you will likely need to keep making an earned income to convert that income into passive income by purchasing residential rental properties, and so on.

As soon as your passive income is more than your expenses, you can decide to quit making a gained income and live the rest of your life financially free.

Retirement Income Tips - Sane Strategies For an Insane Market

The excellent crash of '08 (as I like to call it) has left millions of American people and companies strapped for money. Worst but, it has left many that believed they were close to retirement scrounging to figure out what is next. A recent problem of consumer reports publication quoted a pair who summed it up when they said, "we did what everybody said we're supposed to do. It worked for a long time, but it's not working anymore."

Since we were young, the formula has been pretty clear: Save cash, diversify investments, put money in stock investments, in 40 years we will have enough to retire. Financial advisors have provided convenience through their words "over a 20-year duration the market always goes up". And worst, what happens when the market goes down, and it's time to draw out my money?

What is it "The Donald" knows that every day people do not? He recognizes what is enough to grow money. Now I'm going to share three tricks to making money in a crisis.

1) Start Buying Income Producing Assets

For too long, people have focused on buying assets that sit in an account somewhere doing very little. An example of this would be bank CDs, ultra-safe mutual funds, etc., if you desire to expand any wealth quickly, it should be placed in assets that generate income. Some examples would be a small automatic organization like a laundry floor covering or an auto laundry, if that's too expensive, consider acquiring some vending devices and positioning them in good locations. 10 Gum sphere equipment posted in the right places ought to generate about $1000/month effortless, passive income.

2) Buy Real Estate Cheap

Now that the Real Estate bubble has burst stowing away some money into an affordable residential property is a great way to create passive regular monthly cash circulation. Month-to-month rental on a residential property like this must yield $700-$ 1000/month passive cash circulation.

3) Change your stock market techniques

Sure your stock portfolio might look down, but using the leverages of options, you can rent your stock out using covered call options and make some good monthly income (Usually about 10% of your stocks value each month). Visit your broker to and how you can compose some covered calls on the stocks in your portfolio to lessen your losses.

How to Survive Today's Stock Market With Your IRA Or 401k

The stock market at its present problem is even worse than the crash of 1987 (aka "Black Monday"). The United States Secretary of Treasury, Henry Paulson, along with some government bodies, have tried to rescue the troubling stock market with several treatments. Still, these efforts have resulted in little change.

Before we go any further on the topic of how to take control of your investments, we need to assess some standard information about"private retirement accounts" established by the government. Retirement hopefuls were able to place their IRA's and 401k's in financial investments such as shared funds, stocks, and bonds. These investments appeared to give a good range of investment choices with an excellent range of risk against tolerance and likewise used diversity to spread out the risk of investing

A lot of IRA participants know little about how to purchase these safeties because investing in the market is not precisely scientific research. You can research the business's balance sheet, anticipate what its expected possibility earnings will be, and after that, come up with a stock cost that someone may be ready to pay for in the future. I do not think that there is more than 10% of people that participate in their IRA can create this price estimate, and even if they can, there is no assurance that the company will perform to expectation, and somebody will buy that stock in the future for a higher return. That is why most people that save for retirement using an IRA or 401k do so by purchasing stock funds that rely on fund supervisors to manage the portfolio. Hopefully, these fund managers will surely outperform and get a higher return than people can do on their own. Also, these fund managers who are professionals can fail at times. On October 10, 2008, the stock industrial Dow Jones market took a 3000 point swing to the negative to a reduced of 8,300. That is a decline of about 5,700 points from the Dow Jones high of 14,000 throughout the previous year on October 10, 2007. Hedge Funds are closing left and right due to investors requesting for the investment back before suffering more looses. If professional fund managers can not give an excellent investment return to investors, how are individual investors who are saving for their retirement able to do any better?

They can do so by using a self routed IRA, which enables people to spend in a wide variety of various investment vehicles. Some of the options that retirement participants can take advantage of in a "self-directed IRA" are: accounts receivables, constructing bonds, agreements for sale, gold bullion, real estate, and of course, stocks.

Of the options offered in a self-directed IRA, stock is the option I think most financiers will know, and that is precisely what they ought to be investing in their retirement account.

CHAPTER TEN

How to Trade Momentum Stocks?

What are momentum stocks?

Momentum investing is one of the hardest to define all the conventional trading approaches, but simply put, it's based on looking for companies whose stocks have been getting more potent over the previous three months to a year. The rule below is, "buy high, sell high."

Why People ChooseMomentum Investing

Buying momentum stocks is simply a proven-effective strategy. Two people credited with identifying momentum investing, Narasimhan Jegadeesh and Sheridan Titman, showed this strategy returns average returns of 1% monthly for the three to twelve months following a given trigger occasion that signifies when to buy the stock. Their first record was released in 1993 by the American Finance Association and one more record that validated their earlier research study was published in the Journal of Finance

The advantages of trading momentum stocks

--The first is profitability. Statistics show trading momentum stocks areas around profitable strategy provided you do your study and check your timing.

--When choosing stocks, another advantage for some is that the system doesn't need absolute precision; instead, momentum investors seek considerable incentives to take the chance of proportions. For every stock that loses a small quantity, they find at least one other several that generates a 50% or higher earnings.

--Relative simplicity is one more benefit of this approach. Many trading systems need self-control, which many people simply don't have. The method of trading momentum stocks is entirely based on accurate information that's very easy to locate, so your emotions will not take you off course.

Many people assume the turn over in this way would be extremely high, but in the majority of instances, it isn't especially poor. Frequent turning over seems to be around 90%, and while steep, it's still less than with particular other strategies.

The downsides of trading momentum stocks

Momentum financiers do not buy stocks to hold. The stocks they hire are very unpredictable, and while the investors anticipate their momentum stocks to do well in the short-term, they're ready to sell as soon as the stock starts declining. That means if you don't get your timing right, you will not make money much.

Another complaint against the momentum trading is that economists can't seem to figure out precisely how this technique works, which makes it look like it's based on nothing but dumb luck. Some financial experts think it works because the high returns offset the risk, while others assume it's an instance of smart investors taking advantage of the mistakes of other investors, such as overreaction to hot stocks.

Many stock investors know that momentum trading can be a profitable business. You can make large amounts of money in a short period.

That's why the essential aspect of momentum trading is the understanding FILTER you employ to make your buy and sell options. There are several "superb" stock systems and trading techniques out there, yet you need to evaluate them to uncover which ones help you the more. That's part of your research as a stock trader—test, test, and test again.

The worst point that can happen to a beginner momentum investor is to get information overload. It's better to step by step and evaluate a straightforward stock trading strategy that can show you how to focus on concrete plans to generate income and pick better hot stock trading opportunities once at a time.

Fortunately, there are good sites online today that can show you how to sell a sharp and efficient means.

This momentum trading is all about trading stocks according to your expertise FILTER. You can expect to begin making a considerable amount of money regularly when you known and follow your tried and tested filter specifications like a clock.

Momentum Stock Trading - Entry Points Are Tip to Earning From Momentum Trading

Momentum stock investment is the art of taking earnings from the stock exchange with short-term professions developed to benefit from a stock's upward or downward day-to-day momentum. Lots of capitalists consider this to be a low-risk trading approach since, done correctly. With self-control, you just enter a trade when the targeted stock's momentum is already relocating in your direction.

There are a handful of crucial aspects of active momentum trading.

This book takes a look at the significance of entry points. An entrance point is a factor at which you want to enter a profession.

Why bother setup details entry points?

Because you want to catch the momentum once it has started, instead of buying and hoping your prediction comes true. For example, let's say Stock XYZ closed at $58, with a new hi/lo range of $55-60. Currently, you've obtained first down momentum working against you and, rather possibly, a losing trade on your hands. The trick to active trading on energy is not playing around within the new hi/lo variety.

How do I select an entry point?

Establishing an entry factor above the current hi (if you mean to go long) or below the current low (if you plan to go small) helps you catch bigger, much more substantial momentum in your professions. In our example, Stock XYZ was showing resistance at $60, i.e., the rate has not recently reviewed $60. I would establish an entry factor at something over $60, like claim $60.30. By setting your access factor over the most current resistance degree, your profession will only set off, given the momentum is currently entering the instructions you predicted.

If, however, there is first descending momentum, your profession will not activate, and you have protected your resources for other trades. Setting proper entrance points is, as a result, necessary to your success in momentum trading.

How to Spot the Best Momentum Stocks

The stock momentum has a high turn over rate in the past 3 to 12 months. Momentum investors typically hold a stock for a few months and check their holdings daily.

There are many stocks out there that accelerate in price and go on to make 100% to 300% returns in less than a year or perhaps in a few months.

Nevertheless, for the investors who are just beginning, momentum investing can be a confusing and discouraging experience to discover these stocks.

How to sight momentum stocks.

Among the things to find momentum, stocks are the relative stamina of the stock compared to the overall market over a given timeframe. A lot of momentum investors look at a stock that has outperformed at least 90% of all stocks over the 12 months, when significant indices decline, an excellent momentum stock exhibit strength by holding or perhaps exceeding their highs. When the significant indices rally, momentum stocks generally lead the rally and make new highs outmatching the market.

Possible momentum stocks ought to show in the equilibrium sheet that they are growing at a high up rate.

Also, a favorable forecast by at least some analysts on the Company's profits in necessary for determining momentum stocks; even more momentum financiers also check out whether the reported incomes exceeded the experts'forecasts compared to the last quarter.

A business can not expand its profits quicker than its Return on Equity, which is the Company's earnings divided by the variety of shares held by investors, without increasing money by borrowing or selling even more shares. Some companies raise money by issuing stock or loaning, yet both alternatives decrease earnings-per-share development. For momentum investors, a potential stock ought to show an ROE of 17% or far better.

-Meager trading quantities show the markets do not have an interest. Typically, momentum investors seek those with a minimum amount of 100,000 shares, or at least see their average everyday quantity increases as the value of the stock rises.

-Start keeping a list of prospective momentum stocks and track their performance out there. With time, you will have the ability to spot the stocks that go make-up to 100% to 300% returns in less than a year, or even in a few months

Over the last 16 months, a lot of stock markets have declined over 50%, and some private companies have been washed out thoroughly. The result of many portfolios has been devastating.

So, how does a financier or trader know when to sell?

Well, my point of view is from someone that focuses mainly on price and volume instead of the fundamentals of the underlying business. Undoubtedly, I've had some shares that have fallen a little bit. I intended to hold them as long term investments, but it has been quite painful to watch them decline to current levels. This market has clearly shown that the buy and hold technique can devastate your portfolio if you do not make use of a form of protection, such as choices, stock index futures, and shorting strategies.

Now, back to the question of when to sell. Nevertheless, some hedge funds and Commodity Trading Advisors made a whole lot of cash recently. Some made large bank on a collapsing credit market and shorted the financial stocks. Investors that I am more familiar with having substantial success in trading in the commodity and money markets.

Generally talking, the majority of Commodity Trading Advisors (CTAs), traders that make a living by managing funds with the trading of futures markets and options on futures, can be regarded as trend followers.

Trend following investors exploits the broad patterns that happen in the financial markets from time to time. Recently, there were many significant patterns in the markets, and probably the only best trend that these investors made easy money has been in the sag in Crude Oil.

Pattern complying with traders does not try to choose bases or tops. They await a market to tell them when a design might be starting, and they will leave when the mark suggests that trend might more than. During the period where the markets are rough, these traders do not make money and tend to experience some substantial drawdowns on their equity. With the rigorous application of risk management in their portfolios, some of the far better-performing investors will reduce the volatility of their portfolios.

So how does this apply to stocks?

Well, most people wish to be able to capture that warm stock when it moves 500% or more. The professional trader will have separated his/her feelings from the stock and left when indicators were that the trend was over.

However, there is no one specific price level, or indicator that the specialist counts to leave his setting at the same time. Instead, he will go at different cost factors within the fad.

How to identify when it is time to start taking earnings in your stock, and when to leave altogether.

Let's assume you bought shares of JRCC as it was breaking out to the upside from a small base back in April of 2008. This breakout occurred at about the $20 level. The stock then rallied over 300% in less than three months to a high close over $60. The astute investor would not have exited his entire placement at that level, considering that it is impossible to pick a top. The smart investor would have started discharging some shares around that $55 level and would have left the position between $45 and $50.

The stock had shot higher on four consecutive trading days, with a gain of over 30% during that time structure. The stock was going to the moon, and at the same, when a stock goes to the moon, it needs to come down to earth.

On June 19th, the stock opened over $2 at the open, after that shut down practically $3 for the session.

On that day, its trading range reduced considerably, as its volume, compared with previous trading days. The next day, on June 24th, the stock shut down virtually $6, and nearly 9%, its biggest down day of the trend. Traders following this stock must have left all settings by the end of trading on this day.

Currently, if you want an even more idea for leaving a high momentum stock such as this, simply go 50% of the position when it makes a ten-day lower in cost and the rest when it makes a twenty-day lower in price. This is an unemotional way of exiting a stock placement. Sometimes, you will leave a positioning way to early in a trend since stocks will trade out shorter-term investors, yet a 20 day lower is a good sign that current, intermediate-term trend is over. Longer-term investors who might make use of a methodology such as the CANSLIM technique to entre momentum stocks at 52-week highs might instead exit a position if the stock makes a ten-week low and after that a 20 week low. You will provide up considerable unrealized gains by waiting for a 20- week lower, so it is a great idea to pay attention to the cost and volume relationships talked about formerly. Or, you can leave at a five-week low and ten-week low.

These are simply some ideas on when to exit stock positions after they have made significant relocations. There is nobody perfect exit technique. If you trade in this way regularly, you will experience good profits in the long run, and you will be forced into 100% money when the market suffers the type of bear market we see now.

Momentum Stock Trading - Stop Losses Are Essential To Capital Preservation

In momentum stock trading or any other approaches of day trading, a trader requires a means to decrease the risk of losing trades. Making use of stop losses is crucial to an investor's resources conservation in that stop losses limit the size of a losing trade. A stop loss is a pre-designated price factor at which a trader chooses to exit a business with very little damage.

Why Use Stop Losses?

There are two primary reasons to use quit losses.

-Firstly, establishing a quit loss help to manage your trading risk and maintain your capital for future trades. The reality for day traders is that not every trader is a winning trader.

-Stop losses enable a small activity in the cost going against you but cap the quantity of adverse motion you are willing to soak up. By leaving a trade that is breaking you with only a little loss, you will have protected your trading capital for future professions.

- Secondly, stop losses assist in eliminating emotional trading.

As an investor, you need to guard against being in a trade too long while wishing for a turnaround. Set correctly, your stop loss will allow for small changes in cost but protect you from more effective momentum violating you.

How to Set an Effective Stop Loss

Let's use the following example: Assume my research reveals that Stock XYZ is poised to the run-up. It closed the previous day at $41.53, with a daily high for that day of $41.95. I generally establish an entry point at least $0.10 greater than the previous day's high, so in this situation, my access point maybe $42.05. Using a reward to take the chance of the proportion of 2:1, I would certainly put a stop loss at $41.75 and an exit price of $42.65. This trading plan stocks a prospective benefit gain of $0.60 and minimizes any loss to $0.30.

When setting stop losses, bear in mind to take into consideration a stock's current resistance levels in addition to a stock's recent trading variety.

Tracking Stops - Adjusting Stop Losses Within a Winning Trade

Experienced day traders have found that about 1 in 10 trades surpasses expectations, i.e., the stock's momentum carries the price beyond the targeted exit price. I advise using routing stops when this happens. In the above example, let's state that Stock XYZ exceeded our assumptions, going past $42.65. In this instance, I would change my stop loss approximately $42.65 to secure in the first $0.60 of earnings and keep changing the stop loss upward in $0.10 or $0.15 increments to "trail" the higher momentum.

CHAPTER ELEVEN

Insider Tricks Used by Professional Traders

Insiders who sell or buy stock must submit reports that document their trading task with the Securities and Exchange Commission (SEC), which makes the records readily available to the public. You can see these records either at the SEC workplace or at the Web site of the SEC, which preserves the EDGAR (Electronic Data Gathering, Analysis, and Retrieval) data source

www.sec. Gov/Edgar. HTML

-Form 3: This form is the first statement that experts give. Experts should file Form 3 within ten days of obtaining expert status. An expert submits this record also if he hasn't purchased yet; the report establishes the expert's status.

-Form 4: Form 4 is a document that reveals the expert's activity. For instance, Form 4 would include a change in the expert's position as a shareholder-- the number of shares the person dealt with or other relevant variations. Any type of activity in a specific month should be reported on Form 4 by the 10th of the following month. If, for example, an expert markets stock throughout January, the SEC must obtain the record by February 10.

-Form 5: This yearly record covers transactions that are tiny and not needed on Form 4. Deals might consist of minor, interior transfers of stock or other arrangements.

-Form 144: This form offers as the public statement by an insider of the intention to sell a limited stock. After an insider decides to sell, he submits Form 144 and then must sell within 90 days or else submit a new Form 144. The insider must provide the type on or before the stock's sale date.

Companies are needed to show the papers that track their trading work. The SEC's website provides restricted access to these papers, but also for higher access, check out among some company that reports expert trading information, such as www.marketwatch.com and www.bloomberg.com.

Sarbanes-Oxley Act

In the stock market mania of 1997-- 2000, this misuse had not been simply limited to insider purchasing and selling of stock; it also covered the relevant abuse of bookkeeping scams. Because insiders are primarily the top administration, they tricked investors about the financial conditions of the business and subsequently were able to raise the perceived

The stock might, after that, be sold at a rate that was higher than market value. SOX established a public audit oversight board and tightened the policies on company economic reporting.

The insider must wait at least six months before getting it once more. The rule is likewise real if an expert sells the stock. An expert can't sell it at a higher cost within six months.

Checking Out Insider Transactions
Analyzing insider acquiring against expert marketing can be as different as day and night. Expert buying is comfortable, while insider marketing can be complicated.

Knowing from insider buying

Expert purchasing is usually a distinct signal about how an insider feels about his company. Besides, the key reason that all investors buy a stock is that they expect it to do well. That's generally not a considerable occasion if one expert is buying inventory. But if more experts are getting, those acquisitions should capture your attention.

Expert acquiring is usually a positive omen and advantageous for the stock's rate. When insiders buy stock, less stock is offered to the public. If the investing public meets this lowered stock with enhanced demand, then the

stock price surges. Keep these factor in mind when analyzing expert buying:

Knowing who is buying the stock.

The CEO is buying 5,000 shares. Is that reason enough for you to jump in? Maybe. After all, the CEO knows how well the performance of the company. What if before this purchase, she had no stock in the company at all? Maybe the stock is part of her employment package.

The truth that a new business executive is making her first stock acquisition isn't as strong a signal urging you to buy as the fact that a veteran CEO is doubling her holdings. If significant numbers of insiders are buying, that sends out a more reliable signal than if a single expert is buying.

See how much is being bought.

In the instance in the previous section, the CEO bought 5,000 shares, which is a whole lot of stock, no matter how you count it. But is it enough for you to base a financial investment decision on? Maybe, but a closer look may reveal more. Getting 5,000 additional shares would not be h a good signal of a pending stock increase if she currently owned 1 million shares at the time of the purchase. In this instance, 5,000 shares are a small step-by-step step and don't offer much to get excited able.

What if this insider has possessed just 5,000 shares for the past three years and is now getting 1 million shares? Generally, a significant acquisition tells you that a particular insider has a solid sense of the firm's leads and that she's making a substantial increase in her share of stock possession.

100,000 shares each. Once more, if someone is purchasing, that might or may not be a secure sign of a future increase. If many people are getting, consider it an incredible indicator.

"The more, the merrier!" is an excellent regulation for judging expert buying. All these people have their unique viewpoints on the business and its leads for the near future. Mass buying means mass positivity for the future of the company. If the treasurer, the head of state, the vice-president of sales, and many other principals are placing their extensive range on the line and investing it in a business that they know carefully, that's an excellent sign for your stock investment also.

Notice the timing of the purchase. The timing of expert stock purchases is vital too. If I inform you that five insiders got stock at various points in 2014, you might say, "Hmm." But if I tell you that all the five people got chunks of stock at the same time and right before earnings period, that must make you say, "HMMMMM!".

Picking up tips from Insider marketing.
Insider stock purchasing is hardly an unfavorable event.

Experts may sell their stock for a pair factors: They might assume that the company will not be doing well in the close to future-- an unfavorable sign for you-- or they might simply need the money for a range of individual factors that have nothing to do with the firm's possibility. Some typical reasons experts may sell stock include the following:

To diversify their holdings. If an insider's portfolio is slowly heavy with one firm's stock, a monetary consultant may recommend that he balance his portfolio by marketing a few of that business's stock and purchasing different other protections.

To finance personal emergencies. Often an insider needs money for medical, legal, or family reasons.

To buy a home or make one more major acquisition. An expert may need the cash to make a down settlement or maybe to buy something outright without having to get a car loan.

How do you get information about insider stock selling?

Although experts should report their essential stock sales and acquisitions to the SEC, the information isn't always disclosing.

Always answer these questions before assessing insider marketing:

How numerous insiders are marketing?

If just one expert is marketing, that one deal does not give you enough info to act on.

Is the usual pattern showing on the sales? If one expert offered some stock last month, that sale alone isn't that considered an occasion. However, if ten insiders have made several sales in the past few months, those sales are the reason for the issue. See whether any type of new developments at the business is possibly harmful. Consider placing a stop-loss order on your stock immediately if substantial expert selling has recently happened, and you don't know why.

How much stock is being sold?

That's not a big deal if a CEO markets 5,000 shares of stock but still saves 100,000 shares. If the CEO sells all or a lot of his holdings, that's a possible adverse. Examine to see whether various other business execs have additionally sold the stock.

Do outdoor events or analyst records appear accidental with the sale of the stock? Often, an influential analyst might release a report cautioning about a firm's potential customers. If the company's administration waves aside the record buy the majority of them are bailing out anyhow (marketing their stock), you may wish to do the same. Regularly, when experts understand that dam maturing information looms, they sell the stock before it takes a dip.

In the same way, if the company's management issues positive public declarations or reports that are contradictory to their habits (they're selling their stock holdings), the SEC might investigate to see whether the company is doing anything that may need a charge. The SEC regularly tracks expert sales.

Considering Corporate Stock Buybacks.

When you review the monetary web pages or watch the financial programs on television, you sometimes listen to how a company is getting its very stock.

When companies buy back their stock, they're generally showing that they believe their stock is underestimated, which can increase. If a business reveals strong fundamentals (for instance, excellent economic condition and enhancing earnings and sales) and it's purchasing more of its stock, it's worth exploring it may make a fantastic enhancement to your portfolio.

If you see that a business is buying back its stock while many of the experts are selling their shares, that's not the right signal. It might not necessarily be a wrong signal, yet it's not a favorable indication. Play it risk-free and spend elsewhere.

The following areas present some typical factors a company might redeem its shares from investors in addition to some ideas on the negative results of stock buybacks.

- Enhancing revenues per share

By only redeeming its shares from investors, a business can enhance its revenues per share without having extra money. Sound like an illusionist's technique? Well, it is, type of. A company stock buyback is a monetary deception that investors should know.

Right here's how it works:

NEI has 10 million shares, and it's expected to web profits of $10 million for the 4th quarter. NEI's revenues per share (EPS) would be $1 per share. Thus far, so excellent. However, what happens.

If NEI buys two million of its shares? Total shares impressive shrink to 8 million. The new EPS is $1.25-- the stock buyback synthetically improves the earnings per share by 25 percent!

The crucial sign about stock buybacks is that real company profits do not change-- no essential changes happen in business monitoring or procedures-- so the increase in EPS can be deceptive.

The market can be compulsive about incomes, and because profits are the lifeblood of any company, an earnings increase, even if it's cosmetic, can also increase the stock price.

Also, a stock buyback influences stock and need. With less available stock on the market, demand always sends the stock rate upwards.

Whenever a firm makes a significant purchase, such as acquiring back its stock, think about just how the firm is paying for it and whether it looks like an excellent use of the company's purchasing power. In basic, companies buy their stock for the same factors any investor purchases stock-- they think that the stock is an excellent financial investment and will appreciate in time.

Beating back a takeover quote.

Because acquiring and offering stock are done in a public market or exchange, companies can buy each other's stock. In some cases, the target company likes not to be obtained, in which instance it might buy its shares of stock to protect it against unwanted actions by interested companies.

In most cases, the firm trying the requisition already possesses some of the target business's stock. In this case, the targeted firm may want to repurchase those shares from the aggressor at a premium to prevent the requisition proposal. This kind of deal is frequently described as greenmail.

Takeover usually worries rapid interest in the investing public, driving the stock cost upward and benefiting present stockholders.

Checking out the drawback of buybacks.

If a business pays for the stock with investments from operations, it may comprise of unfavorable effect on the company's ability to fund reasonable and current processes. In general, any mismanagement of money, such as using financial obligation to repurchase stock, influences a company's capability to grow its sales and profits-- two measures that need to keep higher mobility to maintain stock prices climbing.

Why does business split their stock?

Generally, management thinks that the stock's price is high, thus potentially discouraging investors from buying it. The stock split is a way to stir the rate of interest in the stock, and this boost interest regularly leads to an increase in the stock's price.

Getting approved for a stock split is similar to certified to receive a return; you have to be noted as an investor as the date of record.

A stock split is technically a neutral occasion because the supreme market value of the company's stock does not change as a result of the separation.

The following sections give both fundamental kinds of splits: average and reverse stock splits.

- Average stock divides.

When the number of stock shares increases- we usually hear about this, average stock splits--. (For example, a 2-for-1 stock split increases the number of shares.) If you possess 100 shares of Dublin, Inc., stock (at $60 per share), and the investment shows a stock split, what happens? You receive in the mail a stock certification for if you have the stock in certificate kind.

One hundred shares of Dublin, Inc. no, before you think of how your money will double, examine the stock's new price. Each share is changed to a $30 worth.

Not all stock is in certificate kind. Stocks held in a brokerage firm account are taped in book-entry variety. Most stock, in reality, is in book entrance type.

A business only issues stock certificates when necessary or when the investor asks for it. Always consult your broker for the new share total amount to make sure that you're qualified with the original number of shares after the stock split.

A stock split is mainly a neutral occasion, so why does a company bother to do it? One of the most common reasons is that monitoring thinks that the stock is also pricey, so it intends to decrease the stock price to make the stock extra affordable and, for that reason, more attractive to new financiers. Research has shown that stock splits often precede a rise in the stock rate. Although stock divides are thought about a non-event in and of themselves, lots of stock experts see them as favorable signals as a result of the interest they produce among the investing public.

2. Reverse stock splits

A reverse stock split generally happens when a company management wants to increase the rate of its stock. If a stock's cost looks too low, that might discourage passion by specific or institutional investors (such as stock funds). The management intends to drum up more interest in the stock for the advantage of investors (a few of whom are probably insiders).

The firm might also do a reverse split to reduce expenses. When you have to send a yearly record and other correspondence regularly to all the stock- owners, the mailings can get a little expensive, particularly when you have many investors that have a few shares each. Reverse split helps to consolidate the shares to reduced overall management expenses.

A reverse split can best be clarified with an example. TCI introduces a 10-for-1 reverse stock split. If an existing investor had 100 shares at $2 (the old shares), the stockholder currently possesses ten stocks at $20.

Technically, a reverse split is known as a neutral event. Simply as financiers might assume favorable expectations from an ordinary stock split, they may have negative assumptions from a reverse split, because a reverse split tends to happen for negative reasons.

If, on the occasion of a stock split, you have a weird number of shares, the company does not create a "fractional share."Instead, you have to look for the money matching.

Keep good records about your stock splits in case you need to calculate capital gains tax.

CHAPTER TWELVE

How to Identify a Stock that is About to Explode Higher

Essential tools to identify if a stock is about to explode

" Typically, when a stock gets overbought, it is ripe for a pullback because overbought stocks, ones with lots of buyers reaching to absorb the stock, often tend to break back after they have gotten as far away from their longer-term trend line," the CNBC host said.

Financiers can determine whether a stock is overbought or oversold by charting the ratio of higher closes, likewise called the family member power index, or RSI. This is a momentum oscillator that processes the instructions of a given stock and the speed of its step.

To find times in a specific stock's trajectory where its toughness sticks out-- a possible sign of a pending revocation or change in momentum-- Cramer matches the stock's RSI to something else, such as the loved one strength of its sector or a broader index, and afterward determines the past cost action.

But the inverse can also be real, as a stock can fall so quickly that investors should expect it to break back because it is practically oversold, claims the "Mad Money" host. These trends are positive signs that a change in instructions is about to happen and tend to be stellar activity points.

So, for investors that are debating whether they should buy a stock and have done all the research to discover that the said stock is overbought, Cramer recommends waiting on the inescapable pullback that often takes place.

Some stocks, but can break through all the generally determined ceilings and stay overbought for weeks at a time.

" They oppose the notion of the unavoidable gravitational pull of the old stability line and can't be restricted by any of the many ceilings that overbought problems generally bump right into," Cramer said. "When you find these unusual actions, you may have the ability to band yourself into an actual moonshot."

Quantity is one more crucial tool that chartists use to find pivots. It is usually said that number can be a lie detector for investors to inform if a move is real or otherwise. When a little relocation happens in light quantity, service technicians neglect it.

If huge money managers are starting to build or distribute the stock in a hostile means, chartists make use of volume to establish.

Professionals likewise measure something called an accumulation circulation line. This involves charting whether a stock shuts greater on better quantity on any given day, against lower, or on the reduced amount.

Most brokerage firm companies stock this type of charting on their websites. While Cramer considers the method to be somewhat mysterious, he trusts funds because it goes against the grain of conventional thinking and provides a new way to take a look at stock motions.

Cramer saw this happen with shares of Monsanto in July 2012. He didn't worry about the stock of the company at the time; the buildup circulation line showed that the stock had fall days with light volume and rise days with dark volume.

To Cramer, that was a particular sign that more money was streaming into the stock rather than out of it.

It ends up that Monsanto's stock had started correlating with the price of corn, which was going higher due to the new demand for ethanol brought about by government cost assistance. Cramer was too worried about near-term profits and bothered with a deficiency to acknowledge what was happening.

" Powerful relocations can, and commonly do avoid those that are just concentrated on the underlying business and not the activity of the stocks themselves," Cramer said.

CONCLUSION

Thanks for making it with me throughout this publication. I hope it was able and useful to give you the tools you require to accomplish your objectives, whatever they might be on stock investing.

By now, you already have an excellent structure that can lead you to success. The next step is to apply every little thing that you have discovered.

Happy trading!

CPSIA information can be obtained
at www.ICGtesting.com
Printed in the USA
LVHW052056301220
675391LV00014B/690